# Other Books and Series by Jeff Bowen

*Applications for Enrollment of Chickasaw Newborn Act of 1905*
*Volumes I thru VII*

*Cherokee Intermarried White 1906 Volume I thru X*

*Applications for Enrollment of Creek Newborn Act of 1905*
*Volumes I thru XIV*

*Applications for Enrollment of Choctaw Newborn Act of 1905*
*Volume I, II, III, IV, V, VI, VII, VIII, IX & X*

Visit our website at **www.nativestudy.com** to learn more about these and other books and series by Jeff Bowen

# APPLICATIONS FOR ENROLLMENT OF CHOCTAW NEWBORN ACT OF 1905

## VOLUME XI

TRANSCRIBED BY
### JEFF BOWEN

NATIVE STUDY
Gallipolis, Ohio
USA

# Other Books and Series by Jeff Bowen

*1901-1907 Native American Census Seneca, Eastern Shawnee, Miami, Modoc, Ottawa, Peoria, Quapaw, and Wyandotte Indians (Under Seneca School, Indian Territory)*

*1932 Census of The Standing Rock Sioux Reservation with Births And Deaths 1924-1932*

*Census of The Blackfeet, Montana, 1897- 1901 Expanded Edition*

*Eastern Cherokee by Blood, 1906-1910, Volumes I thru XIII*

*Choctaw of Mississippi Indian Census 1929-1932 with Births and Deaths 1924-1931    Volume I*
*Choctaw of Mississippi Indian Census 1933, 1934 & 1937, Supplemental Rolls to 1934 & 1935 with Births and Deaths 1932-1938, and Marriages 1936-1938 Volume II*

*Eastern Cherokee Census Cherokee, North Carolina 1930-1939 Census 1930-1931 with Births And Deaths 1924-1931 Taken By Agent L. W. Page Volume I*
*Eastern Cherokee Census Cherokee, North Carolina 1930-1939 Census 1932-1933 with Births And Deaths 1930-1932 Taken By Agent R. L. Spalsbury    Volume II*
*Eastern Cherokee Census Cherokee, North Carolina 1930-1939 Census 1934-1937 with Births and Deaths 1925-1938 and Marriages 1936 & 1938 Taken by Agents R. L. Spalsbury And Harold W. Foght Volume III*

*Seminole of Florida Indian Census, 1930-1940 with Birth and Death Records, 1930-1938*

*Texas Cherokees 1820-1839  A Document For Litigation 1921*

*Choctaw By Blood Enrollment Cards 1898-1914 Volumes I thru XVII*

*Starr Roll 1894   (Cherokee Payment Rolls)  Districts: Canadian, Cooweescoowee, and Delaware  Volume One*
*Starr Roll 1894 (Cherokee Payment Rolls) Districts: Flint, Going Snake, and Illinois   Volume Two*
*Starr Roll 1894 (Cherokee Payment Rolls) Districts: Saline, Sequoyah, and Tahlequah; Including Orphan Roll  Volume Three*

*Cherokee Intruder Cases  Dockets of Hearings 1901-1909  Volumes I & II*

*Indian Wills, 1911-1921  Records of the Bureau of Indian Affairs Books One thru Seven;*
 *Native American Wills & Probate Records 1911-1921*

# Other Books and Series by Jeff Bowen

*Turtle Mountain Reservation Chippewa Indians 1932 Census with Births & Deaths, 1924-1932*

*Chickasaw By Blood Enrollment Cards 1898-1914 Volume I thru V*

*Cherokee Descendants East An Index to the Guion Miller Applications Volume I*
*Cherokee Descendants West An Index to the Guion Miller Applications Volume II (A-M)*
*Cherokee Descendants West An Index to the Guion Miller Applications Volume III (N-Z)*

*Applications for Enrollment of Seminole Newborn Freedmen, Act of 1905*

*Eastern Cherokee Census, Cherokee, North Carolina, 1915-1922, Taken by Agent James E. Henderson     Volume I (1915-1916)*
*Volume II (1917-1918)*
*Volume III (1919-1920)*
*Volume IV (1921-1922)*

*Complete Delaware Roll of 1898*

*Eastern Cherokee Census, Cherokee, North Carolina, 1923-1929, Taken by Agent James E. Henderson     Volume I (1923-1924)*
*Volume II (1925-1926)*
*Volume III (1927-1929)*

*Applications for Enrollment of Seminole Newborn Act of 1905 Volumes I & II*

*North Carolina Eastern Cherokee Indian Census 1898-1899, 1904, 1906, 1909-1912, 1914 Revised and Expanded Edition*

*1932 Hopi and Navajo Native American Census with Birth & Death Rolls (1925-1931) Volume 1 - Hopi*
*1932 Hopi and Navajo Native American Census with Birth & Death Rolls (1930-1932) Volume 2 - Navajo*

*Western Navajo Reservation Navajo, Hopi and Paiute 1933 Census with Birth & Death Rolls 1925-1933*

*Cherokee Citizenship Commission Dockets 1880-1884 and 1887-1889 Volumes I thru V*

Copyright © 2013
by Jeff Bowen

ALL RIGHTS RESERVED
No part of this publication may be reproduced
or used in any form or manner whatsoever
without previous written permission from the
copyright holder or publisher.

Originally published:
Baltimore, Maryland
2013

Reprinted by:

Native Study LLC
Gallipolis, OH
www.nativestudy.com
2020

Library of Congress Control Number: 2020918113

ISBN: 978-1-64968-104-1

*Made in the United States of America.*

This series is dedicated to the descendants of the
Choctaw newborn listed in these applications.

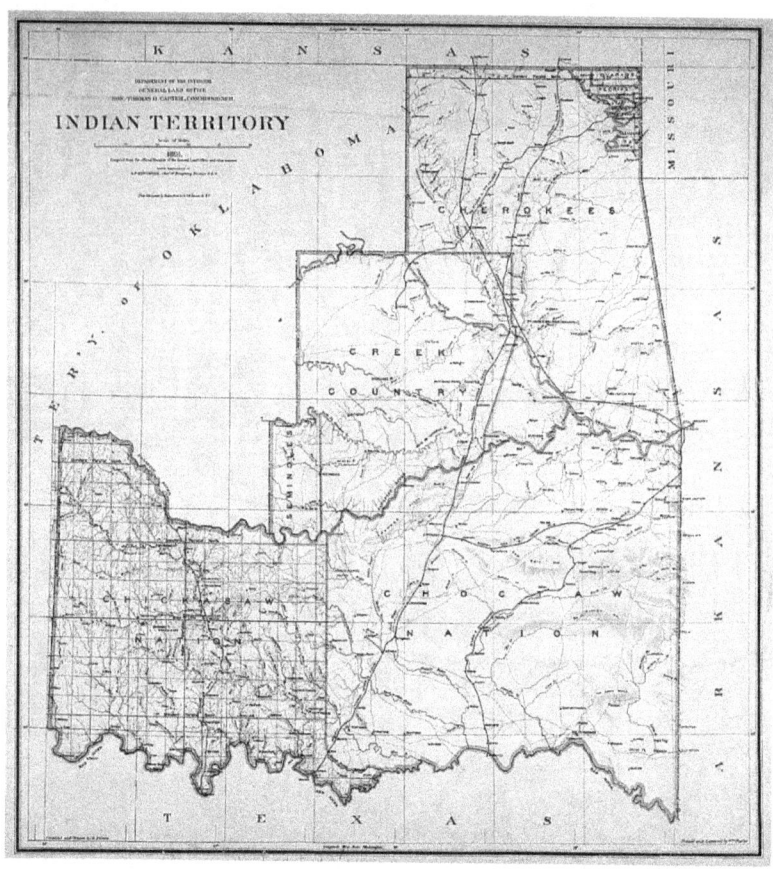

This map of Indian Territory shows how large the Choctaw and Chickasaw Nations' land base was that contained huge deposits of asphalt and coal. Just the size and territory involved was flooded with the "Grafters".

DEPARTMENT OF THE INTERIOR.
Commissioner to the Five Civilized Tribes.

# NOTICE.

## Opening of Land Office at Wewoka,
### IN THE SEMINOLE NATION, INDIAN TERRITORY.

Notice is hereby given that on Monday, September 4, 1905, the Commissioner to the Five Civilized Tribes will establish a land office at Wewoka, in the Seminole Nation, Indian Territory, for the purpose of allowing citizens and freedmen of the Seminole Nation to select allotments of land for their minor children enrolled under the Act of Congress approved March 3, 1905 (33 Stat. L. 1060), and for the further purpose of allowing citizens and freedmen of the Seminole Nation, whose allotments are incomplete, to select additional land in order to bring the value of their allotments up to the standard of $309.09, as nearly as may be practicable.

Each child whose enrollment in accordance with the Act of March 3, 1905, has been duly approved by the Secretary of the Interior, is entitled to receive an alllotment of forty acres without regard to the character or value of the land selected.

Selection of allotments for minor children must be made by their citizen or freedmen parents or by a duly appointed guardian, or curator, or by a duly appointed administrator.

TAMS BIXBY,
Commissioner.

Muskogee, Indian Territory,
July 29, 1905.

*This particular notice for the Seminole and Creek Newborn makes mention of the Act of 1905. It is likely that a similar notice was posted in the Choctaw and Chickasaw Nations for the registration of newborn children.*

DEPARTMENT OF THE INTERIOR,
## Commission to the Five Civilized Tribes.

### Rules and Regulations Governing the Selection of Allotments and the Designation of Homesteads in the Choctaw and Chickasaw Nations.

1. Selections of allotments and designations of homesteads for adult citizens and selections of allotments for adult freedmen must be made in person except as herein otherwise provided.

2. Applications to have land set apart and homesteads designated for duly identified Mississippi Choctaws must be made personally before the Commission to the Five Civilized Tribes. Fathers may apply for their minor children and if the father be dead the mother may apply. Husbands may apply for wives. Applications for orphans, insane persons and persons of unsound mind may be made by duly appointed guardian or curator, and for aged and infirm persons and prisoners by agents duly authorized thereunto by power of attorney, in the discretion of said Commission.

3. At the time of the selection of allotment each citizen and duly identified Mississippi Choctaw shall designate as a homestead out of said selection land equal in value to one hundred and sixty acres of the average allottable land of the Choctaw and Chickasaw Nations, as nearly as may be.

4. Each Choctaw and Chickasaw freedman, at the time of selection shall designate as his or her allotment of the lands of the Choctaw and Chickasaw Nations, land equal in value to forty acres of the average allottable land of the Choctaw and Chickasaw Nations.

5. Citizens, freedmen and identified Mississippi Choctaws who are married, whether they have attained their majority or not, will be regarded as of age for the purpose of making selections.

6. Selections may be made by citizen and freedman parents for unmarried male children under twenty-one years of age and for unmarried female children under eighteen years of age, and a male citizen or freedman may make selection for his wife, if she is entitled to make selection, unless she shall, at the time or previously thereto, protest in writing.

7. Where the father of an unmarried minor citizen, freedman or identified Mississippi Choctaw is a non-citizen, the citizen, freedman or identified Mississippi Choctaw mother of such children must make selection in person in behalf of said children.

8. Selections of allotments and designations of homesteads for minor citizens and selections of allotments for minor freedmen may be made by the citizen father or mother or freedman father or mother, as the case may be, or by a guardian, curator, or an administrator having charge of their estate, in the order named.

9. Selections of allotments and designations of homesteads for citizen, and selections of allotment for freedmen, prisoners, convicts, aged and infirm persons and soldiers and sailors of the United States on duty outside of Indian Territory, may be made by duly appointed agents under power of attorney, and for incompetents by guardians, curators, or other suitable person akin to them.

10. Selections may be made and homesteads designated by duly identified Mississippi Choctaws, who have, within one year after the date of their identification as such, made satisfactory proof of bona fide settlement within the Choctaw-Chickasaw country, at any time within six months after the date of their said identification.

11. Persons authorized to make selections by power of attorney, as provided in rules 2 and 9 hereof, must be the husband or wife, or a relative not further removed than a cousin of the first degree of the person for whom such selection is made.

12. It shall be the duty of the Commission to the Five Civilized Tribes to see that selections of allotments and designations of homesteads for the classes of persons mentioned in rules 2, 6, 7, 8 and 9 hereof, are made for the best interests of such persons.

13. Selections of allotments for citizens, freedmen and identified Mississippi Choctaws who have died subsequent to September 25, 1902, and before making a selection of allotment, shall be made by a duly appointed administrator or executor. If, however, such administrator or executor be not duly and expeditiously appointed, or fails to act promptly when appointed, or for any other cause such selections be not so made within a reasonable and practicable time, the Commission to the Five Civilized Tribes shall designate the lands thus to be allotted.

14. In determining the value of a selection the appraised value of the land selected shall be increased by the appraised value of such pine timber on such land as has heretofore been estimated by the Commission to the Five Civilized Tribes.

15. Selections of allotments may be made only by citizens and freedmen whose enrollment has been approved by the Secretary of the Interior, and by persons duly identified by the Commission to the Five Civilized Tribes as Mississippi Choctaws, and by none others.

16. When a selection of land has been made by a citizen, freedman or identified Mississippi Choctaw, and the land so selected is claimed by a person whose rights as a citizen or freedman have not been finally determined, contest for the land so selected may be instituted by the person claiming the land, formal application for the land being first made as is required by the Rules of Practice in Choctaw and Chickasaw allotment contest cases.

THE COMMISSION TO THE FIVE CIVILIZED TRIBES.
TAMS BIXBY, Chairman.

Muskogee, Indian Territory, March 24, 1903.

The above statement published prior to 1905, was established for what was supposed to be a set of guidelines when it came to allotments. But with supplemental agreements and Congressional legislation, time frames as well as rules and regulations often changed and were not the same for every tribe.

# INTRODUCTION

The *Applications for Enrollment of Choctaw Newborn Act of 1905*, National Archive film M-1301, Rolls 50-57, are found under the heading of Applications for Enrollment of the Commission to the Five Civilized Tribes. For this series, I have transcribed the application forms filled out by individuals applying for enrollment in the Five Civilized Tribes under the Dawes Commission. These applications contain considerably more information than stated on the census cards found in series M-1186. M-1301 possesses its own numerical sequence, separate from M-1186. To find each party's roll number you would have to reference M-1186.

The Choctaw as well as the Chickasaw allotments were likely some of the most sought after properties in Indian Territory. There was supposed to be a 25-year restriction on the sale or lease of any Indian lands so as to insure that the owners wouldn't be swindled, but that isn't what happened. This fact is borne out in the Dawes Commission General Allotment Act, of February 8, 1887, Section 5, which "Provides that after an Indian person is allotted land, the United States will hold the land 'in trust [1] for the sole use and benefit of the Indian' (or his heirs if the Indian landowner dies) for a period of 25 years. (Land held in trust by the United States government cannot be sold or in anyway alienated by the Indian landowner, since the United States government considers the underlying ownership of the land held by itself and not the tribe. After the period of trust ends, the Indian landowner is free to sell the land and is free from any encumbrance from the United States.)"[1] Instead, Native Americans were exploited by the devious. The Choctaw and Chickasaw Districts both had huge asphalt and coal deposits, so there was pressure from outsiders to acquire them from the minute they were discovered. After repeated attacks throughout the years and many legislative changes, President "Roosevelt finally signed the Five Tribes Bill at noon on April 26, 1906, the forces seeking to end all restrictions were disappointed. Section 19 removed restrictions from the sale of all inherited land but directed that no full-bloods could sell their land for twenty-five years. The Act also prohibited leases for more than one year without the approval of the Secretary of the Interior."[2]

Angie Debo described the opportunists that wanted these Native American allotments as, "Grafters". The parents of the newborns enumerated within this series would no sooner receive the approval for their child's allotment than there would be someone there with cash in hand holding a new deed or lease for the parents to sign their child's birthright away. Angie Debo said it best, "As the business incapacity of the allottees became apparent, a horde of despoilers fastened themselves upon their property." According to Debo, "The term 'grafter' was applied as a matter of course to dealers in Indian land, and was frankly accepted by them. The speculative fever also affected Government employees so that it was almost impossible to prevent them from making personal investments."[3]

---

[1] General Allotment Act, Act of Feb. 8, 1887 (24 Stat. 388, ch. 119, 25 USCA 331)
[2] The Dawes Commission and the Allotment of the Five Civilized Tribes, 1893-1914 by Kent Carter, pg. 173
[3] And Still the Waters Run, Angie Debo, p. 92.

# INTRODUCTION

According to the Department of Interior in 1905, "It is estimated that there will be added to the final rolls of the citizens and freedmen of the Choctaw and Chickasaw nations the names of 2,000 persons, including 1,500 new-born children to be enrolled under the provisions of the act of Congress approved March 3, 1905."[4]

The quote below explains, in detail, the requirements for qualifying as a newborn Choctaw, "By the act of Congress approved March 3, 1905 (H.R. 17474), entitled 'An act making appropriations for the current and contingent expenses of the Indian Department and for fulfilling treaty stipulations with various Indian tribes for the fiscal year ending June 30, 1906, and for other purposes,' it was provided as follows:

'That the Commission to the Five Civilized Tribes is hereby authorized for sixty days after the date of the approval of this act to receive and consider applications for enrollment of infant children born prior to September twenty-fifth, nineteen hundred and two, and who were living on said date, to citizens by blood of the Choctaw and Chickasaw tribes of Indians whose enrollment has been approved by the Secretary of the Interior prior to the date of the approval of this act; and to enroll and make allotments to such children.'

'That the Commission to the Five Civilized Tribes is authorized for sixty days after the date of the approval of this act to receive and consider applications for enrollment of children born subsequent to September twenty-fifth, nineteen hundred and two, and prior to March fourth, nineteen hundred and five, and who were living on said latter date, to citizens by blood of the Choctaw and Chickasaw tribes of Indians whose enrollment has been approved by the Secretary of the Interior prior to the date of the approval of this act; and to enroll and make allotments to such children.'

"Notice is hereby given that the Commission to the Five Civilized Tribes will, up to and inclusive of midnight, May 2, 1905, receive applications for the enrollment of infant children born prior to September 25, 1902, and who were living on said date, to citizens by blood of the Choctaw and Chickasaw tribes of Indians whose enrollment has been approved by the Secretary of the Interior prior to March 3, 1905."[5]

Following is the scope of these transcriptions: Besides the applications themselves, researchers will find the identities of other individuals within these applications -- doctors, lawyers, mid-wives, and other relatives -- that may help with you genealogical research.

Jeff Bowen
Gallipolis, Ohio
NativeStudy.com

---

[4] Annual Reports of the Department of the Interior For the Fiscal Year Ended June 30, 1905, p. 609.
[5] Annual Reports of the Department of the Interior For the Fiscal Year Ended June 30, 1905, p. 593.

# Applications for Enrollment of Choctaw Newborn
## Act of 1905   Volume XI

Choc New Born 698
    Olla Huggins   b. 3-15-03

---

**BIRTH AFFIDAVIT.**

DEPARTMENT OF THE INTERIOR.
## COMMISSION TO THE FIVE CIVILIZED TRIBES.

---

IN RE APPLICATION FOR ENROLLMENT, as a citizen of the     Choctaw     Nation, of Olla Huggins     , born on the 15$^{th}$    day of    March   , 1903

Name of Father:  J. J. Huggins             a citizen of the   Choctaw    Nation.
Name of Mother: Lula E. Huggins            a citizen of the   Choctaw    Nation.

                        Postoffice    Utica I.T.

---

**AFFIDAVIT OF MOTHER.**

UNITED STATES OF AMERICA, Indian Territory, }
    Central            DISTRICT.            }

   I,   Lula E Huggins   , on oath state that I am  30   years of age and a citizen by    Blood   , of the    Choctaw   Nation; that I am the lawful wife of    J J Huggins   , who is a citizen, by Inter Marriage  of the    Choctaw   Nation; that a    Female    child was born to me on   15$^{th}$   day of   March   , 1903; that said child has been named   Olla Huggins   , and was living March 4, 1905.

                        Lula E Huggins

Witnesses To Mark:
   {

    Subscribed and sworn to before me this 28$^{th}$   day of   March    , 1905

                        W J ODonby
                            Notary Public.

---

**AFFIDAVIT OF ATTENDING PHYSICIAN OR MID-WIFE.**

UNITED STATES OF AMERICA, Indian Territory, }
    Central           DISTRICT.             }

   I,   H.G. Goben    , a   Physician    , on oath state that I attended on Mrs. Lula E. Huggins    , wife of  J.J. Huggins   on the  15$^{th}$  day of March  , 1903; that there was born to her on said date a    Female    child; that said child was living March 4, 1905, and is said to have been named  Olla Huggins

# Applications for Enrollment of Choctaw Newborn
## Act of 1905   Volume XI

Witnesses To Mark:

H.G. Goben M.D.

{

Subscribed and sworn to before me this   31ˢᵗ   day of   March   , 1905

Dwight Brown
Notary Public.

## NEW-BORN AFFIDAVIT.

Number

### ...Choctaw Enrolling Commission...

IN THE MATTER OF THE APPLICATION FOR ENROLLMENT, as a citizen of the Choctaw   Nation, of   Ola[sic] Huggins

born on the   15   day of   March   190 3

Name of father   J J Huggins            a citizen of   ~~Choctaw~~  *White*
Nation final enrollment No. ——
Name of mother   Lula E Huggins      a citizen of   Choctaw
Nation final enrollment No. 10932

Postoffice   Utica I.T.

### AFFIDAVIT OF MOTHER.

UNITED STATES OF AMERICA
INDIAN TERRITORY
Central        DISTRICT

I   Lula E Huggins   , on oath state that I am 29   years of age and a citizen by   blood   of the   Choctaw   Nation, and as such have been placed upon the final roll of the   Choctaw   Nation, by the Honorable Secretary of the Interior my final enrollment number being   10932   ; that I am the lawful wife of   J J Huggins   , who is a citizen of the   Choctaw   Nation, and as such has been placed upon the final roll of said Nation by the Honorable Secretary of the Interior, his final enrollment number being   ——   and that a   Female   child was born to me on the 15ᵗʰ   day of   March   190 3; that said child has been named   Ola Huggins   , and is now living.

Lula E Huggins

2

# Applications for Enrollment of Choctaw Newborn
## Act of 1905   Volume XI

Witnesseth.

Must be two Witnesses who are Citizens. } Basil L Gardner
William Campbell

Subscribed and sworn to before me this  16  day of  Jan   190 5

W.A. Shoney
Notary Public.

My commission expires:  Jan 10, 1909

---

## *Affidavit of Attending Physician or Midwife*

UNITED STATES OF AMERICA,
INDIAN TERRITORY,
Central     DISTRICT }

I,    H. G. Goben    a    Physician on oath state that I attended on Mrs. Lula E Huggins   wife of   J J Huggins on the  15th  day of  March , 190 3, that there was born to her on said date a   female child, that said child is now living, and is said to have been named   Ola[sic] Huggins

H. G. Goben         M. D.

Subscribed and sworn to before me this the  23  day of  Jan   1905

Dwight Brown
Notary Public.

WITNESSETH:

Must be two witnesses who are citizens and know the child. { Basil L Gardner
William Campbell

We hereby certify that we are well acquainted with    H G Goben a   Physician    and know   him   to be reputable and of good standing in the community.

Must be two citizen witnesses. { Basil L Gardner
William Campbell

# Applications for Enrollment of Choctaw Newborn
## Act of 1905   Volume XI

Choc New Born 699
    Gabe George Parker   b. 4-19-04

                              Choctaw 1629.

              Muskogee, Indian Territory, April 10, 1905.

Gabriel E. Parker,
    Academy, Indian Territory.

Dear Sir:

    Receipt is hereby acknowledged of your letter of April 4, transmitting the affidavits of Louise E. Parker and B. C. Rutherford to the birth of Gabe George Parker, son of Gabriel E. and Louise E. Parker, April 19, 1904, and the same have been filed with our records as an application for the enrollment of said child.

    If further evidence is necessary to determine the right of this child to enrollment you will be notified and it will not be necessary for you to appear before the enrollment party of the Commission in the matter of the enrollment of this child unless you so desire.

                      Respectfully,

                                  Commissioner in Charge.

**BIRTH AFFIDAVIT.**

**DEPARTMENT OF THE INTERIOR.**
**COMMISSION TO THE FIVE CIVILIZED TRIBES.**

    **IN RE APPLICATION FOR ENROLLMENT**, as a citizen of the   Choctaw   Nation, of Gabe George Parker   , born on the 19th   day of Apr   , 1904

Name of Father: Gable E Parker          a citizen of the   Choctaw   Nation.
Name of Mother: Louise E Parker         a citizen of the   Choctaw   Nation.

                    Postoffice   Academy

**AFFIDAVIT OF MOTHER.**

UNITED STATES OF AMERICA, Indian Territory,  }
    Cent                    DISTRICT.

    I,   Louise E Parker   , on oath state that I am   24   years of age and a citizen by   Intermarriage   , of the   Choctaw   Nation; that I am the lawful wife of

## Applications for Enrollment of Choctaw Newborn
## Act of 1905   Volume XI

Gable E Parker, who is a citizen, by blood of the Choctaw Nation; that a male child was born to me on 19$^{th}$ day of April, 1904; that said child has been named Gabe George Parker, and was living March 4, 1905.

Louise E Parker

Witnesses To Mark:
{

Subscribed and sworn to before me this 31$^{st}$ day of Mch, 1905

B.W. Williams
Notary Public.

---

**AFFIDAVIT OF ATTENDING PHYSICIAN OR MID-WIFE.**

UNITED STATES OF AMERICA, Indian Territory,
Cent   DISTRICT.

I, B.C. Rutherford, a Physician, on oath state that I attended on Mrs. Louise E Parker, wife of Gable E Parker on the 19$^{th}$ day of April, 1904; that there was born to her on said date a Male child; that said child was living March 4, 1905, and is said to have been named Gabe George Parker

B.C. Rutherford M.D.

Witnesses To Mark:
{

Subscribed and sworn to before me this 31$^{st}$ day of Mch, 1905

B.W. Williams
Notary Public.

---

Choc New Born 700
  Pearl Verner  b. 6-28-04

## Applications for Enrollment of Choctaw Newborn
## Act of 1905   Volume XI

Choctaw 2371.

Muskogee, Indian Territory, April 10, 1905.

Frank Verner,
    Katie, Indian Territory.

Dear Sir:

    Receipt is hereby acknowledged of your letter of April 3, 1905, transmitting the affidavits of Nettie Verner and W. I. Reese to the birth of Pearl Verner, daughter of Frank and Nettie Verner, June 28, 1904, and the same have been filed with our records as an application for the enrollment of said child.

Respectfully,

Commissioner in Charge.

---

**COPY**

7 N. B. 700

Muskogee, Indian Territory, April 13, 1905.

Frank Verner,
    Katie, Indian Territory.

Dear Sir:

    There is inclosed you herewith for execution application for the enrollment of your infant child, Pearl Verner, born June 28, 1904.

    In having these affidavits executed care should be exercised to see that all names are written in full, as they appear in the body of the affidavit, and in the event that either of the persons signing the affidavit are unable to write, signatures by mark must be attested by two witnesses. Each affidavit must be executed before a Notary Public and the notarial seal and signature of the officer must be attached to each separate affidavit.

Respectfully,

*T. B. Needles.*

LM 13-32                SIGNED    Commissioner in Charge.

## Applications for Enrollment of Choctaw Newborn
## Act of 1905  Volume XI

7 NB 700

Muskogee, Indian Territory, May 5, 1905

Frank Verner,
    Katie, Indian Territory.

Dear Sir:

    Receipt is hereby acknowledged of the affidavits of Nettie Verner and W. I. Reese to the birth of Pearl Verner, daughter of Frank and Nettie Verner, June 28, 1904, and the same have been filed with our records as an application for the enrollment of said child.
    Respectfully,

Commissioner in Charge.

---

**BIRTH AFFIDAVIT.**

### DEPARTMENT OF THE INTERIOR.
### COMMISSION TO THE FIVE CIVILIZED TRIBES.

---

    IN RE APPLICATION FOR ENROLLMENT, as a citizen of the   Choctaw   Nation, of Indians[sic]   , born on the 28" day of  June  , 1904

Name of Father: Frank Verner    a citizen of the Chocktaw[sic]Nation.
Name of Mother: Nettie Verner    a citizen of the   Choctaw   Nation.

    Postoffice   Katie I.T.

---

**AFFIDAVIT OF MOTHER.**

UNITED STATES OF AMERICA, Indian Territory,  
    Southern    DISTRICT.

    I,   Nettie Verner   , on oath state that I am  25   years of age and a citizen by   Blood   , of the   Choctaw   Nation; that I am the lawful wife of   Frank Verner   , who is a citizen, by Marriage   of the   Choctaw   Nation; that a Female   child was born to me on  28" day of  June  , 1904; that said child has been named   Pearl Verner   , and was living March 4, 1905.

                                 her  
                        Nettie x Verner  
Witnesses To Mark:           mark  
    { R.N. Coffer  
      M.A. Fleming

# Applications for Enrollment of Choctaw Newborn
## Act of 1905   Volume XI

Subscribed and sworn to before me this  30" day of   March   , 1905

J T Fleming
Notary Public.
Southern Dist of I.T.
My Term of office Expires Jany 1909

---

**AFFIDAVIT OF ATTENDING PHYSICIAN OR MID-WIFE.**

UNITED STATES OF AMERICA, Indian Territory, }
  Southern       DISTRICT.  }

I,  W.I. Reese  , a  Physician  , on oath state that I attended on Mrs.  Frank Verner  , wife of  Frank Verner  on the  28  day of  June  , 1904; that there was born to her on said date a  Female  child; that said child was living March 4, 1905, and is said to have been named ...........

W.I. Reese M.D.

Witnesses To Mark:
{ (Name Illegible)
{ C.E. Lemons

Subscribed and sworn to before me this  31$^{st}$ day of  March   , 1905

J C Wishart
Notary Public.

---

BIRTH AFFIDAVIT.

**DEPARTMENT OF THE INTERIOR.**
## COMMISSION TO THE FIVE CIVILIZED TRIBES.

---

IN RE APPLICATION FOR ENROLLMENT, as a citizen of the   Choctaw   Nation, of  Pearl Verner  , born on the 28$^{th}$  day of  June  , 1904

Name of Father:  Frank Verner         a citizen of the   Choctaw   Nation.
Name of Mother:  Nettie Verner        a citizen of the   Choctaw   Nation.

Postoffice   Katie I.T.

# Applications for Enrollment of Choctaw Newborn
# Act of 1905 Volume XI

### AFFIDAVIT OF MOTHER.

UNITED STATES OF AMERICA, Indian Territory,
   Southern          DISTRICT.

    I,  Nettie Verner  , on oath state that I am  25  years of age and a citizen by  blood  , of the  Choctaw  Nation; that I am the lawful wife of  Frank Verner  , who is a citizen, by  ———  of the  United States Nation; that a female  child was born to me on  28$^{th}$  day of  June  , 1904; that said child has been named  Pearl Verner  , and was living March 4, 1905.

                                   her
                             Nettie x Verner
Witnesses To Mark:              mark
  { M.A. Fleming
    R.N. Coffer

    Subscribed and sworn to before me this  24"  day of  April  , 1905

                            J T Fleming
                            Notary Public.
            My Time Expires Jany 15 1909

---

### AFFIDAVIT OF ATTENDING PHYSICIAN OR MID-WIFE.

UNITED STATES OF AMERICA, Indian Territory,
..................................................... DISTRICT.

    I,  W.I. Reese  , a  ..............................., on oath state that I attended on Mrs.  Nettie Verner  , wife of  Frank Verner  on the  28$^{th}$  day of  June  , 1904; that there was born to her on said date a  Female  child; that said child was living March 4, 1905, and is said to have been named Pearl Verner

                            W.I. Reese M.D.
Witnesses To Mark:

  {

    Subscribed and sworn to before me this  19$^{th}$  day of  April  , 1905

                            J C Wishart
                            Notary Public.

# Applications for Enrollment of Choctaw Newborn
## Act of 1905   Volume XI

Choc New Born 701
    Ellenor Jane Wilson   b.  3-23-04

**NEW-BORN AFFIDAVIT.**

    Number..................

### ...Choctaw Enrolling Commission...

    IN THE MATTER OF THE APPLICATION FOR ENROLLMENT, as a citizen of the Choctaw     Nation, of     Elenor[sic] Jane Wilson

born on the  23  day of  March   190 4

Name of father    Raphael F Wilson     a citizen of    Choctaw
Nation final enrollment No.  14099
Name of mother    Emma J Wilson     a citizen of    Choctaw
Nation final enrollment No.  2608

           Postoffice    Valliant I T

**AFFIDAVIT OF MOTHER.**

UNITED STATES OF AMERICA
INDIAN TERRITORY
   Central      DISTRICT

       I    Emma J Wilson            , on oath state that I am  28  years of age and a citizen by  blood  of the  Choctaw  Nation, and as such have been placed upon the final roll of the  Choctaw  Nation, by the Honorable Secretary of the Interior my final enrollment number being  2608 ; that I am the lawful wife of  Raphael F Wilson  , who is a citizen of the  Choctaw  Nation, and as such has been placed upon the final roll of said Nation by the Honorable Secretary of the Interior, his final enrollment number being  14099  and that a  female  child was born to me on the  23$^{rd}$  day of  March  190 4; that said child has been named  Elenor Jane Wilson  , and is now living.

                           Emma J Wilson

Witnesseth.
   Must be two  ⎱   EB Herndon
   Witnesses who ⎰
   are Citizens.     D A Fowler

     Subscribed and sworn to before me this  24$^{th}$  day of  Feb  190 5

                         W A Shoney
                               Notary Public.

My commission expires:  Jan 10 1909

# Applications for Enrollment of Choctaw Newborn
## Act of 1905   Volume XI

## AFFIDAVIT OF ATTENDING PHYSICIAN OR MIDWIFE

UNITED STATES OF AMERICA
INDIAN TERRITORY
 Central   DISTRICT

I, M A Lowder a midwife on oath state that I attended on Mrs. Emma J Wilson wife of Raphael F Wilson on the $23^{rd}$ day of March, 190 4, that there was born to her on said date a female child, that said child is now living, and is said to have been named Elenor Jane Wilson

M A Lowder   ~~M.D.~~

WITNESSETH:
Must be two witnesses who are citizens and know the child.
 { EB Herndon
   D A Fowler

Subscribed and sworn to before me this, the 24 day of Feb 190 5

W A Shoney   Notary Public.

We hereby certify that we are well acquainted with M A Lowder a midwife and know her to be reputable and of good standing in the community.

EB Herndon
D A Fowler

BIRTH AFFIDAVIT.

## DEPARTMENT OF THE INTERIOR.
## COMMISSION TO THE FIVE CIVILIZED TRIBES.

IN RE APPLICATION FOR ENROLLMENT, as a citizen of the Choctaw Nation, of Ellenor Jane Wilson, born on the $23^{rd}$ day of March, 1904

Name of Father: Raphael F Wilson   a citizen of the Choctaw Nation.
Name of Mother: Emma J Wilson   a citizen of the Choctaw Nation.

Postoffice   Valliant   I.T.

# Applications for Enrollment of Choctaw Newborn
## Act of 1905   Volume XI

### AFFIDAVIT OF MOTHER.

UNITED STATES OF AMERICA, Indian Territory,  
Central DISTRICT.

I, Emma J Wilson, on oath state that I am 28 years of age and a citizen by blood, of the Choctaw Nation; that I am the lawful wife of Raphael F Wilson, who is a citizen, by blood of the Choctaw Nation; that a female child was born to me on 23rd day of March, 1904; that said child has been named Ellenor Jane Wilson, and was living March 4, 1905.

Emma J Wilson

Witnesses To Mark:

Subscribed and sworn to before me this 27th day of March, 1905

(Name Illegible)<br>Notary Public.

---

### AFFIDAVIT OF ATTENDING PHYSICIAN OR MID-WIFE.

UNITED STATES OF AMERICA, Indian Territory,  
Central DISTRICT.

I, M A Lowder, a midwife, on oath state that I attended on Mrs. Emma J Wilson, wife of Raphael F Wilson on the 23rd day of March, 1904; that there was born to her on said date a female child; that said child was living March 4, 1905, and is said to have been named Ellenor Jane Wilson

M.A. Lowder

Witnesses To Mark:

Subscribed and sworn to before me this 27th day of March, 1905

(Name Illegible)<br>Notary Public.

---

Choc New Born 702  
    John Walton Patterson   b. 12-4-03

# Applications for Enrollment of Choctaw Newborn
## Act of 1905 Volume XI

BIRTH AFFIDAVIT.    No 22

**IN RE-APPLICATION FOR ENROLLMENT**, as a citizen of the Choctaw Nation, of John Walton Patterson, born on the 4th day of December, 1903

Name of Father: Walton Patterson    a citizen of the Choctaw Nation.
Name of Mother: Martha J Patterson    a citizen of the Choctaw Nation.

Postoffice    Ryan I. T.

### AFFIDAVIT OF MOTHER.

UNITED STATES OF AMERICA, INDIAN TERRITORY, }
Southern    District.

I, Martha J. Patterson, on oath state that I am 35 years of age and a citizen by intermarriage, of the Choctaw Nation; that I am the lawful wife of Walton Patterson, who is a citizen, by Blood of the Choctaw Nation; that a male child was born to me on 4th day of Dec., 1903, that said child has been named John Walton Patterson, and is now living.

Martha J Patterson

Witnesses To Mark:

Subscribed and sworn to before me this 11th day of Febry, 1905.

Cham Jones
Notary Public.

### AFFIDAVIT OF ATTENDING PHYSICIAN OR MID-WIFE.

UNITED STATES OF AMERICA, INDIAN TERRITORY, }
Southern    District.

I, S. K. Montgomery, a practicing Physician, on oath state that I attended on Mrs. Martha J Patterson, wife of Walton Patterson on the 4th day of Dec., 1903; that there was born to her on said date a male child; that said child is now living and is said to have been named John Walton Patterson

S.K. Montgomery M.D.

Witnesses To Mark:

# Applications for Enrollment of Choctaw Newborn
## Act of 1905   Volume XI

Subscribed and sworn to before me this   11th   day of   Feby 1905   , 190......

Cham Jones<br>
Notary Public.

---

In re. application for enrollment, as a citizen of the   Choctaw   Nation of   John Walton Patterson   born on the   4$^{th}$   day of   Dec   190 3.

Name of father   Walton Patterson   a citizen of the   Choctaw   Nation.
Name of mother   Martha J Patterson   citizen of the   Choctaw Nation.

Post Office.   Ryan   Ind. Ter.

Affidavit of mother.

UNITED STATES OF AMERICA.

Indian Territory
              SS.
Southern District.

    I,   Martha J Patterson   on oath state that I am   35   years of age and a citizen by   marriage   of the   Choctaw   Nation; That I am the lawful wife of   Walton Patterson   who is a citizen, by   blood   of the   Choctaw   Nation, That a   male   child was born to me on the   4   day of   Dec   190 3. That said child has been named John Walton Patterson   and is now living.

signed,   Martha J Patterson

Subscribed an sworn to before me this   29   day of   March   190 5

Cham Jones<br>Notary Public.

AFFIDAVIT OF ATTENDING PHYSICIAN OR MIDWIFE.

United States of America,
Indian Territory, Southern District, SS.

    I,   S.K. Montgomery   a   Physician   on oath state that attended Mrs.   Martha J Patterson   wife of the[sic]   Walton Patterson   on the   4   day of   Dec   190 3 that there was born to her on said date a   male   child; That said child is now living and is said to have been named   John Walton Patterson

signed,   S.K. Montgomery M.D.

## Applications for Enrollment of Choctaw Newborn
## Act of 1905 Volume XI

Subscribed and sworn to before me this 29 day of March 190 5

Cham Jones<br>Notary Public.

My commission expires Oct 28$^{th}$ 1905

---

Choctaw 2857.

Muskogee, Indian Territory, April 10, 1905.

Walton Patterson,
    Ryan, Indian Territory.

Dear Sir:

    Receipt is hereby acknowledged if the affidavits of Martha J. Patterson and S. K. Montgomery to the birth of John Walton Patterson, son of Walton and Martha J. Patterson, December 4, 1905, and the same have been filed with our records as an application for the enrollment of said child.

Respectfully,

Commissioner in Charge.

---

Choc New Born 703
    Willis Franklin Beal  b. 1-30-03

---

**BIRTH AFFIDAVIT.**

**DEPARTMENT OF THE INTERIOR.**

**COMMISSION TO THE FIVE CIVILIZED TRIBES.**

---

    IN RE APPLICATION FOR ENROLLMENT, as a citizen of the   Choctaw   Nation, of Willis Franklin Beal   , born on the  30  day of  January  , 1903

Name of Father:  George Beal      a citizen of the  Choctaw  Nation.
Name of Mother:  Ada Beal      a citizen of the United States Nation.

Postoffice   Silo, Ind. Ter.

## Applications for Enrollment of Choctaw Newborn
## Act of 1905   Volume XI

**AFFIDAVIT OF MOTHER.**

UNITED STATES OF AMERICA, Indian Territory, }
 Central          DISTRICT.           }

    I,   Ada Beal   , on oath state that I am   24   years of age and a citizen by   Birth  , of the   United States   Nation; that I am the lawful wife of   George Beal , who is a citizen, by Blood   of the   Choctaw   Nation; that a   male   child was born to me on   thirtieth   day of   January   , 1903; that said child has been named   Willis Franklin Beal   , and was living March 4, 1905.

                                        Ada Beal

Witnesses To Mark:
{

    Subscribed and sworn to before me this   3rd   day of   April   , 1905

                                        Luther D Davis
                                        Notary Public.

---

**AFFIDAVIT OF ATTENDING ~~PHYSICIAN OR MID-WIFE.~~   WITNESSES**

UNITED STATES OF AMERICA, Indian Territory, }
 Central          DISTRICT.           }

                                                            we were with
~~I,~~   We (Mrs)N.M. Wingate & (Mrs) D.E. Beal   , on oath state that ~~I attended on~~ Mrs.   Ada Beal   , wife of   George Beal   on the   30   day of   January   , 1903; that there was born to her on said date a   male   child; that said child was living March 4, 1905, and is said to have been named   Willis Franklin Beal

                                        N M Wingate

Witnesses To Mark:                    D E Beal
{

    Subscribed and sworn to before me this   3rd   day of   April   , 1905

                                        Luther D Davis
                                        Notary Public.

## Applications for Enrollment of Choctaw Newborn
## Act of 1905 Volume XI

Choc New Born 704
    Buster Brashears b. 1-8-03
    Viola Brashears b. 10-20-04

---

7-NB-704

Muskogee, Indian Territory, August 12, 1905.

Chief Clerk,
    Choctaw Land Office,
        Atoka, Indian Territory.

Dear Sir:

    Receipt is hereby acknowledged of your letter of August 3, 1905, referring to Choctaw NB card number 704, Buster Brashears et al., in which you state that the name of the father of these children appears on the duplicate card in your office as Fadias Brashears Choctaw roll number 5378 and you ask if the name of the father of said children should not appear as Tobias Brashears.

    In reply to your letter you are advised that the name of the father of Buster and Viola Brashears on Choctaw NB card No. 704 appears upon the original card in this office as Tobias Brashears and the duplicate care in your office should be corrected to conform to the original.

                            Respectfully,

                            Acting Commissioner.

---

**BIRTH AFFIDAVIT.**
### DEPARTMENT OF THE INTERIOR.
### COMMISSION TO THE FIVE CIVILIZED TRIBES.

---

    **IN RE APPLICATION FOR ENROLLMENT**, as a citizen of the     Choctaw     Nation, of Buster Brashears    , born on the   8th   day of   January  , 1903

Name of Father: Tobias Brashears      a citizen of the   Choctaw   Nation.
Name of Mother: Bessie Brashears      a citizen of the   -----------   Nation.

                      Postoffice     Quinton, Indian Territory.

# Applications for Enrollment of Choctaw Newborn
## Act of 1905   Volume XI

**AFFIDAVIT OF MOTHER.**

UNITED STATES OF AMERICA, Indian Territory, }
Western   DISTRICT.

I, Bessie Brashears, on oath state that I am 25 years of age and a citizen by ------------- , of the --------------- Nation; that I am the lawful wife of Tobias Brashears, who is a citizen, by blood of the Choctaw Nation; that a Male child was born to me on 8th day of January, 1903; that said child has been named Buster Brashears, and was living March 4, 1905.

Bessie Brashears

Witnesses To Mark:
{

Subscribed and sworn to before me this 29th day of March, 1905

My Commission expires
Apr 27 - 1907

Guy A Curry
Notary Public.

---

**AFFIDAVIT OF ATTENDING PHYSICIAN OR MID-WIFE.**

UNITED STATES OF AMERICA, Indian Territory, }
Central   DISTRICT.

I, C. H. Mahar, a physician, on oath state that I attended on Mrs. Bessie Brashears, wife of Tobias Brashears on the 8th day of January, 1903; that there was born to her on said date a Male child; that said child was living March 4, 1905, and is said to have been named Buster Brashears

Charles H Mahar M.D.

Witnesses To Mark:
{

Subscribed and sworn to before me this 31st day of March, 1905

Wirt Franklin
Notary Public.

## Applications for Enrollment of Choctaw Newborn
## Act of 1905   Volume XI

BIRTH AFFIDAVIT.

### DEPARTMENT OF THE INTERIOR.
### COMMISSION TO THE FIVE CIVILIZED TRIBES.

IN RE APPLICATION FOR ENROLLMENT, as a citizen of the Choctaw Nation, of Viola Brashears , born on the 29th day of October , 1904

Name of Father: Tobias Brashears        a citizen of the Choctaw Nation.
Name of Mother: Bessie Brashears         a citizen of the ----------- Nation.

Postoffice   Quinton

**AFFIDAVIT OF MOTHER.**

UNITED STATES OF AMERICA, Indian Territory, }
    Western          DISTRICT.

I, Bessie Brashears , on oath state that I am 25 years of age and a citizen by -------------- , of the --------------- Nation; that I am the lawful wife of Tobias Brashears , who is a citizen, by blood of the Choctaw Nation; that a Female child was born to me on 29th day of October , 1904; that said child has been named Viola Brashears , and was living March 4, 1905.

Bessie Brashears

Witnesses To Mark:
{

Subscribed and sworn to before me this 29th day of March , 1905

My Commission expires              Guy A Curry
Apr 27 - 1907                         Notary Public.

**AFFIDAVIT OF ATTENDING PHYSICIAN OR MID-WIFE.**

UNITED STATES OF AMERICA, Indian Territory, }
    Central          DISTRICT.

I, C. H. Mahar , a physician , on oath state that I attended on Mrs. Bessie Brashears , wife of Tobias Brashears on the 29th day of October , 1904; that there was born to her on said date a Female child; that said child was living March 4, 1905, and is said to have been named Viola Brashears

Charles H Mahar M.D.

Witnesses To Mark:
{

## Applications for Enrollment of Choctaw Newborn
## Act of 1905   Volume XI

Subscribed and sworn to before me this 31st day of March, 1905

Wirt Franklin<br>Notary Public.

---

<u>Choc New Born 705</u>
    Ole Johnico   b. 5-19-03

7-NB-705.

Muskogee, Indian Territory, May 29, 1905.

John Johnico,
    Panama, Indian Territory.

Dear Sir:

    Referring to the application for the enrollment of your infant child, Ole Johnico, born May 19, 1903, it is noted from the testimony taken on the 4th ultimo that the mother of the applicant is dead.

    In this event it will be necessary for you to file in this office the affidavits of two parties, who are disinterested and not related to the applicant, who have actual knowledge of the facts that the child was born, the date of her birth; that she was living on March 4, 1905, and that Lucy Johnico was her mother.

Respectfully,

Chairman.

# Applications for Enrollment of Choctaw Newborn
## Act of 1905   Volume XI

Choctaw N B 705

Muskogee, Indian Territory, June 28, 1905.

John Johnico,
    Panama, Indian Territory.

Dear Sir:

    Receipt is hereby acknowledged of the affidavit of Maleunine Honubee to the birth of Ole Johnico, daughter of John and Lucy Johnico, May 19, 1903, and the same has been filed with the record in the matter of the enrollment of said child.

        Respectfully,

            Chairman.

---

7-NB-705

Muskogee, Indian Territory, August 5, 1905.

John Johnico,
    Panama, Indian Territory.

Dear Sir:

    Receipt is hereby acknowledged of your letter of July 17, 1905, in which you ask about filing on land for your daughter Ole Johnico.

    In reply to your letter you are advised that the name of your child Ole Johnico has been placed upon a schedule of citizens by blood of the Choctaw Nation which has been forwarded the Secretary of the Interior and you will be notified when her enrollment is approved by the Department.

    You are further advised that pending the approval of her enrollment no selection of allotment can be made for said child.

        Respectfully,

            Commissioner.

## Applications for Enrollment of Choctaw Newborn
## Act of 1905 Volume XI

BIRTH AFFIDAVIT.

## Department of the Interior,
#### COMMISSION TO THE FIVE CIVILIZED TRIBES.

IN RE APPLICATION FOR ENROLLMENT, as a citizen of the Choctaw Nation, of Ole , born on the 19 day of May , 190 3

Name of Father:   John Johnico     a citizen of the   Choctaw   Nation.
Name of Mother:   Lucy Johnico     a citizen of the   Choctaw   Nation.

Post-Office:   Panama I.T.

AFFIDAVIT OF MOTHER.

UNITED STATES OF AMERICA,
  INDIAN TERRITORY,
  Central    District.

I, _____ Lucy Johnico _____ state that I am _____ years of age and a citizen by _____, of the _____ Died July 24th 1903 _____ Nation; that I am the lawful wife of _____, who is a citizen by _____ of the _____ Nation; that a _____ child was born to me on _____ day of _____, 190_, that said child has been named _____, and is now living.

WITNESSES TO MARK:
  S.W. James
  Jesse Tecumseh

Subscribed and sworn to before me this  20   day of   June  , 190 5

                              Jno H. Goodnight
                                  *Notary Public.*

AFFIDAVIT OF ATTENDING PHYSICIAN OR MID-WIFE.

UNITED STATES OF AMERICA,
  INDIAN TERRITORY,
  _____ District.

I, Malenunine[sic] Honoba[sic] , a Midwife , on oath state that I attended on Mrs.  Lucy Johnico  , wife of  John Johnico   on the  19 day of  May  , 190 3; that there was born to her on said date a  Female   child; that said child is now living and is said to have been named  Ole Johnico

                              Maleunine Honubbee

WITNESSES TO MARK:
  Jesse Tecumseh

Applications for Enrollment of Choctaw Newborn
Act of 1905 Volume XI

Subscribed and sworn to before me this 22 day of June , 1905

Jno. H. Goodnight
*Notary Public.*
My commission expires Jan 19th 1908

# NEW BORN AFFIDAVIT

No ............

## CHOCTAW ENROLLING COMMISSION

IN THE MATTER OF THE APPLICATION FOR ENROLLMENT as a citizen of the Choctaw Nation, of   Ole Johnico   born on the 19 day of May 1903

Name of father   John Johnico   a citizen of   Choctaw   Nation, final enrollment No. 7738

Name of mother   Lucy Johnico (deceased)   a citizen of   Choctaw   Nation, final enrollment No. 7781

Panama I.T.   Postoffice.

**AFFIDAVIT OF MOTHER**

UNITED STATES OF AMERICA
INDIAN TERRITORY
DISTRICT   Central

I Lucy Johnico (deceased)   , on oath state that I am 26   years of age and a citizen by   blood   of the   Choctaw   Nation, and as such have been placed upon the final roll of the   Choctaw   Nation, by the Honorable Secretary of the Interior my final enrollment number being 7781   ; that I am the lawful wife of   John Johnico   , who is a citizen of the   Choctaw   Nation, and as such has been placed upon the final roll of said Nation by the Honorable Secretary of the Interior, his final enrollment number being   7738   and that a   female   child was born to me on the 19 day of May 1903; that said child has been named Ole Johnico   , and is now living.

WITNESSETH:
 Must be two witnesses { Houston Tecumseh
 who are citizens    { W. Watkins

Locay[sic] Johnico (deceased)
by John Johnico

## Applications for Enrollment of Choctaw Newborn
## Act of 1905  Volume XI

Subscribed and sworn to before me this, the 6 day of February, 190 5

James Bower
Notary Public.

My Commission Expires:
Sept 23-1907

---

*Affidavit of Attending Physician or Midwife*

UNITED STATES OF AMERICA,
INDIAN TERRITORY,
Central   DISTRICT

I, Fanine[sic] Honobbee a midwife on oath state that I attended on Mrs. Lucy Johnico wife of John Johnico on the 19 day of May, 190 3, that there was born to her on said date a female child, that said child is now living, and is said to have been named Ole Johnico

Fanny Hounebby[sic]   M. D.

Subscribed and sworn to before me this the 6 day of February 1905

James Bower
Notary Public.

WITNESSETH:

Must be two witnesses who are citizens and know the child. { Houston Tecumseh
W. Watkins

We hereby certify that we are well acquainted with Fannie Honobbee a midwife and know her to be reputable and of good standing in the community.

Must be two citizen witnesses. { Houston Tecumseh
W. Watkins

# Applications for Enrollment of Choctaw Newborn
## Act of 1905   Volume XI

7-7738.

DEPARTMENT OF THE INTERIOR,
COMMISSION TO THE FIVE CIVILIZED TRIBES.
BOKOSHE, INDIAN TERRITORY  APRIL 4, 1905.

In the matter of the application for the enrollment of Ole Johnico as a citizen by blood of the Choctaw Nation.

John Johnico being first duly sworn testifies as follows:

EXAMINATION BY THE COMMISSION:

Q What is your name? A John Johnico.
Q What is your age? A Forty-four.
Q What is your post office address? A Panama.
Q Have you this day made application for your minor child Ole Johnico? A Yes, sir.
Q When was this child born? A 19th of May 1903.
Q Who is the mother of that child? A Lucy Johnico.
Q When did she die? A Last July 1903.
Q She died two or three months after the baby was born? A Yes, sir.
Q Have you made proof of death of the mother of this child? A Yes, sir.
Q This child for whom you have made application today is living? A Yes, sir.

Witness excused.

Dora Sockey being sworn and examined through Loren Cobb interpreter testifies as follows:

EXAMINATION BY THE COMMISSION:

Q What is your name? A Dora Sockey.
Q What is your age? A Twenty-five.
Q What is your post office address? A Panama.
Q Were you acquainted with Lucy Johnico the mother of Ole Johnico for whom application has been made today? A Yes, sir.
Q When was this child Ole Johnico born? A 19th day of May 1903.
Q Is Lucy Johnico living at this time? A No, sir.
Q When did she die? A July 1903.
Q Are you now the wife of John Johnico? A Yes, sir.
Q When did you marry him? A Last March 1904.

Witness excused

Chas. T. Difendafer being first duly sworn states that the above and foregoing is a full, true and correct transcript of his stenographic notes taken in said cause on said date.

Chas. T. Difendafer

# Applications for Enrollment of Choctaw Newborn
## Act of 1905   Volume XI

Subscribed and sworn to before me this 4th day of April 1905.

OL Johnson
Notary Public.

BIRTH AFFIDAVIT.

## DEPARTMENT OF THE INTERIOR.
## COMMISSION TO THE FIVE CIVILIZED TRIBES.

IN RE APPLICATION FOR ENROLLMENT, as a citizen of the     Choctaw     Nation, of          , born on the      day of      , 190

Name of Father:     a citizen of the     Choctaw Nation.
Name of Mother:     a citizen of the     Choctaw Nation.

Postoffice

### AFFIDAVIT OF MOTHER.

UNITED STATES OF AMERICA, Indian Territory,
                                        DISTRICT.

I, _____, on oath state that I am _____ years of age and a citizen by _____, of the _See Testimony_ Nation; that I am the lawful wife of _____, who is a citizen, by _____ of the _____ Nation; that a _____ child was born to me on _____ day of _____, 1___, that said child has been named _____, and was living March 4, 1905.

Witnesses To Mark:

Subscribed and sworn to before me this _____ day of _____, 190___.

Notary Public.

## Applications for Enrollment of Choctaw Newborn
## Act of 1905   Volume XI

**AFFIDAVIT OF ATTENDING PHYSICIAN OR MID-WIFE.**

UNITED STATES OF AMERICA, Indian Territory, }
................................................DISTRICT. }

    I, Melvina[sic] Homubbee[sic] , a midwife , on oath state that I attended on Mrs. Lucy Johnico (deceased) , wife of John Johnico on the 19 day of May , 1903; that there was born to her on said date a female child; that said child was living March 4, 1905, and is said to have been named Ole Johnico

                                      her
                              Melvina x Honubbee
Witnesses To Mark:                      mark
  { Chas. T. Difendafer
  { OL Johnson

    Subscribed and sworn to before me this 4$^{th}$ day of April , 1905

                              OL Johnson
                              Notary Public.

---

<u>Choc New Born 706</u>
    James Otto Parrish   b. 3-19-03

                                            7-3915
             Muskogee, Indian Territory, April 11, 1905.

Ramson Parish[sic],
    Bokchito, Indian Territory.
Dear Sir:

    Receipt is hereby acknowledged of the affidavits of Bethena Parish and Phoeba Labors to the birth of James Otto Parish son of Ramson and Bethena Parish, March 19, 1903, and the same have been filed with our records as an application for the enrollment of said child.

                        Respectfully,

                              Commissioner in Charge.

Applications for Enrollment of Choctaw Newborn
Act of 1905   Volume XI

**NEW-BORN AFFIDAVIT.**

Number..............

## Choctaw Enrolling Commission.

IN THE MATTER OF THE APPLICATION FOR ENROLLMENT, as a citizen of the Choctaw Nation, of  James Ottis[sic] Parrish

born on the  19  day of  March   190 -3

Name of father   Ransom Parrish          a citizen of   Choctaw   Nation final enrollment No ———
Name of mother  Bethena Parrish         a citizen of   Choctaw   Nation final enrollment No  11004

Postoffice   Bokochito[sic] I.T.

**AFFIDAVIT OF MOTHER.**

UNITED STATES OF AMERICA,  
   INDIAN TERRITORY,  
  Central   DISTRICT

I   Bethena Parrish   on oath state that I am  20  years of age and a citizen by  blood  of the  Choctaw  Nation, and as such have been placed upon the final roll of the  Choctaw  Nation, by the Honorable Secretary of the Interior my final enrollment number being   11004   ; that I am the lawful wife of Ransom Parrish  , who is a citizen of the  white  Nation, and as such has been placed upon the final roll of said Nation by the Honorable Secretary of the Interior, his final enrollment number being ——  and that a  male  child was born to me on the  19  day of  March   190 3 ; that said child has been named  James Ottis[sic] Parrish , and is now living.

    Bethana[sic] Parrish

WITNESSETH:
Must be two  ⎫   Wm Labor
Witnesses who ⎬
are Citizens.    ⎭   AB Pusley

Subscribed and sworn to before me this   16   day of   January    190 5

    James Bower
        Notary Public.

My commission expires
  Sept 23 - 1907

## Applications for Enrollment of Choctaw Newborn
## Act of 1905 Volume XI

### *Affidavit of Attending Physician or Midwife*

UNITED STATES OF AMERICA,
INDIAN TERRITORY,
Central   DISTRICT

I,   P. L. Cain   a   Practicing Physician on oath state that I attended on Mrs. Bethena Parrish   wife of Ransom[sic] Parrish on the   19   day of   March   , 190 3, that there was born to her on said date a   male   child, that said child is now living, and is said to have been named   James Ottis[sic] Parrish

P.L. Cain   M. D.

Subscribed and sworn to before me this the   18   day of   January   1905

J.M. Reasor
Notary Public.

WITNESSETH:

Must be two witnesses who are citizens and know the child.   Nora Bybee
*(Name Illegible)*

We hereby certify that we are well acquainted with   P.L. Cain a   Physician   and know   him   to be reputable and of good standing in the community.

Must be two citizen witnesses.   Nora Bybee
Pheby Labor

BIRTH AFFIDAVIT.

### DEPARTMENT OF THE INTERIOR.
### COMMISSION TO THE FIVE CIVILIZED TRIBES.

IN RE APPLICATION FOR ENROLLMENT, as a citizen of the   Choctaw   Nation, of James Otto Parish   , born on the   19 day of March   , 1903

Name of Father:  Ramson Parish         a citizen of the   U. S.   Nation.
Name of Mother:  Bethena Parish        a citizen of the   Choctaw   Nation.

Postoffice   Bokchito I.T.

# Applications for Enrollment of Choctaw Newborn
## Act of 1905  Volume XI

**AFFIDAVIT OF MOTHER.**

UNITED STATES OF AMERICA, Indian Territory, }
Central        DISTRICT.

I, Bethena Parish, on oath state that I am 20 years of age and a citizen by Blood, of the Choctaw Nation; that I am the lawful wife of Ransom Parish, who is a ~~citizen, of~~ U S of the United States Nation; that a Male child was born to me on 19 day of March, 1903; that said child has been named James Otto parish, and was living March 4, 1905.

Bethena Parrish[sic]

Witnesses To Mark:
{

Subscribed and sworn to before me this 4 day of April, 1905

F A McAllen
Notary Public.

---

**AFFIDAVIT OF ATTENDING PHYSICIAN OR MID-WIFE.**

UNITED STATES OF AMERICA, Indian Territory, }
Central        DISTRICT.

I, Phoeba Labors, a Midwife, on oath state that I attended on Mrs. Bethena Parish, wife of Ransom Parish on the 19 day of March, 1903; that there was born to her on said date a Male child; that said child was living March 4, 1905, and is said to have been named James Otto Parish

her
Phoeba x Labors
mark

Witnesses To Mark:
{ J B Lloyd
{ F.F. Long

Subscribed and sworn to before me this 4 day of April, 1905

F A McAllen
Notary Public.

## Applications for Enrollment of Choctaw Newborn
## Act of 1905 Volume XI

Choc New Born 707
    Everet Lee Medell  b. 5-5-03

BIRTH AFFIDAVIT.

### DEPARTMENT OF THE INTERIOR.
### COMMISSION TO THE FIVE CIVILIZED TRIBES.

IN RE APPLICATION FOR ENROLLMENT, as a citizen of the Choctaw Nation, of Everet Lee Medell, born on the $5^{th}$ day of May, 1903

Name of Father: Albert Medell     a citizen of the Choctaw Nation.
Name of Mother: Lula Medell     a citizen of the Choctaw Nation.

    Postoffice  Bennington I.T.

**AFFIDAVIT OF MOTHER.**

UNITED STATES OF AMERICA, Indian Territory,
    Central      DISTRICT.

    I, Lula Medell, on oath state that I am 19 years of age and a citizen by Blood, of the Choctaw Nation; that I am the lawful wife of Albert Medell, who is a citizen, by intermarried of the Choctaw Nation; that a Boy child was born to me on $5^{th}$ day of May, 1903; that said child has been named Everet Lee Medell, and was living March 4, 1905.

                                         Lula Medell

Witnesses To Mark:
{

    Subscribed and sworn to before me this $4^{th}$ day of Apr, 1905

                                    J W Lloyd
                                    Notary Public.

**AFFIDAVIT OF ATTENDING PHYSICIAN OR MID-WIFE.**

UNITED STATES OF AMERICA, Indian Territory,
    Central      DISTRICT.

    I, Emerline Betts, a Mid Wife, on oath state that I attended on Mrs. Lula Medell, wife of Albert Medell on the $5^{th}$ day of May, 1903; that there was born to her on said date a Boy child; that said child was living March 4, 1905, and is said to have been named Everet Lee Medell

## Applications for Enrollment of Choctaw Newborn
## Act of 1905   Volume XI

                                                                her
                                        Emerline x Betts

Witnesses To Mark:                       mark
  { J. V. Meadows
    Joe Lloyd

Subscribed and sworn to before me this 4$^{th}$ day of   Apr   , 1905

                                        JW Lloyd
                                              Notary Public.

---

<u>Choc New Born 708</u>
    Ocia Babb   b. 6-4-04

                                                        Choctaw 4553.

                        Muskogee, Indian Territory, April 10, 1905.

G. L. Babb,
    Nep, Arkansas.

Dear Sir:

    Receipt is hereby acknowledged of the affidavits of Belzora Babb and Amanda Babb to the birth of Ocie[sic] Babb, daughter of G. L. and Belzora Babb, June 4, 1904, and the same have been filed with our records as an application for the enrollment of said child.

                                        Respectfully,

                                                    Commissioner in Charge.

Applications for Enrollment of Choctaw Newborn
Act of 1905 Volume XI

# NEW BORN AFFIDAVIT

No ............

## CHOCTAW ENROLLING COMMISSION

IN THE MATTER OF THE APPLICATION FOR ENROLLMENT as a citizen of the Choctaw Nation, of Ocia Babb born on the 4 day of June 190 4

Name of father G. L. Babb a citizen of Non Nation, final enrollment No. ——
Name of mother Bele Zora[sic] Babb a citizen of Choctaw Nation, final enrollment No. 12611

Nep. Ark. Postoffice.

### AFFIDAVIT OF MOTHER

UNITED STATES OF AMERICA  
INDIAN TERRITORY  
DISTRICT    Central

I    Belzora Babb    , on oath state that I am  18   years of age and a citizen by   blood   of the   Choctaw   Nation, and as such have been placed upon the final roll of the  Choctaw   Nation, by the Honorable Secretary of the Interior my final enrollment number being  12611  ; that I am the lawful wife of   G. L. Babb   , who is a citizen of the   non   Nation, and as such has been placed upon the final roll of said Nation by the Honorable Secretary of the Interior, his final enrollment number being  ——  and that a   female   child was born to me on the   4   day of  June   190 4; that said child has been named   Ocia Babb   , and is now living.

WITNESSETH:                                    Bellzora[sic] Babb
  Must be two witnesses { W.C. Pickens
  who are citizens      { J.L. Pickens

Subscribed and sworn to before me this, the  16  day of  February  , 190 5

                                      James Bower
                                      Notary Public.
My Commission Expires:
    Sept 23-1907

## Applications for Enrollment of Choctaw Newborn
## Act of 1905   Volume XI

### *Affidavit of Attending Physician or Midwife*

UNITED STATES OF AMERICA,
   INDIAN TERRITORY,
Central       DISTRICT

I,   M E M<sup>c</sup>Manus   a   Midwife on oath state that I attended on Mrs. Belzora Babb   wife of  G.L. Babb on the  4   day of  June , 190 4, that there was born to her on said date a   female   child, that said child is now living, and is said to have been named   Ocia Babb

Witness to signature
a L Mathies

M.E. M<sup>c</sup>Manus     M.i D.wife

Subscribed and sworn to before me this the   17<sup>th</sup>   day of   February   1905

C.C. Mathies
Notary Public.

WITNESSETH:
Must be two witnesses who are citizens and know the child.   { W.C. Pickens
                                                                J.L. Pickens

We hereby certify that we are well acquainted with   M E M<sup>c</sup>Manus   a   midwife   and know   her   to be reputable and of good standing in the community.

Must be two citizen witnesses.   { W.C. Pickens
                                   J. L. Pickens

BIRTH AFFIDAVIT.

### DEPARTMENT OF THE INTERIOR.
### COMMISSION TO THE FIVE CIVILIZED TRIBES.

IN RE APPLICATION FOR ENROLLMENT, as a citizen of the   Choctaw   Nation, of Ocie Babb   , born on the  4th  day of  June , 1904

Name of Father: G.L. Babb            a citizen of the United States ~~Nation~~
Name of Mother: Belzora Babb         a citizen of the  Choctaw  Nation.

Postoffice   Nep, Arkansas

## Applications for Enrollment of Choctaw Newborn
## Act of 1905 Volume XI

**AFFIDAVIT OF MOTHER.**

UNITED STATES OF AMERICA, Indian Territory, }
Central  DISTRICT.

I, Belzora Babb, on oath state that I am 18 years of age and a citizen by blood, of the Choctaw Nation; that I am the lawful wife of G L Babb, who is a citizen, ~~by~~ ............ of the United States ~~Nation~~; that a female child was born to me on 4$^{th}$ day of June, 1904; that said child has been named Ocie Babb, and was living March 4, 1905.

Belzora Babb

Witnesses To Mark:
{

Subscribed and sworn to before me this 31st day of March, 1905

Wirt Franklin
Notary Public.

---

**AFFIDAVIT OF ATTENDING PHYSICIAN OR MID-WIFE.**

~~UNITED STATES OF AMERICA, Indian Territory,~~ }
State of Arkansas  ~~DISTRICT.~~
County of Sebastian

I, Amanda Babb, a mid-wife, on oath state that I attended on Mrs. Belzora Babb, wife of G L Babb on the 4th day of June, 1904; that there was born to her on said date a female child; that said child was living March 4, 1905, and is said to have been named Ocie Babb

Amanda Babb

Witnesses To Mark:
{

Subscribed and sworn to before me this 3d day of April, 1905

Albert L Little
my commission   Notary Public.
expires Nov 19, 1908

## Applications for Enrollment of Choctaw Newborn
## Act of 1905  Volume XI

Choc New Born 709
    Adams[sic] Christy  b. 6-15-03

---

Choctaw 2427.

Muskogee, Indian Territory, April 10, 1905.

Wilson Christy,
    Garland, Indian Territory.

Dear Sir:

    Receipt is hereby acknowledged of the affidavits of Miney Christy (Chubbe) and Sallie Christy to the birth of Adam Christy, son of Wilson and Miney Christy, June 15, 1903, and the same have been filed with our records as an application for the enrollment of said child.

                Respectfully,

                Commissioner in Charge.

---

**NEW-BORN AFFIDAVIT.**

    Number..................

...Choctaw Enrolling Commission...

---

    IN THE MATTER OF THE APPLICATION FOR ENROLLMENT, as a citizen of the Choctaw Nation, of   Adam Christy

born on the  15  day of ___June___ 190 3

Name of father  Wilson Christy      a citizen of  Choctaw
Nation final enrollment No.  7015    *married to Wilson Christy*
Name of mother  Miney Chubby      a citizen of  Choctaw
Nation final enrollment No.  7016

                Postoffice      Garland IT

## Applications for Enrollment of Choctaw Newborn
## Act of 1905 Volume XI

### AFFIDAVIT OF MOTHER.

UNITED STATES OF AMERICA
INDIAN TERRITORY
Central   DISTRICT

I   Miney Chubby   , on oath state that I am 16 years of age and a citizen by blood of the Choctaw Nation, and as such have been placed upon the final roll of the Choctaw Nation, by the Honorable Secretary of the Interior my final enrollment number being   7015[sic] ; that I am the lawful wife of   Wilson Christy   , who is a citizen of the   Choctaw   Nation, and as such has been placed upon the final roll of said Nation by the Honorable Secretary of the Interior, his final enrollment number being   7016[sic]   and that a   Male   child was born to me on the   15th   day of   June   190 3; that said child has been named   Adam Christy   , and is now living.

Miney Chubby

Witnesseth.
Must be two Witnesses who are Citizens. } Frank Garland
Mathew Henry

Subscribed and sworn to before me this ........ day of ........................... 190......

Notary Public.
My commission expires:

---

### AFFIDAVIT OF ATTENDING PHYSICIAN OR MIDWIFE

UNITED STATES OF AMERICA
INDIAN TERRITORY
Central   DISTRICT

I,   Sallie Christy   a   midwife on oath state that I attended on Mrs.   Miney Chubby   wife of   Wilson Christy on the   15th   day of   June   , 190 3 , that there was born to her on said date a   male child, that said child is now living, and is said to have been named   Adam Christy

her
Sallie x Christy
mark

Subscribed and sworn to before me this, the ............................. day of ................................. 190.........

Notary Public.

WITNESSETH:
Must be two witnesses who are citizens { Joshua Christy
Osborne Cass

# Applications for Enrollment of Choctaw Newborn
## Act of 1905   Volume XI

We hereby certify that we are well acquainted with        Sallie Christy
a    midwife        and know      her      to be reputable and of good standing in the community.

Joshua Christy                          _____

Osborne Cass                            _____

7-7015        7-7016.
**BIRTH AFFIDAVIT.**

### DEPARTMENT OF THE INTERIOR.
### COMMISSION TO THE FIVE CIVILIZED TRIBES.

IN RE APPLICATION FOR ENROLLMENT, as a citizen of the    Choctaw    Nation, of Adam Christy    , born on the 15th day of June , 1903

Name of Father:    Wilson Christy            a citizen of the  Choctaw  Nation.
Name of Mother: Miney Christy (nee Chubbe)   a citizen of the  Choctaw  Nation.

Postoffice    Garland, Ind. Ter.

**AFFIDAVIT OF MOTHER.**

UNITED STATES OF AMERICA, Indian Territory, }
     Central              DISTRICT.         }

I,   Miney Christy   , on oath state that I am  16  years of age and a citizen by   blood   , of the   Choctaw   Nation; that I am the lawful wife of   Wilson Christy   , who is a citizen, by blood   of the   Choctaw   Nation; that a male   child was born to me on  15th  day of  June  , 1903; that said child has been named   Adam Christy   , and was living March 4, 1905.

                                    Miney Christy
Witnesses To Mark:
  {

Subscribed and sworn to before me this  4  day of  April   , 1905

                                    C C Jones
                                        Notary Public.

38

## Applications for Enrollment of Choctaw Newborn
## Act of 1905   Volume XI

### AFFIDAVIT OF ATTENDING PHYSICIAN OR MID-WIFE.

UNITED STATES OF AMERICA, Indian Territory,
   Central                       DISTRICT.

   I,   Sally Christy   , a   midwife   , on oath state that I attended on Mrs.   Miney Christy   , wife of   Wilson Christy   on the   15th   day of   June  , 1903; that there was born to her on said date a   male   child; that said child was living March 4, 1905, and is said to have been named Adam Christy

                              This is
                              Sally x Christy
                                my mark
Witnesses To Mark:
   { Joshua Christy
   { Cephus Scott

   Subscribed and sworn to before me this  4  day of   April   , 1905

                        C C Jones
                              Notary Public.

---

Choc New Born 710
         Troy Silvister[sic] Impson  b. 3-2-04

BIRTH AFFIDAVIT.
                  DEPARTMENT OF THE INTERIOR.
            **COMMISSION TO THE FIVE CIVILIZED TRIBES.**

      IN RE APPLICATION FOR ENROLLMENT, as a citizen of the   Choctaw   Nation, of Troy Silvester[sic] Impson   , born on the  2  day of  March  , 1904

Name of Father: William D. Impson          a citizen of the   Choctaw   Nation.
Name of Mother: Flora A. Impson            a citizen of the   Choctaw   Nation.

                  Postoffice    Bokchito Ind Ter

# Applications for Enrollment of Choctaw Newborn
## Act of 1905 Volume XI

### AFFIDAVIT OF MOTHER.

UNITED STATES OF AMERICA, Indian Territory, }
Central        DISTRICT.

I, Flora Impson, on oath state that I am 39 years of age and a citizen by intermarriage, of the Choctaw Nation; that I am the lawful wife of William D. Impson, who is a citizen, by blood of the Choctaw Nation; that a male child was born to me on 2 day of March, 1904; that said child has been named Troy Silvester Impson, and was living March 4, 1905.

Flora Impson

Witnesses To Mark:
{

Subscribed and sworn to before me this 10 day of June, 1905

F A McAllen
Notary Public.

---

### AFFIDAVIT OF ATTENDING PHYSICIAN OR MID-WIFE.

UNITED STATES OF AMERICA, Indian Territory, }
Central        DISTRICT.

I, N. J. Hamilton, a Physician, on oath state that I attended on Mrs. Flora Impson, wife of William D Impson on the 2 day of March, 1904; that there was born to her on said date a male child; that said child was living March 4, 1905, and is said to have been named Troy Silvester Impson

N J Hamilton MD

Witnesses To Mark:
{

Subscribed and sworn to before me this 10 day of June, 1905

F A McAllen
Notary Public.

Applications for Enrollment of Choctaw Newborn
Act of 1905   Volume XI

## AFFIDAVIT OF ATTENDING PHYSICIAN OR MIDWIFE

UNITED STATES OF AMERICA
INDIAN TERRITORY
Central   DISTRICT

I, N J Hamilton   a   Practicing Physician on oath state that I attended on Mrs. Flora Impson wife of Wm D. Impson on the 2$^d$ day of March, 190 4, that there was born to her on said date a male child, that said child is now living, and is said to have been named Troy Sylvester Impson

N J Hamilton   M.D.

WITNESSETH:
Must be two witnesses who are citizens and know the child.
{ D H Gardner
  M M Impson

Subscribed and sworn to before me this, the 17 day of February 190 5

A E Folsom   Notary Public.

We hereby certify that we are well acquainted with Dr N J Hamilton a Practicing Physician and know him to be reputable and of good standing in the community.

{ D.H. Gardner
  M. M. Impson

**NEW-BORN AFFIDAVIT.**

Number

...Choctaw Enrolling Commission...

IN THE MATTER OF THE APPLICATION FOR ENROLLMENT, as a citizen of the Choctaw Nation, of Troy Sylvester Impson

born on the 2$^d$ day of March 190 4

Name of father W$^m$ D Impson   a citizen of Choctaw
Nation final enrollment No. 10137
Name of mother Flora Impson   a citizen of Choctaw
Nation final enrollment No.

## Applications for Enrollment of Choctaw Newborn
## Act of 1905   Volume XI

Postoffice   Bokchito IT

### AFFIDAVIT OF MOTHER.

UNITED STATES OF AMERICA
INDIAN TERRITORY
Central   DISTRICT

I   Flora Impson   , on oath state that I am 39 years of age and a citizen by marriage of the Choctaw Nation, and as such have been placed upon the final roll of the Choctaw Nation, by the Honorable Secretary of the Interior my final enrollment number being ..................; that I am the lawful wife of W$^m$ D Impson , who is a citizen of the Choctaw Nation, and as such has been placed upon the final roll of said Nation by the Honorable Secretary of the Interior, his final enrollment number being .................. and that a Male child was born to me on the 2$^d$ day of March 190 4; that said child has been named Troy Sylvester Impson , and is now living.

Flora Impson

Witnesseth.
Must be two Witnesses who are Citizens.   } D H Gardner
   M M Impson

Subscribed and sworn to before me this 17$^{th}$ day of February 190 5

A E Folsom
Notary Public.

My commission expires:
Jan 9 - 1909

---

BIRTH AFFIDAVIT.

### DEPARTMENT OF THE INTERIOR.
### COMMISSION TO THE FIVE CIVILIZED TRIBES.

---

**IN RE APPLICATION FOR ENROLLMENT,** as a citizen of the Choctaw Nation, of Troy Silvester , born on the 2 day of March , 1904

Name of Father: William D Impson   a citizen of the Choctaw Nation.
Name of Mother: Flora A Impson   a citizen of the Choctaw Nation.

Postoffice   Bokchito I.T.

# Applications for Enrollment of Choctaw Newborn
## Act of 1905 Volume XI

### AFFIDAVIT OF MOTHER.

UNITED STATES OF AMERICA, Indian Territory,  
Central DISTRICT.

I, Flora A Impson, on oath state that I am 39 years of age and a citizen by Marriage, of the Choctaw Nation; that I am the lawful wife of William D Impson, who is a citizen, by Blood of the Choctaw Nation; that a Male child was born to me on second day of March, 1904; that said child has been named ........................................., and was living March 4, 1905.

Flora A Impson

Witnesses To Mark:

Subscribed and sworn to before me this 3 day of April, 1905

F A McAllen  
Notary Public.

### AFFIDAVIT OF ATTENDING PHYSICIAN OR MID-WIFE.

UNITED STATES OF AMERICA, Indian Territory,  
Central DISTRICT.

I, N.J. Hamilton, a Physician, on oath state that I attended on Mrs. Flora A Impson, wife of William D Impson on the 2 day of March, 1904; that there was born to her on said date a male child; that said child was living March 4, 1905, and is said to have been named Troy Silvester Impson

N J Hamilton MD

Witnesses To Mark:

Subscribed and sworn to before me this Third day of April, 1905

F A McAllen  
Notary Public.

## Applications for Enrollment of Choctaw Newborn
## Act of 1905   Volume XI

Choctaw 3592.

Muskogee, Indian Territory, April 10, 1905.

William D. Impson,
    Bokchito, Indian Territory.

Dear Sir:

    Receipt is hereby acknowledged of the affidavits of Flora A. Impson and N. J. Hamilton to the birth of Troy Silvester Impson, son of William D. and Flora A. Impson, March 2, 1904, and the same have been filed with our records as an application for the enrollment of said child.

    Respectfully,

Commissioner in Charge.

---

7 N B 710

**COPY**

Muskogee, Indian Territory, April 15, 1905.

William D. Impson,
    Bokchito, Indian Territory.

Dear Sir:

    There is inclosed you herewith for execution application for the enrollment of your infant child, ---- Impson, born March 1, 1904.

    In the affidavit of the mother heretofore filed with the Commission, the name of the child is not given. Please insert the correct name in the inclosed application.

    In having these affidavits executed care should be exercised to see that all names are written in full, as they appear in the body of the affidavit, and in the event that either of the persons signing the affidavit are unable to write, signatures by mark must be attested by two witnesses. Each affidavit must be executed before a Notary Public and the notarial seal and signature of the officer must be attached to each separate affidavit.

    Respectfully,

SIGNED

*Tams Bixby*
Chairman.

LM 15-155

## Applications for Enrollment of Choctaw Newborn
## Act of 1905   Volume XI

7-NB-710.

Muskogee, Indian Territory, June 5, 1905.

Flora Impson,
    Bokchito, Indian Territory.

Dear Madam:

    There is enclosed you herewith for execution application for the enrollment of your infant child, born March 2, 1904.

    In your affidavit heretofore filed with the Commission, the name of the child is not given. Please insert the correct name in the inclosed application.

    In having these affidavits executed care should be exercised to see that all names are written in full, as they appear in the body of the affidavit, and in the event that either of the persons signing the affidavit are unable to write, signatures by mark must be attested by two witnesses. Each affidavit must be executed before a Notary Public and the notarial seal and signature of the officer must be attached to each separate affidavit.

                           Respectfully,

VR 5-1.                                             [sic]

---

7 NB 710

Muskogee, Indian Territory, June 16, 1905.

William B[sic]. Impson,
    Bokchito, Indian Territory.

Dear Sir:

    Receipt is hereby acknowledged of the affidavits of Flora Impson and N. J. Hamilton to the birth of Troy Silvester Impson son of William D. and Flore R[sic]. Impson, March 2, 1904, and the same have been filed with our records in the matter of the enrollment of said child.

                             Respectfully,

                                           Chairman.

# Applications for Enrollment of Choctaw Newborn
## Act of 1905   Volume XI

7-NB-710

Muskogee, Indian Territory, August 24, 1905.

W. D. Impson,
    Bokchito, Indian Territory.

Dear Sir:

    Receipt is hereby acknowledged of your letter of August 19, 1905, asking if Troy Sylvester Impson, minor child of W. D. Impson has been approved so that selection of allotment can now be made.

    In reply to your letter you are advised that the name of your minor child Troy Sylvester Impson has been placed upon a schedule of citizens by blood of the Choctaw Nation which has been forwarded the Secretary of the Interior and you will be advised when his enrollment is approved by the Department.

                    Respectfully,

                            Commissioner.

---

Choc New Born 711
    Sophia Homer  b. 11-15-04

This is to certify that Dana Homer and Nancy Achih are duly married according to law by A. H. Homer this the 17$^{th}$ day of June A.D. 1904

                        A.H. Homer
                      Minister of the Gospel

**BIRTH AFFIDAVIT.**

## DEPARTMENT OF THE INTERIOR.
## COMMISSION TO THE FIVE CIVILIZED TRIBES.

**IN RE APPLICATION FOR ENROLLMENT,** as a citizen of the Choctaw Nation, of Sophia Homer, born on the 15 day of Nov, 1904

Name of Father: Dana Homer      a citizen of the   Choctaw   Nation.
Name of Mother: Nancy Homer   a citizen of the   Choctaw   Nation.

                    Postoffice   Bennington I.T.

# Applications for Enrollment of Choctaw Newborn
## Act of 1905 Volume XI

**AFFIDAVIT OF MOTHER.**

UNITED STATES OF AMERICA, Indian Territory, }
Central DISTRICT. }

I, Nancy Homer , on oath state that I am about 24 years of age and a citizen by Blood , of the Choctaw Nation; that I am the lawful wife of Dana Homer , who is a citizen, by Blood of the Choctaw Nation; that a Girl child was born to me on 15$^{th}$ day of November , 1904; that said child has been named Sophia Homer , and was living March 4, 1905.

             her
          Nancy x Homer
Witnesses To Mark:     mark
 { J V Meadows
   Will Pope

Subscribed and sworn to before me this 4$^{th}$ day of April , 1905

           J W Lloyd
            Notary Public.

**AFFIDAVIT OF ATTENDING PHYSICIAN OR MID-WIFE.**

UNITED STATES OF AMERICA, Indian Territory, }
Central DISTRICT. }

I, Kizzie Homer , a Mid-wife , on oath state that I attended on Mrs. Nancy Homer , wife of Dana Homer on the 15$^{th}$ day of November , 1904; that there was born to her on said date a Girl child; that said child was living March 4, 1905, and is said to have been named Sophia Homer

             her
          Kizzie x Homer
Witnesses To Mark:     mark
 { J V Meadows
   Will Pope

Subscribed and sworn to before me this 4$^{th}$ day of April , 1905

           J W Lloyd
            Notary Public.

## Applications for Enrollment of Choctaw Newborn
## Act of 1905   Volume XI

Choctaw 3506.

Muskogee, Indian Territory, April 10, 1905.

Dana Homer,
    Bennington, Indian Territory.

Dear Sir:

    Receipt is hereby acknowledged of the affidavits of Nancy Homer and Kizzie Homer to the birth of Sophia Homer, daughter of Dana and Nancy Homer, November 15, 1904, and the same have been filed with our records as an application for the enrollment of said child.

    In compliance with your request there is enclosed herewith a blank for the enrollment of an infant child.

        Respectfully,

                Commissioner in Charge.

1 C. B.

---

**COPY**   7 N B 711

Muskogee, Indian Territory, April 15, 1905.

Dana Homer,
    Bennington, Indian Territory.

Dear Sir:

    You are hereby advised that before the application for the enrollment of your infant child, Sophia Homer, can be finally disposed of, it will be necessary for you to furnish the Commission with either the original or a certified copy of the license and certificate of your marriage to her mother, Nancy Homer.

    Please attend to this matter promptly.

        Respectfully,

SIGNED

*Tams Bixby*
Chairman.

## Applications for Enrollment of Choctaw Newborn
## Act of 1905   Volume XI

7 NB 711

**COPY**

Muskogee, Indian Territory, April 27, 1905.

Dana Homer,
    Bennington, Indian Territory.

Dear Sir:

    Receipt is hereby acknowledged of your letter of April 22, 1905, enclosing marriage license and certificate between Dana Homer and Nancy Achih which you offer in support of the application for the enrollment of your child Sophia Homer and the same have been filed with the record in this case.

                  Respectfully,
                  SIGNED

                    *Tams Bixby*
                    Chairman.

---

7-NB-711.

Muskogee, Indian Territory, June 5, 1905.

Dana Homer,
    Bennington, Indian Territory.

Dear Sig:

    It is noted from the application for the enrollment of your infant child, Sophia Homer, born November 15, 1904, heretofore filed in this office, that your wife claims to be a Choctaw by blood.

    If this is correct you will please state when, where and under what name she was listed for enrollment, the names of her parents and any other person who applied for enrollment at the same time, and if she has selected an allotment, give her roll number as the same appears on her allotment certificate.

                    Respectfully,

                          [sic]

# Applications for Enrollment of Choctaw Newborn
## Act of 1905 Volume XI

*(The letter below typed as given.)*

Bennington, I.T. July 7-1905.

Commission to five tribes
    Muskogee, I.T.

Gentlemen:

    In regard to the enrolment of my infant child Sophia Homer. Her mother was Nancy Homer and was a Mississippi Choctaw. Her Roll number as Homestead Designated certificate No. is 70 and allotment no. is 71. I have filed proof of both in your office. You will please advise me what steps are necessary to secure the enrollment of my child.

        Yours truly,
        Dana Homer.

P.S. Please send me blank affidavits for me to fill out for Willie Homer whose mother is dead, his no. is 7-NB-851.

D--H

---

7-NB-711

Muskogee, Indian Territory, July 21, 1905.

Dana Homer,
    Bennington, Indian Territory.

Dear Sir:

    Receipt is hereby acknowledged of your letter of July 7, 1905, stating that the mother of your infant child, Sophia Homer was named Nancy Phillip, and was a Mississippi Choctaw, and this information has enabled us to identify Nancy Homer as a Mississippi Choctaw.

    In compliance with your request there is inclosed herewith affidavits for two witnesses partially filled out, which you are requested to have executed as to the birth of your child Willie Homer, September 10, 1903, and return same to this office.

        Respectfully,

        Commissioner.

LM 3-20

## Applications for Enrollment of Choctaw Newborn
## Act of 1905   Volume XI

Choc New Born 712
  Lisabeth Crowder  b. 6-5-03

Choctaw 3611.

Muskogee, Indian Territory, April 10, 1905.

Martin S. Crowder,
  Bennington, Indian Territory.

Dear Sir:

  Receipt is hereby acknowledged of the affidavits of Emily Crowder and Nettie Rogers to the birth of Lisabeth Crowder daughter of Martin S. and Emily Crowder, June 5, 1903, and the same have been filed with our records as an application for the enrollment of said child.

Respectfully,

Commissioner in Charge.

**BIRTH AFFIDAVIT.**

### DEPARTMENT OF THE INTERIOR.
### COMMISSION TO THE FIVE CIVILIZED TRIBES.

  **IN RE APPLICATION FOR ENROLLMENT,** as a citizen of the     Choctaw     Nation, of Lisabeth Crowder     , born on the  5   day of  June  , 1903

Name of Father: Martin S. Crowder      a citizen of the  Choctaw  Nation.
Name of Mother: Emily Crowder           a citizen of the  Choctaw  Nation.

Postoffice   Bennington Ind Ter

**AFFIDAVIT OF MOTHER.**

UNITED STATES OF AMERICA, Indian Territory, }
   Central            DISTRICT. }

  I,  Emily Crowder   , on oath state that I am  about 40   years of age and a citizen by   Birth   , of the   Choctaw   Nation; that I am the lawful wife of Martin S. Crowder       , who is a citizen, by  Birth   of the     Choctaw Nation; that a   female    child was born to me on  5th   day of  June   , 1903; that said child has been named  Lisabeth Crowder    , and was living March 4, 1905.

                            her
                     Emily x Crowder
                            mark

# Applications for Enrollment of Choctaw Newborn
## Act of 1905   Volume XI

Witnesses To Mark:
- P.C. Crowder
- Rena Crowder

Subscribed and sworn to before me this  3  day of  April  , 1905

T.M. Sullivan
Notary Public.

---

**AFFIDAVIT OF ATTENDING PHYSICIAN OR MID-WIFE.**

UNITED STATES OF AMERICA, Indian Territory,
Central           DISTRICT.

I,   Nettie Roggers[sic]   , a  mid wife  , on oath state that I attended on Mrs.  Emily Crowder  , wife of  Martin S Crowder   on the  5  day of   June , 1903; that there was born to her on said date a   female   child; that said child was living March 4, 1905, and is said to have been named   Lisabeth Crowder

Nettie Rogers

Witnesses To Mark:

Subscribed and sworn to before me this  3  day of  April  , 1905

T.M. Sullivan
Notary Public.

---

Choc New Born 713
Sarah Annie Garland   b. 10-7-03

Applications for Enrollment of Choctaw Newborn
Act of 1905 Volume XI

Choctaw 637.

Muskogee, Indian Territory, April 10, 1905.

John Arthur Garland,
    Parsons, Indian Territory.

Dear Sir:

    Receipt is hereby acknowledged of the affidavits of Quay Garland and Demmer Follmar to the birth of Sarah Annie Garland, daughter of John Arthur Garland and Quay Garland, October 7, 1903, and the same have been filed with our records as an

Respectfully,

Commissioner in Charge.

---

**NEW-BORN AFFIDAVIT.**

Number

**...Choctaw Enrolling Commission...**

---

    IN THE MATTER OF THE APPLICATION FOR ENROLLMENT, as a citizen of the Choctaw     Nation, of     Sarah Annie Garland

born on the   7$^{th}$   day of _____October_____ 190 3

Name of father     John A Garland         a citizen of     Choctaw
Nation final enrollment No.   1487
Name of mother   Quay Garland           a citizen of     Choctaw
Nation final enrollment No.   628

                                                Postoffice         Parson[sic] IT

**AFFIDAVIT OF MOTHER.**

UNITED STATES OF AMERICA
INDIAN TERRITORY
    Central         DISTRICT

              I     Quay Garland                , on oath state that I am
    22         years of age and a citizen by   Intermarriage   of the     Choctaw
Nation, and as such have been placed upon the final roll of the   Choctaw   Nation, by the Honorable Secretary of the Interior my final enrollment number being   628   ; that I am the lawful wife of   John A Garland     , who is a citizen of the   Choctaw     Nation, and

## Applications for Enrollment of Choctaw Newborn
## Act of 1905  Volume XI

as such has been placed upon the final roll of said Nation by the Honorable Secretary of the Interior, his final enrollment number being    1487    and that a    female    child was born to me on the    7th    day of    October    190 3; that said child has been named    Sarah Annie Garland    , and is now living.

                                           Quay Garland

Witnesseth.
Must be two Witnesses who are Citizens. } George Washington
Isaac Harkins

       Subscribed and sworn to before me this    21    day of    Feb    190 5

                                   W A Shoney
                                          Notary Public.

My commission expires:    Jan 10 1909

---

## AFFIDAVIT OF ATTENDING PHYSICIAN OR MIDWIFE

UNITED STATES OF AMERICA
INDIAN TERRITORY
   Central    DISTRICT

    I,    Susan John    a    midwife
on oath state that I attended on Mrs.  Quay Garland    wife of  John A Garland
on the    7th    day of    October , 190 3, that there was born to her on said date a    female child, that said child is now living, and is said to have been named    Sarah Annie Garland

                                   her
                              Susan x John    ~~M.D~~.
WITNESSETH:                  mark
Must be two witnesses who are citizens and know the child. { George Washington
Isaac Harkins

             Subscribed and sworn to before me this, the    21st    day of    Feb    190 5

                          W A Shoney    Notary Public.

    We hereby certify that we are well acquainted with    Susan John    a    midwife    and know    her    to be reputable and of good standing in the community.

                          { George Washington
                            Isaac Harkins

# Applications for Enrollment of Choctaw Newborn
## Act of 1905 Volume XI

BIRTH AFFIDAVIT.

## DEPARTMENT OF THE INTERIOR.
## COMMISSION TO THE FIVE CIVILIZED TRIBES.

IN RE APPLICATION FOR ENROLLMENT, as a citizen of the Choctaw Nation, of Sarah Annie Garland, born on the 7 day of October, 1903

Name of Father: John Arthur Garland    a citizen of the Choctaw Nation.
Name of Mother: Quay Garland    a citizen of the Choctaw Nation.

Postoffice    Parsons I.T.

### AFFIDAVIT OF MOTHER.

UNITED STATES OF AMERICA, Indian Territory,}
Central    DISTRICT.

I, Quay Garland, on oath state that I am 22 years of age and a citizen by Intermarriage, of the Choctaw Nation; that I am the lawful wife of John Arthur Garland, who is a citizen, by Blood of the Choctaw Nation; that a Female child was born to me on 7$^{th}$ day of October, 1903; that said child has been named Sarah Annie Garland, and was living March 4, 1905.

Quay Garland

Witnesses To Mark:
{

Subscribed and sworn to before me this 1 day of April, 1905

T G Carr
Notary Public.

### AFFIDAVIT OF ATTENDING PHYSICIAN OR MID-WIFE.

UNITED STATES OF AMERICA, Indian Territory,}
Central    DISTRICT.

I, Demmer Follmar, a Midwife, on oath state that I attended on Mrs. Quay Garland, wife of John A Garland on the 7$^{th}$ day of October, 1903; that there was born to her on said date a female child; that said child was living March 4, 1905, and is said to have been named Sarrah[sic] Annie Garland

Demmer Fallmar

Witnesses To Mark:
{

## Applications for Enrollment of Choctaw Newborn
## Act of 1905 Volume XI

Subscribed and sworn to before me this 3$^d$ day of  April  , 1905

E.J. Gardner
Notary Public.

---

Choc New Born 714
    Milton Nelson Taylor  b. 12-28-02
    Absalom James Taylor  b. 9-29-04

**NEW-BORN AFFIDAVIT.**

Number..................

## Choctaw Enrolling Commission.

IN THE MATTER OF THE APPLICATION FOR ENROLLMENT, as a citizen of the Choctaw   Nation, of   Milton Nelson Taylor

born on the  28$^{th}$   day of   December   190 2

Name of father   Simon Taylor   a citizen of   Choctaw
Nation final enrollment No   2513[sic]
Name of mother   Melvina Taylor   a citizen of   Choctaw
Nation final enrollment No   2513

Postoffice   Garvin IT

**AFFIDAVIT OF MOTHER.**

UNITED STATES OF AMERICA,  ⎫
    INDIAN TERRITORY,  ⎬
  Central   DISTRICT  ⎭

    I   Melvina Taylor   on oath state that I am  24  years of age and a citizen by   Blood   of the   Choctaw   Nation, and as such have been placed upon the final roll of the   Choctaw   Nation, by the Honorable Secretary of the Interior my final enrollment number being  ——  ; that I am the lawful wife of   Simon Taylor   , who is a citizen of the   Choctaw   Nation, and as such has been placed upon the final roll of said Nation by the Honorable Secretary of the Interior, his final enrollment number being  —  and that a   Male   child was born to me on the  28$^{th}$  day of   December   190 2 ; that said child has been named   Milton Nelson Taylor   , and is now living.

Melvina Taylor

## Applications for Enrollment of Choctaw Newborn
## Act of 1905   Volume XI

WITNESSETH:

Must be two Witnesses who are Citizens.  } Chas R Holman

Ellis Taylor

Subscribed and sworn to before me this  25  day of  Jan  190 5

G.C. Spaulding
~~Notary Public~~

My commission expires ................................   U.S. Cou

---

*Affidavit of Attending Physician or Midwife*

UNITED STATES OF AMERICA,
INDIAN TERRITORY,
Central   DISTRICT  }

I,  Mary Mitchell   a   Midwife  on oath state that I attended on Mrs.  Melvina Taylor   wife of  Simon Taylor  on the  28$^{th}$   day of  December  , 190 2, that there was born to her on said date a  Male  child, that said child is now living, and is said to have been named  Milton Nelson Taylor

Mary x Mitchell   M. D.
her / mark

Subscribed and sworn to before me this the  20  day of  Jan   1905

G.C. Spaulding
~~Notary Public~~

WITNESSETH:    U.S. Cou

Must be two witnesses who are citizens and know the child.  { Chas R Holman

Ellis Taylor

We hereby certify that we are well acquainted with   Mary Mitchell  a  Midwife   and know  her   to be reputable and of good standing in the community.

Must be two citizen witnesses.  { Chas R Holman

Ellis Taylor

Applications for Enrollment of Choctaw Newborn
Act of 1905   Volume XI

**NEW-BORN AFFIDAVIT.**

Number..........

## Choctaw Enrolling Commission.

IN THE MATTER OF THE APPLICATION FOR ENROLLMENT, as a citizen of the Choctaw    Nation, of      Absolom James Taylor

born on the  29$^{th}$  day of  September       190 4

Name of father    Simon Taylor            a citizen of     Choctaw
Nation final enrollment No    2513[sic]
Name of mother    Melvina Taylor         a citizen of     Choctaw
Nation final enrollment No   2513
                            Postoffice      Garvin IT

**AFFIDAVIT OF MOTHER.**

UNITED STATES OF AMERICA,
   INDIAN TERRITORY,
   Central      DISTRICT

   I          Melvina Taylor                    on oath state that I am  24  years of age and a citizen by   Blood      of the  Choctaw    Nation, and as such have been placed upon the final roll of the    Choctaw      Nation, by the Honorable Secretary of the Interior my final enrollment number being  ——  ; that I am the lawful wife of    Simon Taylor     , who is a citizen of the   Choctaw       Nation, and as such has been placed upon the final roll of said Nation by the Honorable Secretary of the Interior, his final enrollment number being — and that a   Male    child was born to me on the  29$^{th}$ day of  September    190 4 ; that said child has been named    Absalom James Taylor    , and is now living.

                           Melvina Taylor

WITNESSETH:
   Must be two  } Chas R Holman
   Witnesses who
   are Citizens.    Ellis Taylor

   Subscribed and sworn to before me this  25   day of  Jan        190 5

                      G.C. Spaulding
                           ~~Notary Public.~~
My commission expires ..........     U.S. Cou

## Applications for Enrollment of Choctaw Newborn
## Act of 1905   Volume XI

### *Affidavit of Attending Physician or Midwife*

UNITED STATES OF AMERICA,  
INDIAN TERRITORY,  
Central   DISTRICT

I, Mary Mitchell   a   Midwife on oath state that I attended on Mrs. Melvina Taylor   wife of   Simon Taylor on the 29$^{th}$ day of September , 190 4, that there was born to her on said date a   Male child, that said child is now living, and is said to have been named   Absalom James Taylor

                                            her  
                                  Mary x Mitchell   M. D.  
                                    mark

Subscribed and sworn to before me this the   20   day of   Jan   1905

                                      G.C. Spaulding  
                                      ~~Notary Public.~~  
                                      U.S. Court

WITNESSETH:  
Must be two witnesses who are citizens and know the child.   { Chas R Holman  
                               Ellis Taylor

We hereby certify that we are well acquainted with   Mary Mitchell a   Midwife   and know   her   to be reputable and of good standing in the community.

                            Must be two citizen witnesses.   { Chas R Holman  
                                                 Ellis Taylor

BIRTH AFFIDAVIT.

## DEPARTMENT OF THE INTERIOR,
### COMMISSION TO THE FIVE CIVILIZED TRIBES.

**In Re Application for Enrollment,** as a citizen of the   Choctaw   Nation, of   Absalom James Taylor , born on the   29   day of September   , 1904

Name of Father: Simon Taylor          a citizen of the   Choctaw   Nation.  
Name of Mother: Melvina Taylor      a citizen of the   Choctaw   Nation.

                             Post-office   Garvin Ind Ter.

# Applications for Enrollment of Choctaw Newborn
## Act of 1905   Volume XI

**AFFIDAVIT OF MOTHER.**

UNITED STATES OF AMERICA,  
INDIAN TERRITORY,  
Central   District.

I, Melvina Taylor, on oath state that I am 24 years of age and a citizen by Blood, of the Choctaw Nation; that I am the lawful wife of Simon Taylor, who is a citizen, by Blood of the Choctaw Nation; that a Male child was born to me on 29$^{th}$ day of September, 1904, that said child has been named Absalom James Taylor, and is now living.

Melvina Taylor

**WITNESSES TO MARK:**

Subscribed and sworn to before me this 3$^{rd}$ day of April, 1905.

T.J. Barnes  
**NOTARY PUBLIC.**

**AFFIDAVIT OF ATTENDING PHYSICIAN OR MID-WIFE.**

UNITED STATES OF AMERICA,  
INDIAN TERRITORY,  
Central   District.

I, Mary Mitchell, a Midwife, on oath state that I attended on Mrs. Melvina Taylor, wife of Simon Taylor on the 29$^{th}$ day of September, 1904; that there was born to her on said date a Male child; that said child is now living and is said to have been named Absalom James Taylor

her  
Mary x Mitchell  
mark

**WITNESSES TO MARK:**  
Nellie Ida Forbes  
Cele Kanictobe

Subscribed and sworn to before me this 3$^{rd}$ day of April, 1905.

T.J. Barnes  
**NOTARY PUBLIC.**

## Applications for Enrollment of Choctaw Newborn
## Act of 1905   Volume XI

BIRTH AFFIDAVIT.

## DEPARTMENT OF THE INTERIOR,
### COMMISSION TO THE FIVE CIVILIZED TRIBES.

**In Re Application for Enrollment,** as a citizen of the Choctaw Nation, of Milton Nelson Taylor , born on the 28" day of December , 1902

Name of Father: Simon Taylor     a citizen of the Choctaw Nation.
Name of Mother: Melvina Taylor     a citizen of the Choctaw Nation.

Post-office     Garvin Ind Ter.

**AFFIDAVIT OF MOTHER.**

UNITED STATES OF AMERICA, }
    INDIAN TERRITORY,
    Central     District.

I, Melvina Taylor , on oath state that I am 24 years of age and a citizen by Blood , of the Choctaw Nation; that I am the lawful wife of Simon Taylor, who is a citizen, by Blood of the Choctaw Nation; that a Male child was born to me on 28th day of December , 1902, that said child has been named Milton James Taylor , and is now living.

                                               Melvina Taylor

WITNESSES TO MARK:
{

Subscribed and sworn to before me this 3rd day of April , 1905.

                                            T.J. Barnes
                                                 NOTARY PUBLIC.

**AFFIDAVIT OF ATTENDING PHYSICIAN OR MID-WIFE.**

UNITED STATES OF AMERICA, }
    INDIAN TERRITORY,
    Central     District.

I, Mary Mitchell , a Midwife , on oath state that I attended on Mrs. Melvina Taylor , wife of Simon Taylor on the 28" day of December , 1902 ; that there was born to her on said date a Male child; that said child is now living and is said to have been named Milton Nelson Taylor

                                                       her
                                            Mary x Mitchell
                                               mark

## Applications for Enrollment of Choctaw Newborn
## Act of 1905 Volume XI

**WITNESSES TO MARK:**
{ Nellie Ida Forbes
{ Cele Kanictobe

Subscribed and sworn to before me this 3$^{rd}$ day of April , 1905.

T.J. Barnes
**NOTARY PUBLIC.**

---

Choc New Born 715
    Charlie R. Williams  b. 10-3-04

---

Choctaw 2515.

Muskogee, Indian Territory, April 10, 1905.

Foster & Dalton,
    Attorneys at Law,
        Stigler, Indian Territory.

Gentlemen:

    Receipt is hereby acknowledged of your letter of April 4, transmitting the affidavits of Mrs. Mamie Williams and Elum M. Russell to the birth of Charlie R. Williams, son of Kelsey and Mamie Williams, October 3, 1904, and the same have been filed with our records as an application for the enrollment of said child.

Respectfully,

Commissioner in Charge.

---

## Applications for Enrollment of Choctaw Newborn
## Act of 1905   Volume XI

7-NB-715.

Muskogee, Indian Territory, May 29, 1905.

Kelsey Williams,
    Stigler, Indian Territory.

Dear Sir:

    Referring to the application for the enrollment of your infant child, Charlie R. Williams, born October 3, 1904, it is noted from the affidavits heretofore filed in this office that the applicant claims through you.

    It will therefore be necessary for you to file in this office either the original or a certified copy of the license and certificate of your marriage to the applicant's mother, Mamie Williams.

                Respectfully,

                             Chairman.

---

7 NB 715

Muskogee, Indian Territory, June 16, 1905.

Kelsey Williams,
    Stigler, Indian Territory.

Dear Sir:

    Receipt is hereby acknowledged of your letter of June 10, 1905, enclosing marriage license and certificate between yourself and Mamie Finton which you offer in support of the application for the enrollment of your child Charley R. Williams and the same have been filed with the records in this case.

                Respectfully,

                             Chairman.

# Applications for Enrollment of Choctaw Newborn
## Act of 1905   Volume XI

7-NB-715

Muskogee, Indian Territory, February 9, 1907.

Kelsey Williams,
    Stigler, Indian Territory.

Dear Sir:

    Receipt is hereby acknowledged of your letter of January 24, 1907, stating that you forwarded to this office your marriage license and certificate and have never received it and you ask that it be returned to you.

    In reply to your letter you are advised that this office has been directed by the Department to retain all papers filed with its records in enrollment matters, and it is therefore impracticable to comply with your request for the return of your marriage license and certificate.

                             Respectfully,

                                                Commissioner.

Applications for Enrollment of Choctaw Newborn
Act of 1905   Volume XI

No. 2008

## Certificate of Record of Marriages.

United States of America,
**The Indian Territory,** } sct.
Central    District.

I,   E.J. Fannin   Clerk of the United States Court, in the Indian Territory and District aforesaid, do hereby CERTIFY, that the License for and Certificate of the Marriage of

Mr.   Kelsey Williams   and

Miss Mamie Finton   was

filed in my office in said Territory and District the 26 day of January A.D., 190 4, and duly recorded in Book 2 of Marriage Record, Page 386

WITNESS my hand and Seal of said Court, at at Poteau this 26 day of January A.D. 190 4

*E. J. Fannin*
                                Clerk.
By   T.T. Varner              Deputy.

P. O.

DEPARTMENT OF THE INTERIOR,
COMMISSION TO THE FIVE CIVILIZED TRIBES.
**FILED**
JUN 15 1905
*Turns Bixley*

Applications for Enrollment of Choctaw Newborn
Act of 1905 Volume XI

No.

## MARRIAGE LICENSE

United States of America,     The Indian Territory,
                              Central DISTRICT, SS.

**To any Person Authorized by Law to Solemnize Marriage, Greeting:**

You are hereby commanded to Solemnize the Rite and publish the Banns of Matrimony between Mr.     Kelsey Williams
of     Stigler          in the Indian Territory, aged     22     years,
and Miss Mamie Finton               of     Stigler
in the Indian Territory., aged     20     years, according to law, and do you officially sign and return this License to the parties therein named.

WITNESS my hand and official seal, this     6th     day
of     January          A. D. 190 4

E.J. Fannin
Clerk of the United States Court.

By T.T. Varner     Deputy

---

### Certificate of Marriage.

United States of America, ⎫
**The Indian Territory,** ⎬ ss.
Central     District. ⎭          I,     M.J. Martin

a     Minister of the Gospel     , do hereby certify, that on the     10     day of
January     A. D. 190 4 , I did, duly and according to law, as commanded in the foregoing License, solemnize the Rite and publish the Banns of Matrimony between the parties therein named.

Witness my hand, this     10     day of     January     A. D. 190 4

My credentials are recorded in the office of the Clerk of ⎫
the United States Court in the Indian Territory, ⎬     M J Martin
~~Central District~~, Book     B     , Page     149 ⎭     a     Minister of the gospel
South McAlester

Note—This License and Certificate of Marriage must be returned to the Office of the Clerk of the United States Court of the Indian Territory, from whence it was issued, within sixty days from the date thereof, or the party to whom the License was issued will be liable in the amount of the One Hundred Dollars ($100.00).

## Applications for Enrollment of Choctaw Newborn
## Act of 1905   Volume XI

**NEW-BORN AFFIDAVIT.**

Number..................

### ...Choctaw Enrolling Commission...

IN THE MATTER OF THE APPLICATION FOR ENROLLMENT, as a citizen of the Choctaw Nation, of Charley R Williams

born on the 3 day of ___October___ 190 4

Name of father   Kelsey Williams             a citizen of   Choctaw
Nation final enrollment No.   15426
Name of mother   Mamie Williams            a citizen of   White
Nation final enrollment No.   ——

Postoffice   Stigler I.T.

**AFFIDAVIT OF MOTHER.**

UNITED STATES OF AMERICA
INDIAN TERRITORY
Central   DISTRICT

I   Mamie Williams   , on oath state that I am 20 years of age and a citizen by White of the —— Nation, and as such have been placed upon the final roll of the Choctaw Nation, by the Honorable Secretary of the Interior my final enrollment number being — ; that I am the lawful wife of Kelsey Williams , who is a citizen of the Choctaw Nation, and as such has been placed upon the final roll of said Nation by the Honorable Secretary of the Interior, his final enrollment number being 15426 and that a Male child was born to me on the 3 day of October 190 4; that said child has been named Charley R Williams , and is now living.

Mamie Williams

Witnesseth.
Must be two Witnesses who are Citizens.   John E Foster
   James Bower

Subscribed and sworn to before me this 2 day of Jan 190 5

James Bower
Notary Public.

My commission expires:
Sept 23 - 1907

# Applications for Enrollment of Choctaw Newborn
## Act of 1905 Volume XI

## AFFIDAVIT OF ATTENDING PHYSICIAN OR MIDWIFE

UNITED STATES OF AMERICA
INDIAN TERRITORY
................................DISTRICT

I, Elum M. Russell   a   Practicing Physician on oath state that I attended on Mrs. Mamie Williams   wife of Kelsey Williams on the 3 day of October, 190 4, that there was born to her on said date a Male child, that said child is now living, and is said to have been named Charles R Williams

Elum M. Russell

Subscribed and sworn to before me this, the   2   day of January 190 5

James Bower   Notary Public.

WITNESSETH:
Must be two witnesses who are citizens { JS Stigler
James Bower

We hereby certify that we are well acquainted with Elum M Russell a Practicing Physician and know him to be reputable and of good standing in the community.

Abel Cooper

J S Stigler

BIRTH AFFIDAVIT.

## DEPARTMENT OF THE INTERIOR.
### COMMISSION TO THE FIVE CIVILIZED TRIBES.

IN RE APPLICATION FOR ENROLLMENT, as a citizen of the Choctaw Nation, of Charlie R Williams, born on the 3 day of Oct, 1904

Name of Father: Kelsey Williams   a citizen of the Choctaw Nation.
Name of Mother: Mamie Williams   a citizen of the Choctaw Nation.

Postoffice   Stigler I T

# Applications for Enrollment of Choctaw Newborn
## Act of 1905 Volume XI

### AFFIDAVIT OF MOTHER.

UNITED STATES OF AMERICA, Indian Territory, }
Central    DISTRICT. }

    I, Mamie Williams, on oath state that I am 22 years of age and a citizen by blood, of the White race ~~Nation~~; that I am the lawful wife of Kelsey Williams, who is a citizen, by blood of the Choctaw Nation; that a male child was born to me on 3rd day of Oct, 1904; that said child has been named Charlie R Williams, and was living March 4, 1905.

                                Mrs Mamie Williams

Witnesses To Mark:
{

    Subscribed and sworn to before me this 4$^{th}$ day of April, 1905

                              E.M. Dalton
                              Notary Public.
          My commission expires Oct 29 1908

---

### AFFIDAVIT OF ATTENDING PHYSICIAN OR MID-WIFE.

UNITED STATES OF AMERICA, Indian Territory, }
............................................ DISTRICT. }

    I, Elum M. Russell, a physician, on oath state that I attended on Mrs. Mamie Williams, wife of Kelsey Williams on the Third day of October, 1904; that there was born to her on said date a male child; that said child was living March 4, 1905, and is said to have been named Charlie R Williams

                              Elum M. Russell, M.D.

Witnesses To Mark:
{

    Subscribed and sworn to before me this 5$^{th}$ day of April, 1905

                              E.M. Dalton
                              Notary Public.
          My commission expires Oct 29 1908

# Applications for Enrollment of Choctaw Newborn
## Act of 1905    Volume XI

Choc New Born 716
Walter Leonard Pruner   b. 7-22-04

The mother of this child is enrolled as Barney Etta Anderson, Choctaw Roll, by blood, No. 14306.

JE Williams

**BIRTH AFFIDAVIT.**

### DEPARTMENT OF THE INTERIOR.
### COMMISSION TO THE FIVE CIVILIZED TRIBES.

**IN RE APPLICATION FOR ENROLLMENT,** as a citizen of the Choctaw Nation, of Walter Leonard Pruner, born on the 22$^{nd}$ day of July, 1904

Name of Father: Charles B. Pruner      a citizen of the Caddo Nation.
Name of Mother: Burney Etta Pruner      a citizen of the Choctaw Nation.

Postoffice    Verden Oklahoma Ter.

**AFFIDAVIT OF MOTHER.**

UNITED STATES OF AMERICA, Indian Territory,
Southern   DISTRICT.

I, Burney Etta Pruner, on oath state that I am  years of age and a citizen by blood, of the Choctaw Nation; that I am the lawful wife of Charles B Pruner, who is a citizen, by blood of the Caddo Nation; that a male child was born to me on 22$^{nd}$ day of July, 1904, that said child has been named Walter Leonard Pruner, and is now living.

Burney Etta Pruner

Witnesses To Mark:

Subscribed and sworn to before me this 3$^{rd}$ day of April, 1905.

S.W. Hayes
Notary Public.

My commission
expires Feb 19, 1908

## Applications for Enrollment of Choctaw Newborn
## Act of 1905 Volume XI

### AFFIDAVIT OF ATTENDING PHYSICIAN OR MID-WIFE.

UNITED STATES OF AMERICA, Indian Territory,
Southern DISTRICT.

I, J.H. Kitzmiller, a physician, on oath state that I attended on Mrs. Burney Etta Pruner, wife of Charles B. Pruner on the $22^{nd}$ day of July, 1904; that there was born to her on said date a male child; that said child is now living and is said to have been named Walter Leonard Pruner

J.H. Kitzmiller MD

Witnesses To Mark:
{

Subscribed and sworn to before me this $3^{rd}$ day of April, 1905.

S.W. Hayes
Notary Public.

My commission
expires Feb 19, 1908

---

Choc New Born 717
    Albert D. Dobson  b. 2-17-04

7-7385       7-644
**BIRTH AFFIDAVIT.**

### DEPARTMENT OF THE INTERIOR.
### COMMISSION TO THE FIVE CIVILIZED TRIBES.

IN RE APPLICATION FOR ENROLLMENT, as a citizen of the Choctaw Nation, of Albert D. Dobson, born on the 17th day of February, 1904

Name of Father: Thomas M. Dobson     a citizen of the Choctaw Nation.
Name of Mother: Ollia Dobson     a citizen of the Choctaw Nation.

Postoffice   Milton, Ind. Ter.

# Applications for Enrollment of Choctaw Newborn
## Act of 1905  Volume XI

**AFFIDAVIT OF MOTHER.**

UNITED STATES OF AMERICA, Indian Territory, }
Central   DISTRICT.

I, Ollia Dobson, on oath state that I am 20 years of age and a citizen by intermarriage, of the Choctaw Nation; that I am the lawful wife of Thomas M. Dobson, who is a citizen, by blood of the Choctaw Nation; that a male child was born to me on 17th day of February, 1904; that said child has been named Albert D. Dobson, and was living March 4, 1905.

Ollia Dobson

Witnesses To Mark:
{

Subscribed and sworn to before me this 4th day of April, 1905

OL Johnson
Notary Public.

---

**AFFIDAVIT OF ATTENDING PHYSICIAN OR MID-WIFE.**

UNITED STATES OF AMERICA, Indian Territory, }
Central   DISTRICT.

I, E. F. Hodges, a physician, on oath state that I attended on Mrs. Ollia Dobson, wife of Thomas M Dobson on the 17th day of February, 1904; that there was born to her on said date a male child; that said child was living March 4, 1905, and is said to have been named Albert D. Dobson.

E.F. Hodges, M.D.

Witnesses To Mark:
{

Subscribed and sworn to before me this 4$^{th}$ day of April, 1905

OL Johnson
Notary Public.

## Applications for Enrollment of Choctaw Newborn
## Act of 1905   Volume XI

Choc New Born 718
    Della May Hines   b. 8-14-03

7-3921

Muskogee, Indian Territory, April 10, 1905.

G. M. Hines,
    Alma, Indian Territory.

Dear Sir:

    Receipt is hereby acknowledged of the affidavits of Oma Hines and R. P. Dickey to the birth of Della May Hines, daughter of G. M. and Oma McLellan Hines, August 14, 1903, and the same have been filed with our records as an application for the enrollment of said child.

                    Respectfully,

                    Commissioner in Charge.

Choctaw N B 718

Muskogee, Indian Territory, May 19, 1905.

G. M. Hines,
    Alma, Indian Territory.

Dear Sir:

    Receipt is hereby acknowledged of your letter of May 15, asking when you can file for your child for whom you made application a short time ago.

    In reply to your letter you are advised that the affidavits heretofore forwarded to the birth of your child, Della May Hines, have been filed with our records as an application for her enrollment but no selection of allotment can be permitted for children for whose enrollment application is made under the act of Congress approved March 3, 1905, until their enrollment has been approved by the Secretary of the Interior.

                Respectfully,

                    Chairman.

## Applications for Enrollment of Choctaw Newborn
## Act of 1905   Volume XI

BIRTH AFFIDAVIT.

### DEPARTMENT OF THE INTERIOR.
### COMMISSION TO THE FIVE CIVILIZED TRIBES.

IN RE APPLICATION FOR ENROLLMENT, as a citizen of the Choctaw Nation, of Della May Hines, born on the 14 day of August, 1903

Name of Father: G.M. Hines ~~a citizen of the~~ *non citizen* Nation.
Name of Mother: Oma M^{c}lellan-Hines   a citizen of the Choctaw Nation.

Postoffice   Alma Ind Tery

### AFFIDAVIT OF MOTHER.

UNITED STATES OF AMERICA, Indian Territory,
Southern   DISTRICT.

I, Oma M^{c}lellan-Hines, on oath state that I am 27 years of age and a citizen by Blood, of the Choctaw Nation; that I am the lawful wife of G.M. Hines, who is ~~a citizen, by~~ *non citizen* of the ............ Nation; that a female child was born to me on 14 day of August, 1903; that said child has been named Della May Hines, and was living March 4, 1905.

Oma Hines

Witnesses To Mark:

Subscribed and sworn to before me this 3 day of April, 1905

J.E. Harbison
Notary Public.
My commission expires <u>Dec-6-08</u>

### AFFIDAVIT OF ATTENDING PHYSICIAN OR MID-WIFE.

UNITED STATES OF AMERICA, Indian Territory,
Central   DISTRICT.

I, R.P. Dickey, a physician, on oath state that I attended on Mrs. Oma M^{c}lellan-Hines, wife of G.M. Hines on the 14 day of August, 1903; that there was born to her on said date a female child; that said child was living March 4, 1905, and is said to have been named Della May Hines

R.P. Dickey

## Applications for Enrollment of Choctaw Newborn
## Act of 1905   Volume XI

Witnesses To Mark:
{

   Subscribed and sworn to before me this 27  day of   March    , 1905

                              J.G. Reeder
                                   Notary Public.
                    My commission expires 1908

---

Choc New Born 719
   Julius Beal   b. 11-18-03

                                        7-3489

              Muskogee, Indian Territory, April 10, 1905.

Pinkney Beal,
   Albany, Indian Territory.

Dear Sir:

   Receipt is hereby acknowledged of the affidavits of Ailsie Beal and P. L. Cain to the birth of Julius Beal, son of Pinkney and Ailsey[sic] Beal, November 18, 1903, and the same have been filed with our records as an application for the enrollment of said child.

                     Respectfully,

                              Commissioner in Charge.

                                        7-NB-719.

              Muskogee, Indian Territory, May 29, 1905.

Pinkney Beal,
   Albany, Indian Territory.

Dear Sir:

   There is enclosed you herewith for execution application for the enrollment of your infant child, Julius Beal.

# Applications for Enrollment of Choctaw Newborn
## Act of 1905   Volume XI

In the affidavits of January 16, 1905, heretofore filed in this office the date of the applicant's birth is given as November 19, 1903, while in those of the 4th ultimo the date is given as November 18, 1903. In the enclosed application the date of birth has been left blank. Please insert the correct date and, when the affidavits are properly executed, return them to this office.

It is also noted in these affidavits that the applicant claims through you. If this is correct it will be necessary for you to file in this office either the original or a certified copy of the license and certificate of your marriage to the mother of this applicant, Ailsey Beal.

In having these affidavits executed care should be exercised to see that all names are written in full, as they appear in the body of the affidavit, and in the event that either of the persons signing the affidavit are unable to write, signatures by mark must be attested by two witnesses. Each affidavit must be executed before a Notary Public and the notarial seal and signature of the officer must be attached to each separate affidavit.

Respectfully,

VR 29-4.                                        Chairman.

---

7 NB 719

Muskogee, Indian Territory, June 30, 1905.

Pinkney Beal,
    Albany, Indian Territory.

Dear Sir:

Receipt is hereby acknowledged of the affidavits of Ailsie Beal and P. S. Cain to the birth of Julius Beal, son of Pinkney and Ailsie Beal, November 18, 1903; receipt is also acknowledged of the marriage license and certificate between Pinckney[sic] Beal and Ailcy[sic] Cooper and the same have been filed with our records in the matter of the enrollment of said child.

Respectfully,

Chairman.

**Applications for Enrollment of Choctaw Newborn**
**Act of 1905   Volume XI**

*Mr* Pinckney Beal

AND

*Miss* Ailsey Cooper

## Marriage Certificate

DEPARTMENT OF THE INTERIOR,
COMMISSION TO THE FIVE CIVILIZED TRIBES.
**FILED**

JUN 29 1905

*Tams Bixby* CHAIRMAN.

*Issued*   June 12   *190*

Pat Henry   *Clerk*

*By* _____ *Deputy*

*Fee $1.00*

## Marriage Certificate

STATE OF TEXAS

COUNTY OF Fannin

This Instrument Witnesseth that on the 24th day of July A.D. ~~190~~ 1882 there was issued out of the office of the Clerk of the County Court of said County a License for the Marriage of

*Mr* **Pinckney Beal**

## Applications for Enrollment of Choctaw Newborn
## Act of 1905 Volume XI

and Miss Ailey Cooper and on the 30th day of July A.D. ~~190~~ 1882 said parties were legally united in Marriage by a properly authorized person, named in said License and due return thereof made to this office in the manner and form required by law, all of which is duly entered upon the Marriage Records of my office in Vol D. Page 424

Witness my hand and official seal at my office in Bonham Texas on this the 12th day of June A.D. 1905.

Pat Henry
Clerk County Court **Fannin** County Texas
By ............................................. Deputy

---

**NEW-BORN AFFIDAVIT.**

Number..............

## Choctaw Enrolling Commission.

IN THE MATTER OF THE APPLICATION FOR ENROLLMENT, as a citizen of the Choctaw Nation, of Julious[sic] Beal

born on the 19[sic] day of November 190 3

Name of father  Pinkney Beal          a citizen of   Choctaw
Nation final enrollment No  9931
Name of mother  Ailsie Beal           a citizen of   white
Nation final enrollment No    9931

Postoffice   Albany I.T.

## Applications for Enrollment of Choctaw Newborn
## Act of 1905  Volume XI

### AFFIDAVIT OF MOTHER.

UNITED STATES OF AMERICA,
INDIAN TERRITORY,
Central   DISTRICT

I  Alsie[sic] Beal  on oath state that I am 40 years of age and a citizen by white of the Choctaw Nation, and as such have been placed upon the final roll of the _____ Nation, by the Honorable Secretary of the Interior my final enrollment number being _____ ; that I am the lawful wife of Pinkney Beal, who is a citizen of the Choctaw Nation, and as such has been placed upon the final roll of said Nation by the Honorable Secretary of the Interior, his final enrollment number being 9931 and that a male child was born to me on the 19 day of November 190 3 ; that said child has been named Julious Beal, and is now living.

Ailsie Beal

WITNESSETH:
Must be two Witnesses who are Citizens.
Thomas T Beal
Andrew P Beal

Subscribed and sworn to before me this 16# day of January 190 5

J M Reaser
Notary Public.

My commission expires May 1908

---

### AFFIDAVIT OF ATTENDING PHYSICIAN OR MIDWIFE

UNITED STATES OF AMERICA
INDIAN TERRITORY
Central   DISTRICT

I, P.L. Cain a Physician on oath state that I attended on Mrs. Ailsie Beal wife of Pinkney Beal on the 19# day of November, 190 3, that there was born to her on said date a Male child, that said child is now living, and is said to have been named Julious Beal

P.L. Cain  M.D.

Subscribed and sworn to before me this, the 16# day of January 190 5

J.M. Reaser
Notary Public.

WITNESSETH:
Must be two witnesses who are citizens and know the child.
Thomas T Beal
Andrew P Beal

## Applications for Enrollment of Choctaw Newborn
## Act of 1905   Volume XI

We hereby certify that we are well acquainted with P.L. Cain a _____ and know him to be reputable and of good standing in the community.

> Thomas T Beal
> Andrew P Beal

**BIRTH AFFIDAVIT.**

## DEPARTMENT OF THE INTERIOR.
## COMMISSION TO THE FIVE CIVILIZED TRIBES.

IN RE APPLICATION FOR ENROLLMENT, as a citizen of the Choctaw Nation, of Julius Beal, born on the 18 day of November, 1903

Name of Father: Pinkney Beal      a citizen of the Choctaw Nation.
Name of Mother: Ailsey Beal       a citizen of the United States Nation.

Postoffice   Albany, I. T.

**AFFIDAVIT OF MOTHER.**

UNITED STATES OF AMERICA, Indian Territory,
Central   DISTRICT.

I, Ailsey Beal, on oath state that I am ___ years of age and a citizen by ____, of the United States ~~Nation~~; that I am the lawful wife of Pinkney Beal, who is a citizen, by blood of the Choctaw Nation; that a male child was born to me on 18 day of November, 1903; that said child has been named Julius Beal, and was living March 4, 1905.

Ailsie Beal

Witnesses To Mark:

Subscribed and sworn to before me this 4# day of April, 1905

J.M. Reaser
Notary Public.

# Applications for Enrollment of Choctaw Newborn
## Act of 1905   Volume XI

**AFFIDAVIT OF ATTENDING PHYSICIAN OR MID-WIFE.**

UNITED STATES OF AMERICA, Indian Territory, }
   Central            DISTRICT.

I, P.L. Cain, a physician, on oath state that I attended on Mrs. Ailsey Beal, wife of Pinkney Beal on the 18# day of November, 1903; that there was born to her on said date a male child; that said child was living March 4, 1905, and is said to have been named Julius Beal

                              P.L. Cain

Witnesses To Mark:
{

Subscribed and sworn to before me this 4$^{th}$ day of April, 1905.

                              J.M. Reaser
                              Notary Public.

**BIRTH AFFIDAVIT.**

## DEPARTMENT OF THE INTERIOR.
## COMMISSION TO THE FIVE CIVILIZED TRIBES.

IN RE APPLICATION FOR ENROLLMENT, as a citizen of the Choctaw Nation, of Julius Beal, born on the 18 day of November, 1903

Name of Father: Pinkney Beal      a citizen of the Choctaw Nation.
Name of Mother: Ailsey Beal      a citizen of the United States Nation.

                     Postoffice    Albany, I. T.

**AFFIDAVIT OF MOTHER.**

UNITED STATES OF AMERICA, Indian Territory, }
   Central            DISTRICT.

I, Ailsey Beal, on oath state that I am 40 years of age and a citizen by ———, of the United States Nation; that I am the lawful wife of Pinkney Beal, who is a citizen, by blood of the Choctaw Nation; that a male child was born to me on 18 day of November, 1903; that said child has been named Julius Beal, and was living March 4, 1905.

                              Ailsie Beal

Witnesses To Mark:
{

# Applications for Enrollment of Choctaw Newborn
## Act of 1905   Volume XI

Subscribed and sworn to before me this 23  day of   June  , 1905

> P.L. Cain
> Notary Public.

---

**AFFIDAVIT OF ATTENDING PHYSICIAN OR MID-WIFE.**

UNITED STATES OF AMERICA, Indian Territory, }
Central                DISTRICT.

I,  P.L. Cain  , a  Physician  , on oath state that I attended on Mrs.  Ailsey Beal  , wife of  Pinkney Beal  on the 18 day of November , 1903; that there was born to her on said date a  male  child; that said child was living March 4, 1905, and is said to have been named Julius Beal

> P.L. Cain

Witnesses To Mark:
{

Subscribed and sworn to before me this 23$^{rd}$  day of   June  , 1905

> W.J. O'Donby
> Notary Public.

---

Choc New Born 720
  Charles Coley  b. 2-19-04

7-2825

Muskogee, Indian Territory, April 10, 1905.

Anderson Coley,
  Redoak, Indian Territory.

Dear Sir:

Receipt is hereby acknowledged of the affidavits of Biney Coley and John J. Gill to the birth of Carlos[sic] Coley, son of Anderson and Biney Coley, February 19, 1904, and the same have been filed with our records as an application for the enrollment of said child.

Applications for Enrollment of Choctaw Newborn
Act of 1905   Volume XI

Respectfully,

Commissioner in Charge.

# NEW BORN AFFIDAVIT

No ............

## CHOCTAW ENROLLING COMMISSION

IN THE MATTER OF THE APPLICATION FOR ENROLLMENT as a citizen of the Choctaw Nation, of    Charlie Coley          born on the  19   day of  February    190 4

Name of father   Anderson Coley       a citizen of   Choctaw    Nation, final enrollment No.  8300
Name of mother   Biney Coley          a citizen of   Choctaw    Nation, final enrollment No.  8301

Red Oak, I.T.                Postoffice.

### AFFIDAVIT OF MOTHER

UNITED STATES OF AMERICA }
INDIAN TERRITORY
DISTRICT   Central

I    Biney Coley          , on oath state that I am   33   years of age and a citizen by   blood   of the   Choctaw   Nation, and as such have been placed upon the final roll of the   Choctaw   Nation, by the Honorable Secretary of the Interior my final enrollment number being   8301   ; that I am the lawful wife of   Anderson Coley  , who is a citizen of the   Choctaw   Nation, and as such has been placed upon the final roll of said Nation by the Honorable Secretary of the Interior, his final enrollment number being  8300   and that a   male   child was born to me on the   19   day of  February  190 4; that said child has been named   Charlie Coley   , and is now living.

                                                her
WITNESSETH:                         Biney  x  Coley
  Must be two witnesses { Morris Sam            mark
  who are citizens      { Mack H LeFlore

83

## Applications for Enrollment of Choctaw Newborn
## Act of 1905  Volume XI

Subscribed and sworn to before me this, the 21 day of February, 1905

Robert E Lee
Notary Public.

My Commission Expires: Jan 11 1906

*Affidavit of Attending Physician or Midwife*

UNITED STATES OF AMERICA,  
INDIAN TERRITORY,  
Central DISTRICT

I, Jno J Gill a physician on oath state that I attended on Mrs. Biney Coley wife of Anderson Coley on the 19 day of February, 1904, that there was born to her on said date a male child, that said child is now living, and is said to have been named Charlie Coley

Jno J Gill   M. D.

Subscribed and sworn to before me this the 21 day of February 1905

Robert E Lee
Notary Public.

WITNESSETH:
Must be two witnesses who are citizens and know the child.
- Morris Sam
- Mack H Leflore

We hereby certify that we are well acquainted with John J Gill a physician and know him to be reputable and of good standing in the community.

Must be two citizen witnesses.
- Simon Atoka
- Ned Sockey

---

BIRTH AFFIDAVIT.

## DEPARTMENT OF THE INTERIOR,
### COMMISSION TO THE FIVE CIVILIZED TRIBES.

*IN RE Application for Enrollment,* as a citizen of the Choctaw Nation, of Carles[sic] Coley, born on the 19 day of Feb, 1904

Name of Father: Anderson Coley   a citizen of the Choctaw Nation.
Name of Mother: Biney Coley   a citizen of the Choctaw Nation.

## Applications for Enrollment of Choctaw Newborn
## Act of 1905   Volume XI

Post-Office:   Red Oak

**AFFIDAVIT OF MOTHER.**

UNITED STATES OF AMERICA,  
**INDIAN TERRITORY.**  
Central   District.

I, Biney Coley, on oath state that I am about 34 years of age and a citizen by birth, of the Choctaw Nation; that I am the lawful wife of Anderson Coley, who is a citizen, by birth of the Choctaw Nation; that a male child was born to me on 19 day of Feb, 1904, that said child has been named Charles Coley, and is now living.

                                                              her  
                                              Biney x Coley  
**WITNESSES TO MARK:**                      mark  
{ M.D. Carney  
  Thomas Jefferson

Subscribed and sworn to before me this 4 day of April, 1905.

*(Name Illegible)*  
**NOTARY PUBLIC.**

**AFFIDAVIT OF ATTENDING PHYSICIAN OR MID-WIFE.**

UNITED STATES OF AMERICA,  
**INDIAN TERRITORY.**  
Central   District.

I, J J Gill MD, a MD, on oath state that I attended on Mrs. Biney Coley, wife of Anderson Coley on the 19 day of Feb, 1904; that there was born to her on said date a male child; that said child is now living and is said to have been named Charles Coley

                                              Jno J Gill M.D.  
**WITNESSES TO MARK:**  
{

Subscribed and sworn to before me this 4 day of April, 1905.

*(Name Illegible)*  
**NOTARY PUBLIC.**

## Applications for Enrollment of Choctaw Newborn
## Act of 1905   Volume XI

Choc New Born 721
   Joseph Jefferson b. 2-6-03

7-2891

Muskogee, Indian Territory, April 10, 1905.

Thomas Jefferson,
   Redoak, Indian Territory.

Dear Sir:

   Receipt is hereby acknowledged of the affidavits of Bicey Jefferson and Elsie Carney to the birth of Joseph Jefferson, son of Thomas and Bicey Jefferson, February 6, 1903, and the same have been filed with our records as an application for the enrollment of said child.

                        Respectfully,

                        Commissioner in Charge.

**BIRTH AFFIDAVIT.**

## DEPARTMENT OF THE INTERIOR,
### COMMISSION TO THE FIVE CIVILIZED TRIBES.

   *IN RE Application for Enrollment,* as a citizen of the   Choctaw   Nation, of   Joseph Jefferson   , born on the   6   day of   Feb   , 1903

Name of Father: Thomas Jefferson      a citizen of the   Choctaw   Nation.
Name of Mother: Bicey Jefferson      a citizen of the   Choctaw   Nation.

                Post-Office:   Red Oak

### AFFIDAVIT OF MOTHER.

UNITED STATES OF AMERICA, ⎫
    INDIAN TERRITORY.      ⎬
  Central      District.     ⎭

   I,   Bicey Jefferson   , on oath state that I am   about 34   years of age and a citizen by   birth   , of the   Choctaw   Nation; that I am the lawful wife of   Thomas Jefferson   , who is a citizen, by   birth   of the   Choctaw   Nation; that a   male   child

## Applications for Enrollment of Choctaw Newborn
## Act of 1905   Volume XI

was born to me on   6   day of   Feb  , 1903 , that said child has been named   Joseph Jefferson   , and is now living.

her<br>Bicey x Jefferson<br>mark

WITNESSES TO MARK:
{ M.D. Carney
  Elsie Carney

Subscribed and sworn to before me this   4   day of   Aprl[sic]   , 1905.

W.W. Ish<br>NOTARY PUBLIC.

---

### AFFIDAVIT OF ATTENDING PHYSICIAN OR MID-WIFE.

UNITED STATES OF AMERICA, }
    INDIAN TERRITORY.
  Central       District. }

I,   Elsie Carney   , a   Nurse   , on oath state that I attended on Mrs.   Bicey Jefferson   , wife of   Thomas Jefferson   on the   6   day of   Feb  , 1903 ; that there was born to her on said date a   male   child; that said child is now living and is said to have been named   Joseph Jefferson

Elsie Carney

WITNESSES TO MARK:
{

Subscribed and sworn to before me this   4   day of   April   , 1905.

W.W. Ish<br>NOTARY PUBLIC.

---

<u>Choc New Born 722</u>
   Zora Goings   b. 11-18-04

# Applications for Enrollment of Choctaw Newborn
## Act of 1905 Volume XI

7-3633

Muskogee, Indian Territory, April 10, 1905.

Nicholas Goings,
Boswell, Indian Territory.

Dear Sir:

Receipt is hereby acknowledged of the affidavits of Lena Goings and Mary Stephens to the birth of Zora Goings, daughter of Nicholas[sic] and Lena Goings, November 18, 1904, and the same have been filed with our records as an application for the enrollment of said child.

Respectfully,

Commissioner in Charge.

---

**BIRTH AFFIDAVIT.**

### DEPARTMENT OF THE INTERIOR.
### COMMISSION TO THE FIVE CIVILIZED TRIBES.

---

**IN RE APPLICATION FOR ENROLLMENT,** as a citizen of the Choctaw Nation, of Zora Goings , born on the 18 day of November , 1904

Name of Father: Nicholas Goings    a citizen of the Choctaw Nation.
Name of Mother: Lena Goings    a citizen of the Choctaw Nation.

Postoffice    Boswell I.T.

---

**AFFIDAVIT OF MOTHER.**

UNITED STATES OF AMERICA, Indian Territory, }
Central    DISTRICT. }

I, Lena Goings , on oath state that I am 27 years of age and a citizen by intermarage[sic] , of the Choctaw Nation; that I am the lawful wife of Nicholas Goings , who is a citizen, by blood of the Choctaw Nation; that a Female child was born to me on 18" day of November , 1904; that said child has been named Zora Goings , and was living March 4, 1905.

Lena Goings

Witnesses To Mark:
{

## Applications for Enrollment of Choctaw Newborn
## Act of 1905   Volume XI

Subscribed and sworn to before me this 5" day of   April   , 1905

S H Downing
Notary Public.

---

**AFFIDAVIT OF ATTENDING PHYSICIAN OR MID-WIFE.**

UNITED STATES OF AMERICA, Indian Territory, }
Central                            DISTRICT. }

I,   Mary Stephens   , a   midwife   , on oath state that I attended on Mrs.   Lena Goings   , wife of   Nicholas Goings   on the   18"   day of   November   , 1904; that there was born to her on said date a   Female   child; that said child was living March 4, 1905, and is said to have been named   Zora Goings

Mary Stephens

Witnesses To Mark:
{

Subscribed and sworn to before me this 5" day of   April   , 1905

S H Downing
Notary Public.

---

Choc New Born 723
    Clarence Edward Caudill   b. 5-19-03

7-3472

Muskogee, Indian Territory, April 10, 1905.

Henry A. Caudill,
    Durant, Indian Territory.

Dear Sir:

    Receipt is hereby acknowledged of the affidavits of Bertha Caudill and Mary Lane to the birth of Clarence Edward Caudill son of Henry A. and Bertha Caudill, May 19, 1903, and the same have been filed with our records as an application for the enrollment of said child.

# Applications for Enrollment of Choctaw Newborn
## Act of 1905  Volume XI

Respectfully,

Commissioner in Charge.

7-NB-723.

Muskogee, Indian Territory, May 29, 1905.

Henry A. Candill[sic],
   Durant, Indian Territory.

Dear Sir:

There is enclosed you herewith for execution application for the enrollment of your infant child, Clarence Edward Caudill.

In the affidavits of January 16, 1905, heretofore filed in this office, the date of the applicant's birth is given as May 9, 1903, while in the affidavits of the 5th ultimo it is given as May 19, 1903. In the enclosed application the date of birth is left blank. Please insert the correct date and, when the affidavits are properly executed, return them to this office.

In having these affidavits executed care should be exercised to see that all names are written in full, as they appear in the body of the affidavit, and in the event that either of the persons signing the affidavit are unable to write, signatures by mark must be attested by two witnesses. Each affidavit must be executed before a Notary Public and the notarial seal and signature of the officer must be attached to each separate affidavit.

Respectfully,

VR 29-5.                                                            Chairman.

7-N.B. 723.

Muskogee, Indian Territory, June 5, 1905.

Henry A. Caudill,
   Durant, Indian Territory.

Dear Sir:

Receipt is hereby acknowledged of the affidavits of Bertha Cadill[sic] and Mary Lane to the birth of Clarence Edward Caudill, son of Henry A. and Bertha Caudill, May 19, 1903, and the same have been filed with our records in the matter of the enrollment of said child.

## Applications for Enrollment of Choctaw Newborn
## Act of 1905   Volume XI

Respectfully,

Commissioner in Charge.

BIRTH AFFIDAVIT.

### DEPARTMENT OF THE INTERIOR.
### COMMISSION TO THE FIVE CIVILIZED TRIBES.

IN RE APPLICATION FOR ENROLLMENT, as a citizen of the Choctaw Nation, of Clarence Edward Caudill, born on the 19$^{th}$ day of May A.D., 1903

Name of Father: Henry A Caudill     a citizen of the U.S. Nation.
Name of Mother: Bertha Caudill     a citizen of the Choctaw Nation.

Postoffice    Durant Ind Ter

**AFFIDAVIT OF MOTHER.**

UNITED STATES OF AMERICA, Indian Territory,
Central     DISTRICT.

I, Bertha Caudill, on oath state that I am 22 years of age and a citizen by blood, of the Choctaw Nation; that I am the lawful wife of Henry A Caudill, who is a citizen, ~~by~~ —— of the United States Nation; that a male child was born to me on 19$^{th}$ day of May A.D., 1903; that said child has been named Clarence Edward Caudill, and was living March 4, 1905.

Bertha Caudill

Witnesses To Mark:

Subscribed and sworn to before me this 2$^{nd}$ day of June, 1905

T.M. Hinsley
Commission     Notary Public.
Expires 12-5-06

# Applications for Enrollment of Choctaw Newborn
# Act of 1905   Volume XI

### AFFIDAVIT OF ATTENDING PHYSICIAN OR MID-WIFE.

UNITED STATES OF AMERICA, Indian Territory,
Central           DISTRICT.

I, Mary Lane, a Female, on oath state that I attended on Mrs. Bertha Caudill, wife of Henry A Caudill on the 19$^{th}$ day of May A.D., 1903; that there was born to her on said date a male child; that said child was living March 4, 1905, and is said to have been named Clarence Edward Caudill

Mary Lane

Witnesses To Mark:

{

Subscribed and sworn to before me this 2$^{nd}$ day of June, 1905

T.M. Hinsley<br>Notary Public.

Commission expires 12-5-06

---

## AFFIDAVIT OF ATTENDING PHYSICIAN OR MIDWIFE

UNITED STATES OF AMERICA
INDIAN TERRITORY
Central   DISTRICT

I, Mary Lane   a   midwife   on oath state that I attended on Mrs. Bertha Caudill   wife of   Anderson Caudill on the   9$^{th}$[sic]   day of   May, 190 3, that there was born to her on said date a Male child, that said child is now living, and is said to have been named Clarence Caudill

Mary Lane   M.D.

Subscribed and sworn to before me this, the 16$^{th}$ day of Jan   190 5

W.A. Shoney<br>Notary Public.

WITNESSETH:

Must be two witnesses who are citizens and know the child.
{ Horatio Veach
  (Name Illegible)

We hereby certify that we are well acquainted with   Mary Lane   a   midwife   and know   her   to be reputable and of good standing in the community.

{ Horatio Veach
  (Name Illegible)

Applications for Enrollment of Choctaw Newborn
Act of 1905   Volume XI

**NEW-BORN AFFIDAVIT.**

Number..............

## Choctaw Enrolling Commission.

IN THE MATTER OF THE APPLICATION FOR ENROLLMENT, as a citizen of the Choctaw Nation, of    Clarence Caudill

born on the   $9^{th}$[sic] day of   May   190 3

Name of father   Anderson Caudill        a citizen of   Choctaw   Nation final enrollment No —
Name of mother   Bertha Caudill        a citizen of   Choctaw   Nation final enrollment No  9896

Postoffice   Durant I.T.

**AFFIDAVIT OF MOTHER.**

UNITED STATES OF AMERICA,
INDIAN TERRITORY,
Central   DISTRICT

I   Bertha Caudill   on oath state that I am   21   years of age and a citizen by   blood   of the   Choctaw   Nation, and as such have been placed upon the final roll of the   Choctaw   Nation, by the Honorable Secretary of the Interior my final enrollment number being   9896   ; that I am the lawful wife of   Anderson Caudill   , who is a citizen of the   White   Nation, and as such has been placed upon the final roll of said Nation by the Honorable Secretary of the Interior, his final enrollment number being   —and that a   male   child was born to me on the   $9^{th}$   day of   May   190 3; that said child has been named   Clarence Caudill   , and is now living.

Bertha Caudill

WITNESSETH:
Must be two
Witnesses who
are Citizens.   } Horatio Veach

*(Name Illegible)*

Subscribed and sworn to before me this   $16^{th}$   day of   January   190 5

W.A. Shoney
Notary Public.

My commission expires   Jan 10 1909

## Applications for Enrollment of Choctaw Newborn
## Act of 1905 Volume XI

BIRTH AFFIDAVIT.

### DEPARTMENT OF THE INTERIOR.
### COMMISSION TO THE FIVE CIVILIZED TRIBES.

IN RE APPLICATION FOR ENROLLMENT, as a citizen of the Choctaw Nation, of Clarence Edward Caudill, born on the 19 day of May, 1903

Name of Father: Henry A Caudill    a citizen of the U.S. Nation.
Name of Mother: Bertha Caudill    a citizen of the Choctaw Nation.

Postoffice    Durant Ind Ter

**AFFIDAVIT OF MOTHER.**

UNITED STATES OF AMERICA, Indian Territory,
Central    DISTRICT.

I, Bertha Caudill, on oath state that I am 22 years of age and a citizen by blood, of the Choctaw Nation; that I am the lawful wife of Henry A Caudill, who is a citizen, ~~by~~ ——— of the U. S. Nation; that a male child was born to me on 19 day of May, 1903; that said child has been named Clarence Edward Caudill, and was living March 4, 1905.

                                       Bertha Caudill

Witnesses To Mark:
{

Subscribed and sworn to before me this 5$^{th}$ day of April, 1905

                                       T.M. Hinsley
                                       Notary Public.

**AFFIDAVIT OF ATTENDING PHYSICIAN OR MID-WIFE.**

UNITED STATES OF AMERICA, Indian Territory,
Central    DISTRICT.

I, Mary Lane, a Midwife, on oath state that I attended on Mrs. Bertha Caudill, wife of Henry A Caudill on the 19 day of May, 1903; that there was born to her on said date a male child; that said child was living March 4, 1905, and is said to have been named Clarence Edward Caudill

                                       Mary Lane

Witnesses To Mark:
{

## Applications for Enrollment of Choctaw Newborn
## Act of 1905   Volume XI

Subscribed and sworn to before me this 5th day of April, 1905

T.M. Hinsley
Notary Public.

---

Choc New Born 724
Wilburn Hunt   b. 3-1-05

7-NB-724

Muskogee, Indian Territory, February 9, 1906.

Charles T. Mitchell,
Attorney at Law,
McCurtain, Indian Territory.

Dear Sir:

Receipt is hereby acknowledged of your letter of February 6, 1906, asking the roll number of Wilburn Hunt a new born Choctaw, child of James and Ennett[sic] Hunt.

In reply to your letter you are advised that the name of Wilburn Hunt, child of James and Annette Hunt appears upon the approved roll of new born citizens of the Choctaw Nation, opposite No. 693.

Respectfully,

Acting Commissioner.

**BIRTH AFFIDAVIT.**
**DEPARTMENT OF THE INTERIOR.**
**COMMISSION TO THE FIVE CIVILIZED TRIBES.**

IN RE APPLICATION FOR ENROLLMENT, as a citizen of the    Choctaw    Nation, of Wilburn Hunt, born on the 1st day of March, 1905

Name of Father: James Hunt                a citizen of the   Choctaw   Nation.
Name of Mother: Annette Hunt (nee Kanehta)   a citizen of the   Choctaw   Nation.

Postoffice   McCurtain, Ind. Ter.

# Applications for Enrollment of Choctaw Newborn
## Act of 1905   Volume XI

**AFFIDAVIT OF MOTHER.**

UNITED STATES OF AMERICA, Indian Territory, }
Central                           DISTRICT.

I, Annette Hunt, on oath state that I am 17 years of age and a citizen by blood, of the Choctaw Nation; that I am the lawful wife of James Hunt, who is a citizen, by blood of the Choctaw Nation; that a male child was born to me on 1st day of March, 1905; that said child has been named Wilburn Hunt, and was living March 4, 1905.

Annette Hunt

Witnesses To Mark:
{

Subscribed and sworn to before me this 5 day of April, 1905

My commission Exp 2/2/08

Frank E Parke
Notary Public.

---

**AFFIDAVIT OF ATTENDING PHYSICIAN OR MID-WIFE.**

UNITED STATES OF AMERICA, Indian Territory, }
Central                           DISTRICT.

I, Louisa Hunt, a midwife, on oath state that I attended on Mrs. Annette Hunt, wife of James Hunt on the 1st day of March, 1905; that there was born to her on said date a male child; that said child was living March 4, 1905, and is said to have been named Wilburn Hunt

her
Louisa x Hunt
mark

Witnesses To Mark:
{ Roy Parke
{ A.R. Davis

Subscribed and sworn to before me this 5 day of April, 1905

My Com Exp 2/2/08

Frank E Parke
Notary Public.

---

<u>Choc New Born 725</u>
   Bennie Alfred Darneal   b. 3-31-04

## Applications for Enrollment of Choctaw Newborn
## Act of 1905  Volume XI

7-2778

Muskogee, Indian Territory, April 10, 1905.

Stephen Darneal,
    Kinta, Indian Territory.

Dear Sir:

    Receipt is hereby acknowledged of the affidavits of Mary Darneal and E. Johnson, to the birth of Bennie Alfred Darneal, son of Stephen and Mary Darneal, March 31, 1904, and the same have been filed with our records as an application for the enrollment of said child.

                Respectfully,

                Commissioner in Charge.

---

### AFFIDAVIT OF ATTENDING PHYSICIAN OR MIDWIFE

UNITED STATES OF AMERICA
INDIAN TERRITORY
  Western    DISTRICT

    I,  E. Johnson  a  Practicing Physician on oath state that I attended on Mrs.  Mary Darneal  wife of  Steven[sic] Darneal on the  31  day of  March  , 190 4, that there was born to her on said date a  male child, that said child is now living, and is said to have been named  Bennie Alfred Darneal

                E. Johnson  *M.D.*

    Subscribed and sworn to before me this, the  6  day of  Jan  190 5

WITNESSETH:                L C Tuey      Notary Public.

Must be two witnesses who are citizens { Roger Cooper
                        James Darneal

    We hereby certify that we are well acquainted with  Dr E Johnson  a  Practicing Physician  and know  him  to be reputable and of good standing in the community.

    Robert Cooper                        _____

    Dave Coley                           _____

# Applications for Enrollment of Choctaw Newborn
## Act of 1905   Volume XI

**BIRTH AFFIDAVIT.**

DEPARTMENT OF THE INTERIOR.
## COMMISSION TO THE FIVE CIVILIZED TRIBES.

IN RE APPLICATION FOR ENROLLMENT, as a citizen of the Choctaw Nation, of Bennie Alfred Darneal, born on the 31 day of March, 1904

Name of Father: Stephen C Darneal   a citizen of the Choctaw Nation.
Name of Mother: Mary Darneal   a citizen of the Choctaw Nation.

Postoffice   Kinta I.T.

**AFFIDAVIT OF MOTHER.**

UNITED STATES OF AMERICA, Indian Territory,
Western   DISTRICT.

I, Mary Darneal, on oath state that I am 36 years of age and a citizen by Intermarried, of the Choctaw Nation; that I am the lawful wife of Stephen C Darneal, who is a citizen, by blood of the Choctaw Nation; that a male child was born to me on 31 day of March, 1904, that said child has been named Bennie Alfred Darneal, and is now living.

Mary Darnll[sic]

Witnesses To Mark:
{

Subscribed and sworn to before me this 5th day of April, 1905.

L D Allen
Notary Public.

**AFFIDAVIT OF ATTENDING PHYSICIAN OR MID-WIFE.**

UNITED STATES OF AMERICA, Indian Territory,
Western   DISTRICT.

I, E Johnson, a Physician, on oath state that I attended on Mrs. Mary Darneal, wife of Stephen C Darneal on the 31 day of March, 1904; that there was born to her on said date a male child; that said child is now living and is said to have been named Bennie Alfred Darneal

E Johnson MD

Witnesses To Mark:
{

## Applications for Enrollment of Choctaw Newborn
## Act of 1905  Volume XI

Subscribed and sworn to before me this 5th day of April, 1905.

L D Allen
Notary Public.

My commission expires Feb 27/07

**NEW-BORN AFFIDAVIT.**

Number..................

...Choctaw Enrolling Commission...

IN THE MATTER OF THE APPLICATION FOR ENROLLMENT, as a citizen of the Choctaw Nation, of  Bennie Alfred Darneal

born on the 31 day of __March__ 190 4

Name of father  Stephen Darneal       a citizen of  Choctaw
Nation final enrollment No.  8145
Name of mother  Mary Darneal          a citizen of  Choctaw
Nation final enrollment No.  127

Postoffice    Kinta IT

**AFFIDAVIT OF MOTHER.**

UNITED STATES OF AMERICA
INDIAN TERRITORY
  Western    DISTRICT

I    Mary Darneal    , on oath state that I am 35 years of age and a citizen by Marriage of the Choctaw Nation, and as such have been placed upon the final roll of the Choctaw Nation, by the Honorable Secretary of the Interior my final enrollment number being 127 ; that I am the lawful wife of  Steven[sic] Darneal , who is a citizen of the Choctaw Nation, and as such has been placed upon the final roll of said Nation by the Honorable Secretary of the Interior, his final enrollment number being 8145 and that a Male child was born to me on the 31 day of March 190 4; that said child has been named Bennie Alfred Darneal , and is now living.

Mary Darneal

Witnesseth.
  Must be two  } Robert Cooper
  Witnesses who
  are Citizens.   James Darneal

## Applications for Enrollment of Choctaw Newborn
## Act of 1905   Volume XI

Subscribed and sworn to before me this   6   day of   Jan      190 5

                                    L C Tuey

My commission expires:   Jan 17 1907             Notary Public.

---

Choc New Born 726
        Scopia Russell   b. 3-4-05
                Cancelled

    Record Transferred to Choc NB No 170
                7-13-06

                empty

---

Choc New Born 727
        Lula Pearl Williams   b. 9-22-03

7-913 I.W.      7-730
**BIRTH AFFIDAVIT.**

                DEPARTMENT OF THE INTERIOR.
        **COMMISSION TO THE FIVE CIVILIZED TRIBES.**

    **IN RE APPLICATION FOR ENROLLMENT,** as a citizen of the   Choctaw   Nation, of Lula Pearl Williams   , born on the   22   day of   September   , 1903

Name of Father: Senora W Williams     a citizen of the   Choctaw   Nation.
Name of Mother: Sarah E Williams     a citizen of the   Choctaw   Nation.

                Postoffice   Ward Ind Ter

# Applications for Enrollment of Choctaw Newborn
## Act of 1905   Volume XI

**AFFIDAVIT OF MOTHER.**

UNITED STATES OF AMERICA, Indian Territory, }
................................................ DISTRICT. }

    I, Sarah E Williams, on oath state that I am 23 years of age and a citizen by intermarriage, of the Choctaw Nation; that I am the lawful wife of Senora W Williams, who is a citizen, by blood of the Choctaw Nation; that a female child was born to me on 22 day of September, 1903; that said child has been named Lula Pearl Williams, and was living March 4, 1905.

                                      her
                            Sarah E x Williams
Witnesses To Mark:          mark
  { FP Allen
    O O Jenkins

    Subscribed and sworn to before me this 3$^{rd}$ day of April, 1905

                            OL Johnson
                            Notary Public.

---

**AFFIDAVIT OF ATTENDING PHYSICIAN OR MID-WIFE.**

UNITED STATES OF AMERICA, Indian Territory, }
................................................ DISTRICT. }

    I, J B Beckett, a physician, on oath state that I attended on Mrs. Sarah E Williams, wife of Senora W Williams on the 22 day of September, 1903; that there was born to her on said date a ................ child; that said child was living March 4, 1905, and is said to have been named Lula Pearl Williams

                            J.B. Beckett M.D.
Witnesses To Mark:

  {

    Subscribed and sworn to before me this 5 day of April, 1905

                            A H Crouthamel
                            Notary Public.
My Com ex 2-3-1907

## Applications for Enrollment of Choctaw Newborn
## Act of 1905   Volume XI

Choc New Born 728
Ollie Lee Munkus   b. 8-2-04

7-2802

Muskogee, Indian Territory, April 11, 1905.

Walter McFerran,
Walls, Indian Territory.

Dear Sir:

Receipt is hereby acknowledged of the affidavits of Isabel McFerran and Isham C. Talley to the birth of Bennie McFerran, son of Walter and Isabel McFerran, October 3, 1903, and the same have been filed with our records as an application for the enrollment of said child.

Respectfully,

Commissioner in Charge.

**BIRTH AFFIDAVIT.**
### DEPARTMENT OF THE INTERIOR.
### COMMISSION TO THE FIVE CIVILIZED TRIBES.

IN RE APPLICATION FOR ENROLLMENT, as a citizen of the   Choctaw   Nation, of Ollie Lee Munkus   , born on the 2   day of   Aug   , 1904

Name of Father: Beverly D Munkus   a citizen of the   Choctaw   Nation.
Name of Mother: Sillie[sic] May Munkus   a citizen of the   Choctaw   Nation.

Postoffice   Harrisburg I.T.

**AFFIDAVIT OF MOTHER.**

UNITED STATES OF AMERICA, Indian Territory,
Southern                   DISTRICT.

I,   Lillie May Munkus   , on oath state that I am   25   years of age and a citizen by   blood   , of the   Choctaw   Nation; that I am the lawful wife of Beverly C Munkus   , who is a citizen, by   Intermarriage   of the   Choctaw Nation; that a   female   child was born to me on   2   day of   August   , 1904; that said child has been named   Ollie Lee Munkus   , and was living March 4, 1905.

## Applications for Enrollment of Choctaw Newborn
## Act of 1905   Volume XI

                                                  her
                                        Lillie  x  May Munkus
Witnesses To Mark:                    mark
  { W.J. Gilbert
    J H Skaggs

      Subscribed and sworn to before me this   5   day of     April         , 1905

                                                E.H. Bond
                                                      Notary Public.

---

### AFFIDAVIT OF ATTENDING PHYSICIAN OR MID-WIFE.

UNITED STATES OF AMERICA, Indian Territory, }
   Southern             DISTRICT.

     I,    Maggie F Richerson   , a    midwife      , on oath state that I attended on Mrs.   Lillie May Munkus      , wife of    Beverly C Munkus    on the  2  day of  August    , 1904; that there was born to her on said date a    female     child; that said child was living March 4, 1905, and is said to have been named   Ollie Lee Munkus

                                                her
                                      Maggie F.  x  Richerson
Witnesses To Mark:                    mark
  { W.J. Gilbert
    J H Skaggs

      Subscribed and sworn to before me this   5   day of     April         , 1905

                                                E.H. Bond
                                                 Notary Public.

---

<u>Choc New Born 729</u>
        Dave Hodges   b.  2-17-05

# Applications for Enrollment of Choctaw Newborn
## Act of 1905   Volume XI

7 N B 729

**COPY**

Muskogee, Indian Territory, April 17, 1905.

Henry C. Hodges,
    Coalgate, Indian Territory.

Dear Sir:

    You are hereby advised that before the application for the enrollment of your infant child, Dave Hodges, can be finally disposed of, it will be necessary for you to furnish the Commission with either the original or a certified copy of the license and certificate of your marriage to his mother, Myrtle Hodges.

    Please give this matter your immediate attention.

                      Respectfully,

              SIGNED
                *Tams Bixby*
                Chairman.

---

7 N.B. 729.

Muskogee, Indian Territory, May 4, 1905.

P. E. Wilhelm,
    Attorney at Law,
        Coalgate, Indian Territory.

Dear Sir:

    Receipt is hereby acknowledged of your letter of April 29, transmitting the marriage license and certificate between Henry Hodges and Myrtle Sneed, which you offer in support of the application for the enrollment of Dave Hodges, and the same have been filed in the matter of the enrollment of said child.

                  Respectfully,

                                  Chairman.

## Applications for Enrollment of Choctaw Newborn
### Act of 1905 Volume XI

DEPARTMENT OF THE INTERIOR,
Commission to the Five Civilized Tribes.

**FILED**

MAY 3 1905

*Tams Bixby* CHAIRMAN.

No. 1616

## Certificate of Record of Marriages.

UNITED STATES OF AMERICA, ⎫
   INDIAN TERRITORY, ⎬ SCT:
   Central       DISTRICT. ⎭

I,   E.J. Fannin   , Clerk of the United States Court in the Indian Territory and District aforesaid, do hereby CERTIFY, that the License for and Certificate of the Marriage of

Mr.   Henry Hodges   and

M iss Myrtle Sneed   was

filed in my office in said Territory and District the 25 day of Oct A.D., 190 2 and duly recorded in Book 2 of Marriage Record, Page 190

WITNESS my hand and seal of said Court, at   Atoka   , this 25 day of Oct   , A.D. 190 2

*E.J. Fannin*
Clerk.

By   J D Collins   Deputy.

Applications for Enrollment of Choctaw Newborn
Act of 1905 Volume XI

No. 1616

FORM NO. 598.

# MARRIAGE LICENSE.

UNITES STATES OF AMERICA, }
   THE INDIAN TERRITORY, } ss:
   Central     DISTRICT. }

To any Person Authorized by Law to Solemnize Marriage—Greeting:

*You are hereby commanded to solemnize the Rite and publish the* Banns of Matrimony *between* Mr. Henry Hodges *of* Coalgate *in the Indian Territory, aged* 21 *years, and Miss* Myrtle Sneed *of* Coalgate *in the Indian Territory, aged* 16 *years, according to law, and do you officially sign and return this License to the parties therein named.*

WITNESS my hand and official seal, this 6 day of Oct A. D. 190 2

                           E.J. Fannin
                           Clerk of the United States Court.

JD Collins         Deputy

---

## CERTIFICATE OF MARRIAGE.

UNITES STATES OF AMERICA, }
   THE INDIAN TERRITORY, } ss:     I,    F.B. McEntire D.D.
   .................... DISTRICT. }     a .................................................................................

do hereby CERTIFY, that on the 10 day of Oct A, D. 190 2 ; I did duly and according to law, as commanded in the foregoing License, solemnize the Rite and publish the BANNS OF MATRIMONY between the parties therein named.

Witness my hand this 10 day of Oct. , A. D. 190 2

My credentials are recorded in the office of the Clerk of the United States Court in the Indian Territory, Central District, Book B    Page 271

                         F. B. McEntire

                         a     D. D.

## Applications for Enrollment of Choctaw Newborn
## Act of 1905 Volume XI

BIRTH AFFIDAVIT.

### DEPARTMENT OF THE INTERIOR.
### COMMISSION TO THE FIVE CIVILIZED TRIBES.

IN RE APPLICATION FOR ENROLLMENT, as a citizen of the Choctaw Nation, of Dave Hodges, born on the 17 day of Feb, 1905

Name of Father: Henry C Hodges    a citizen of the Choctaw Nation.
Name of Mother: Myrtle Hodges    a citizen of the U.S. Nation.

Postoffice    Coal-Gate I.T.

**AFFIDAVIT OF MOTHER.**

UNITED STATES OF AMERICA, Indian Territory, }
Central    DISTRICT.

I, Myrtle Hodges, on oath state that I am 18 years of age and a citizen by —, of the U.S. Nation; that I am the lawful wife of Henry C Hodges, who is a citizen, by Blood of the Choctaw Nation; that a Male child was born to me on 17 day of Feb, 1905; that said child has been named Dave Hodges, and was living March 4, 1905.

Myrtle Hodges

Witnesses To Mark:
{

Subscribed and sworn to before me this 4 day of April, 1905

John H Cross
Notary Public.

**AFFIDAVIT OF ATTENDING PHYSICIAN OR MID-WIFE.**

UNITED STATES OF AMERICA, Indian Territory, }
Central    DISTRICT.

I, R.D. Cody, a Physician, on oath state that I attended on Mrs. Myrtle Hodges, wife of Henry C Hodges on the 17 day of Feb, 1905; that there was born to her on said date a Male child; that said child was living March 4, 1905, and is said to have been named Dave Hodges

R.D. Cody M.D.

Witnesses To Mark:
{

## Applications for Enrollment of Choctaw Newborn
## Act of 1905   Volume XI

Subscribed and sworn to before me this   4 day of     April      , 1905

John H Cross
Notary Public.

---

Choc New Born 730
    Arthur Marmeduke Allen   b. 2-16-05
    Sylvia Eltine Allen   b. 12-23-02

7-N.B.-730.

Muskogee, Indian Territory, May 12, 1905.

John C. Allen,
    Ada, Indian Territory.

Dear Sir:

    Receipt is hereby acknowledged of the affidavit of Jennie McCarty to the birth of Silvy Eltine Allen, daughter of John C. and Mary I. Allen, December 23, 1902, and the same has been filed in the matter of the enrollment of said child.

Respectfully,

Chairman.

**AFFIDAVIT OF ATTENDING PHYSICIAN OR MID-WIFE.**

UNITED STATES OF AMERICA, Indian Territory,
    Southern              DISTRICT.

    I,   Jennie M$^c$Carty        , a   Mid-Wife     , on oath state that I attended on Mrs.  Mary I Allen     , wife of   John C Allen      on the   23$^d$ day of   Dec   , 1902; that there was born to her on said date a     Female    child; that said child was living March 4, 1905, and is said to have been named  Sylvy[sic] Eltine Allen

Jennie McCarty

Witnesses To Mark:
    { W A Turner
      R B Beatty

## Applications for Enrollment of Choctaw Newborn
## Act of 1905   Volume XI

Subscribed and sworn to before me this 2$^{nd}$ day of May , 1905

EJ Mitchell<br>Notary Public.

---

**BIRTH AFFIDAVIT.**

**DEPARTMENT OF THE INTERIOR.**
**COMMISSION TO THE FIVE CIVILIZED TRIBES.**

---

**IN RE APPLICATION FOR ENROLLMENT,** as a citizen of the Choctaw Nation, of Sylvia Eltine Allen , born on the 23 day of December , 1902

Name of Father: John C Allen        a citizen of the Choctaw Nation.
Name of Mother: Mary I Allen        a citizen of the Choctaw Nation.

Postoffice   Ada I.T.

---

**AFFIDAVIT OF MOTHER.**

UNITED STATES OF AMERICA, Indian Territory, }
   Southern            DISTRICT.

I, Mary I Allen , on oath state that I am 27 years of age and a citizen by blood , of the Choctaw Nation; that I am the lawful wife of John C Allen , who is a citizen, by intermarriage of the Choctaw Nation; that a female child was born to me on the 23 day of December , 1902; that said child has been named Sylvia Eltine Allen , and was living March 4, 1905.

Mary I Allen

Witnesses To Mark:
{

Subscribed and sworn to before me this 29 day of April , 1905

J E Williams<br>Notary Public.

# Applications for Enrollment of Choctaw Newborn
## Act of 1905   Volume XI

**AFFIDAVIT OF ATTENDING PHYSICIAN OR MID-WIFE.**

UNITED STATES OF AMERICA, Indian Territory, }
................................................ DISTRICT. }

*Affidavit of mid-wife will be furnished later.*

I, ................., a ......................, on oath state that I attended on Mrs. ................, wife of ................ on the ........ day of ............, 1......; that there was born to her on said date a ............... child; that said child was living March 4, 1905, and is said to have been named ..................................

Witnesses To Mark:
{ ..............................
  .............................. }

Subscribed and sworn to before me this ........ day of ..............., 1905.

................................................
Notary Public.

---

**BIRTH AFFIDAVIT.**

### DEPARTMENT OF THE INTERIOR.
### COMMISSION TO THE FIVE CIVILIZED TRIBES.

---

IN RE APPLICATION FOR ENROLLMENT, as a citizen of the   Choctaw   Nation, of Arthur Marmeduke Allen   , born on the   16$^{th}$   day of   February   , 1905

Name of Father: John C Allen            a citizen of the   Choctaw   Nation.
Name of Mother: Mary I Allen            a citizen of the   Choctaw   Nation.

Postoffice   Ada I.T.

---

**AFFIDAVIT OF MOTHER.**

UNITED STATES OF AMERICA, Indian Territory, }
   Southern           DISTRICT. }

I, Mary I Allen   , on oath state that I am   27   years of age and a citizen by blood   , of the   Choctaw   Nation; that I am the lawful wife of   John C Allen   , who is a citizen, by   Intermarriage   of the   Choctaw   Nation; that a   male   child was born to me on   16$^{th}$   day of   February   , 1905 , that said child has been named   Arthur Marmeduke Allen   , and is now living.

                                Mary I Allen

Witnesses To Mark:
{

## Applications for Enrollment of Choctaw Newborn
## Act of 1905   Volume XI

Subscribed and sworn to before me this 5th day of April , 1905.

>Tom D. McKeown
>Notary Public.

### AFFIDAVIT OF ATTENDING PHYSICIAN OR MID-WIFE.

**UNITED STATES OF AMERICA, Indian Territory,**
Southern   **DISTRICT.**

I,   L.M. Weaver   , a  Mid-wife  , on oath state that I attended on Mrs. Mary I Allen , wife of  John C Allen  on the  16th  day of February , 1905; that there was born to her on said date a   male   child; that said child is now living and is said to have been named   Arthur Marmeduke Allen

>her
>L. M.  x  Weaver
>mark

Witnesses To Mark:
{ WH Bealey
{ Tom D McKeown

Subscribed and sworn to before me this 5th day of April , 1905.

>Tom D. McKeown
>Notary Public.

---

Choc New Born 731
   John E. Tucker Jr  b. 8-24-04

### NEW-BORN AFFIDAVIT.

Number............

## Choctaw Enrolling Commission.

IN THE MATTER OF THE APPLICATION FOR ENROLLMENT, as a citizen of the   Choctaw   Nation, of     John J[sic] Tucker

born on the  24th   day of  August    190 4

Name of father   Ernest Tucker        a citizen of   Choctaw Nation final enrollment No    6964

# Applications for Enrollment of Choctaw Newborn
## Act of 1905   Volume XI

Name of mother   Bertha Tucker                    a citizen of   ───────
Nation final enrollment No............................

Postoffice

**AFFIDAVIT OF MOTHER.**

UNITED STATES OF AMERICA, ⎱
   INDIAN TERRITORY,    ⎰
  Central      DISTRICT

    I     Bertha Tucker                 on oath state that I am   19   years of age and a citizen by   Marriage     of the   Choctaw    Nation, and as such have been placed upon the final roll of the    Choctaw     Nation, by the Honorable Secretary of the Interior my final enrollment number being.........................; that I am the lawful wife of    Ernest Tucker        , who is a citizen of the    Choctaw       Nation, and as such has been placed upon the final roll of said Nation by the Honorable Secretary of the Interior, his final enrollment number being   6964    and that a    Male     child was born to me on the   24   day of   August    190 4 ; that said child has been named    John J Tucker       , and is now living.

Bertha Tucker

WITNESSETH:
  Must be two   ⎱  C Rogers
  Witnesses who  ⎰
  are Citizens.      O Thomas

    Subscribed and sworn to before me this   13   day of   June      190 5

A E Folsom<br>Notary Public.

My commission expires
9 - Jan 1905[sic]

## AFFIDAVIT OF ATTENDING PHYSICIAN OR MIDWIFE

UNITED STATES OF AMERICA
INDIAN TERRITORY
  Central      DISTRICT

    I,    J. A. Dabney             a          Practicing Physician on oath state that I attended on Mrs.   Bertha Tucker    wife of   Ernest Tucker   on the   24   day of    August  , 190 4, that there was born to her on said date a    Male   child, that said child is now living, and is said to have been named   John J Tucker

J A Dabney       M.D.

    Subscribed and sworn to before me this, the   13$^{th}$  day of    January     190 5

O C Elkins<br>Notary Public.

## Applications for Enrollment of Choctaw Newborn
## Act of 1905   Volume XI

WITNESSETH:

Must be two witnesses who are citizens and know the child.
{ C Rogers
  O Thomas

We hereby certify that we are well acquainted with Dr J A Dabney a Practicing Physician and know him to be reputable and of good standing in the community.

{ C Rogers
  O Thomas

My commission expires Jan $3^d$ 1909

---

No.

## Certificate of Record of Marriages.

UNITED STATES OF AMERICA,
INDIAN TERRITORY,
Central  DISTRICT. } SCT:

I, E.J. Fannin , Clerk of the United States Court in the Indian Territory and District aforesaid, do hereby CERTIFY, that the License for and Certificate of the Marriage of

Mr. Ernest Tucker and

Miss Bertha Ward was

filed in my office in said Territory and District the 7 day of Sept A.D., 190 3 and duly recorded in Book 2 of Marriage Record, Page 333

WITNESS my hand and seal of said Court, at Atoka , this 7 day of Sept , A.D. 190 3

E.J. Fannin
*Clerk.*
By  J D Cathie  *Deputy.*

DEPARTMENT OF THE INTERIOR,
Commission to the Five Civilized Tribes.

**FILED**

APR 11 1905

*Tams Bixby* CHAIRMAN.

**Applications for Enrollment of Choctaw Newborn
Act of 1905   Volume XI**

No. 1902                    FORM NO. 598.

# MARRIAGE LICENSE.

UNITES STATES OF AMERICA,
   THE INDIAN TERRITORY,  } ss:
  Central        DISTRICT.

To any Person Authorized by Law to Solemnize Marriage—Greeting:

You are hereby commanded to solemnize the Rite and publish the Banns of Matrimony between Mr. Ernest Tucker of Stringtown in the Indian Territory, aged 26 years, and Miss Bertha Ward of Atoka in the Indian Territory, aged 18 years, according to law, and do you officially sign and return this License to the parties therein named.

WITNESS my hand and official seal, this 2 day of Sept A. D. 190 3

*E. J. Fannin*
Clerk of the United States Court.

JD Cathie
      Deputy

---

## CERTIFICATE OF MARRIAGE.

UNITES STATES OF AMERICA,
   THE INDIAN TERRITORY,  } ss:
  ............................ DISTRICT.

I, Rev W. M. Davis
a n Elder of the M. E. Church, South

do hereby CERTIFY, that on the 6 day of September A, D. 190 3 ; I did duly and according to law, as commanded in the foregoing License, solemnize the Rite and publish the BANNS OF MATRIMONY between the parties therein named.

Witness my hand this 6 day of September , A. D. 190 3

My credentials are recorded in the office of the Clerk of the United States Court in the Indian Territory, Central District, Book A   Page 6

Rev W.M. Davis

a n Elder of the M.E. Church,
South

## Applications for Enrollment of Choctaw Newborn
## Act of 1905   Volume XI

BIRTH AFFIDAVIT.

## DEPARTMENT OF THE INTERIOR.
## COMMISSION TO THE FIVE CIVILIZED TRIBES.

    IN RE APPLICATION FOR ENROLLMENT, as a citizen of the    Choctaw    Nation, of    John E Tucker    , born on the   24$^{th}$   day of   August   , 1904

Name of Father: Earnest Tucker      a citizen of the   Choctaw   Nation.
Name of Mother: Bertha Tucker      a citizen of the United States Nation.

         Postoffice    Stringtown, I.T.

**AFFIDAVIT OF MOTHER.**

UNITED STATES OF AMERICA, Indian Territory, }
    Central            DISTRICT.

    I,  Bertha Tucker   , on oath state that I am  20   years of age and a citizen by ———   , of the   United States   ~~Nation~~; that I am the lawful wife of   Earnest Tucker   , who is a citizen, by blood   of the   Choctaw   Nation; that a   male   child was born to me on   24$^{th}$   day of   August   , 1904; that said child has been named   John E Tucker   , and was living March 4, 1905.

                                       Bertha Tucker

Witnesses To Mark:
{

     Subscribed and sworn to before me this  5$^{th}$  day of   April   , 1905

                                 W.H. Angell
                                    Notary Public.

**AFFIDAVIT OF ATTENDING PHYSICIAN OR MID-WIFE.**

UNITED STATES OF AMERICA, Indian Territory, }
    Central            DISTRICT.

    I,   J A Dabney   , a  Physician   , on oath state that I attended on Mrs.  Bertha Tucker   , wife of   Earnest Tucker   on the  24$^{th}$  day of  August , 1904; that there was born to her on said date a   male   child; that said child was living March 4, 1905, and is said to have been named  John E Tucker

                                 J A Dabney MD

Witnesses To Mark:
{

## Applications for Enrollment of Choctaw Newborn
## Act of 1905   Volume XI

Subscribed and sworn to before me this 6th day of   April   , 1905

O C Elkins<br>Notary Public.

---

Choc New Born 732
    Henry C. Butler   b. 10-23-04

7-NB-732.

Muskogee, Indian Territory, May 29, 1905.

J. M. Butler,
    Atoka, Indian Territory.

Dear Sir:

    There is enclosed you herewith for execution application for the enrollment of your infant child, Henry C. Butler.

    In the affidavits of February 21, 1905, heretofore filed in this office, the date of the applicant's birth is given as January 23, 1904, while the affidavits of the 5th ultimo give it as October 23, 1904. In the enclosed application the date of birth has been left blank. Please insert the correct date and, when the affidavits are properly executed, return them to this office.

    In having these affidavits executed care should be exercised to see that all names are written in full, as they appear in the body of the affidavit, and in the event that either of the persons signing the affidavit are unable to write, signatures by mark must be attested by two witnesses. Each affidavit must be executed before a Notary Public and the notarial seal and signature of the officer must be attached to each separate affidavit.

Respectfully,

VR 29-3.                                                                                                  Chairman.

Applications for Enrollment of Choctaw Newborn
Act of 1905   Volume XI

7 NB 732

Muskogee, Indian Territory, June 8, 1905.

J. M. Butler,
    Atoka, Indian Territory.

Dear Sir:

    Receipt is hereby acknowledged of the affidavits of Maggie E. Butler and T. J. Long to the birth of Henry C. Butler, son of J. M. Butler and Maggie E. Butler (Black) October 23, 1904, and the same have been filed in the matter of the enrollment of said child.

Respectfully,

Chairman.

# NEW BORN AFFIDAVIT

No ...............

## CHOCTAW ENROLLING COMMISSION

IN THE MATTER OF THE APPLICATION FOR ENROLLMENT as a citizen of the Choctaw Nation, of    Henry Clide Butler    born on the   $23^d$   day of   October    190 4

Name of father   James M Butler      a citizen of   ——  ——   Nation, final enrollment No.   ——   ——      now Butler

Name of mother   Maggie E Black      a citizen of   Choctaw   Nation, final enrollment No.   11752

Atoka IT      Postoffice.

**AFFIDAVIT OF MOTHER**

UNITED STATES OF AMERICA
    INDIAN TERRITORY
DISTRICT   Central

    I   Maggie E Black   now Butler        , on oath state that I am   21   years of age and a citizen by   blood   of the   Choctaw   Nation, and as such have been placed upon the final roll of the   Choctaw   Nation, by the Honorable Secretary of the

# Applications for Enrollment of Choctaw Newborn
## Act of 1905   Volume XI

Interior my final enrollment number being 11752 ; that I am the lawful wife of James M. Butler , who is a citizen of the Choctaw Nation, and as such has been placed upon the final roll of said Nation by the Honorable Secretary of the Interior, his final enrollment number being —— and that a male child was born to me on the 23$^d$ day of January[sic] 190 4; that said child has been named Henry Clide Butler , and is now living.

Maggie E Black now Butler

WITNESSETH:
Must be two witnesses { Robert B Brinkley
who are citizens    { Elias Thompson

Subscribed and sworn to before me this, the 21$^{st}$ day of February , 190 5

A E Folsom
Notary Public.

My Commission Expires:
Jan 9 - 1909

## AFFIDAVIT OF ATTENDING PHYSICIAN OR MIDWIFE

UNITED STATES OF AMERICA
INDIAN TERRITORY
Central   DISTRICT

I, Thomas Long a Practicing Physician on oath state that I attended on Mrs. Maggie E Black now Butler wife of James M Butler on the 23$^d$ day of January[sic] , 190 4, that there was born to her on said date a male child, that said child is now living, and is said to have been named Henry Clide Butler

T.J. Long   M.D.

WITNESSETH:
Must be two witnesses { Robert B Brinkley
who are citizens and  {
know the child.       { Elias Thompson

Subscribed and sworn to before me this, the 21$^{st}$ day of February 190 5

A E Folsom   Notary Public.

We hereby certify that we are well acquainted with D$^r$ Thomas Long a Practicing Physician and know him to be reputable and of good standing in the community.

Robert B Brinkley
Elias Thompson

# Applications for Enrollment of Choctaw Newborn
## Act of 1905   Volume XI

BIRTH AFFIDAVIT.

### DEPARTMENT OF THE INTERIOR.
## COMMISSION TO THE FIVE CIVILIZED TRIBES.

**IN RE APPLICATION FOR ENROLLMENT,** as a citizen of the Choctaw Nation, of Henry C Butler, born on the 23$^{rd}$ day of October, 1904

Name of Father: J M Butler   a citizen of the United States ~~Nation~~.
Name of Mother: Maggie E Butler nee Black   a citizen of the Choctaw Nation.

Postoffice   Atoka, I.T.

#### AFFIDAVIT OF MOTHER.

UNITED STATES OF AMERICA, Indian Territory, }
Central           DISTRICT.

I, Maggie E. Butler, on oath state that I am 21 years of age and a citizen by blood, of the Choctaw Nation; that I am the lawful wife of J M Butler, who is a citizen, ~~by~~ —— of the United States ~~Nation~~; that a male child was born to me on 23$^{rd}$ day of October, 1904; that said child has been named Henry C. Butler, and was living March 4, 1905.

Maggie E Butler

Witnesses To Mark:
{

Subscribed and sworn to before me this 5$^{th}$ day of April, 1905

W.H. Angell
Notary Public.

#### AFFIDAVIT OF ATTENDING PHYSICIAN OR MID-WIFE.

UNITED STATES OF AMERICA, Indian Territory, }
Central           DISTRICT.

I, T. J. Long, a physician, on oath state that I attended on Mrs. Maggie E. Butler, wife of J. M. Butler on the 23$^{rd}$ day of October, 1904; that there was born to her on said date a male child; that said child was living March 4, 1905, and is said to have been named Henry C. Butler

T J Long

Witnesses To Mark:
{

## Applications for Enrollment of Choctaw Newborn
## Act of 1905  Volume XI

Subscribed and sworn to before me this 5th day of April, 1905

W.H. Angell
Notary Public.

---

**BIRTH AFFIDAVIT.**

DEPARTMENT OF THE INTERIOR.
**COMMISSION TO THE FIVE CIVILIZED TRIBES.**

---

IN RE APPLICATION FOR ENROLLMENT, as a citizen of the    Choctaw    Nation, of Henry C Butler    , born on the 23rd    day of    October , 1904

Name of Father: J M Butler    a citizen of the    U.S.    Nation.
Name of Mother: Maggie E Butler  (Black)    a citizen of the    Choctaw    Nation.

Postoffice    Atoka, Ind. Ter.

---

**AFFIDAVIT OF MOTHER.**

UNITED STATES OF AMERICA, Indian Territory,
Central    DISTRICT.

I,  Maggie E. Butler    , on oath state that I am  21    years of age and a citizen by    blood  , of the    Choctaw    Nation; that I am the lawful wife of   J M Butler  , who is a citizen, ~~by~~ ——of the    United States    Nation; that a    male    child was born to me on  23rd    day of    October    , 1904; that said child has been named Henry C. Butler    , and was living March 4, 1905.

Maggie E Butler

Witnesses To Mark:
{

Subscribed and sworn to before me this 5th day of June , 1905 *at Atoka Ind Ter*

A.G. Etheredge
My commission expires    Notary Public.
Oct. 15, 1907.

# Applications for Enrollment of Choctaw Newborn
## Act of 1905 Volume XI

### AFFIDAVIT OF ATTENDING PHYSICIAN OR MID-WIFE.

UNITED STATES OF AMERICA, Indian Territory,
Central DISTRICT.

I, T. J. Long, a physician, on oath state that I attended on Mrs. Maggie E. Butler, wife of J. M. Butler on the 23rd day of October, 1904; that there was born to her on said date a male child; that said child was living March 4, 1905, and is said to have been named Henry C. Butler

T J Long MD

Witnesses To Mark:

Subscribed and sworn to before me this 5$^{th}$ day of June, 1905

A.G. Etheredge
My commission expires Notary Public.
Oct. 15, 1907.

---

Choc New Born 733
Emily McGee b. 12-3-03

7- 12978

**BIRTH AFFIDAVIT.**

### DEPARTMENT OF THE INTERIOR.
### COMMISSION TO THE FIVE CIVILIZED TRIBES.

**IN RE APPLICATION FOR ENROLLMENT,** as a citizen of the Choctaw Nation, of Emily McGee, born on the 3 day of December, 1903

Name of Father: Swinney McGee a citizen of the Choctaw Nation.
Name of Mother: Lizzie McGee formerly King a citizen of the Choctaw Nation.

Postoffice McCurtain I.T.

# Applications for Enrollment of Choctaw Newborn
## Act of 1905   Volume XI

### AFFIDAVIT OF MOTHER.

UNITED STATES OF AMERICA, Indian Territory, }
Central    DISTRICT.

I, Lizzie McGee formerly King, on oath state that I am 24 years of age and a citizen by blood, of the Choctaw Nation; that I am the lawful wife of Swinney McGee, who is a citizen, by blood of the Choctaw Nation; that a female child was born to me on 3 day of December, 1903; that said child has been named Emily McGee, and was living March 4, 1905.

                                                her
                                    Lizzie x McGee
Witnesses To Mark:                mark
{ Chas T. Difendafer
{ OL Johnson

Subscribed and sworn to before me this 6 day of April, 1905

                                    OL Johnson
                                         Notary Public.

---

### AFFIDAVIT OF ATTENDING PHYSICIAN OR MID-WIFE.

UNITED STATES OF AMERICA, Indian Territory, }
Central    DISTRICT.

I, Caroline Durant, a midwife, on oath state that I attended on Mrs. Lizzie McGee, wife of Swinney McGee on the 3rd day of December, 1903; that there was born to her on said date a female child; that said child was living March 4, 1905, and is said to have been named Emily McGee

                                    Caroline Durant
Witnesses To Mark:
{

Subscribed and sworn to before me this 6 day of April, 1905

                                    OL Johnson
                                         Notary Public.

## Applications for Enrollment of Choctaw Newborn
## Act of 1905   Volume XI

Choc New Born 734
  Ruth Juanita Harrison  b. 3-25-04

$W^m O.B.$

COMMISSIONERS:
TAMS BIXBY,
THOMAS B. NEEDLES,
C.R. BRECKINBRIDGE.

**DEPARTMENT OF THE INTERIOR,**
**COMMISSIONER TO THE FIVE CIVILIZED TRIBES.**

REFER IN REPLY TO THE FOLLOWING:

7 N B 734

WM. O. BEALL
Secretary

ADDRESS ONLY THE
COMMISSION TO THE FIVE CIVILIZED TRIBES.

Muskogee, Indian Territory, April 17, 1905.

Joseph Colbert Harrison,
  Coalgate, Indian Territory.

Dear Sir:

You are hereby advised that before the application for the enrollment of your infant child, Ruth Juanita Harrison, can be finally disposed of, it will be necessary for you to furnish the Commission with either the original or a certified copy of the license and certificate of your marriage to her mother, Leola Harrison.

Your immediate attention should be given this matter.

Respectfully,
Tams Bixby
Chairman.

# Applications for Enrollment of Choctaw Newborn
## Act of 1905   Volume XI

COMMISSIONERS:
TAMS BIXBY,
THOMAS B. NEEDLES,
C.R. BRECKINRIDGE.

WM. O. BEALL
Secretary

DEPARTMENT OF THE INTERIOR,
COMMISSIONER TO THE FIVE CIVILIZED TRIBES.

W$^m$O.B.

REFER IN REPLY TO THE FOLLOWING:

7-NB-734.

ADDRESS ONLY THE
COMMISSION TO THE FIVE CIVILIZED TRIBES.

Muskogee, Indian Territory, May 29, 1905.

Leola Harrison,
    Coalgate, Indian Territory.

Dear Madam:

    Referring to the application for the enrollment of your infant child, Ruth Juanita Harrison, born March 25, 1904, it is noted that the applicant claims through her father.

    In this event it will be necessary for you to furnish the Commission with the original or a certified copy of the license and certificate of your marriage to the applicant's father, Joseph Colbert Harrison.

                                   Respectfully,
                                     Tams Bixby
                                        Chairman.

7-NB-734

                           Muskogee, Indian Territory, November 1, 1905.

Joseph C. Harrison,
    Bailey, Indian Territory.

Dear Sir:

    Receipt is hereby acknowledged of your letter of October 21, 1905, asking if the name of Ruth Juanita Harrison has been approved.

    In reply to your letter you are advised that the name of your child Ruth Juanita Harrison has not yet been placed upon a schedule of citizens by blood of the Choctaw Nation prepared for forwarding to the Secretary of the Interior and before disposition can be made of the application for the enrollment of said child it will be necessary for you to furnish either the original or a certified copy of the license or certificate showing the marriage between yourself and Leola Harrison.  This matter should receive your immediate attention.

## Applications for Enrollment of Choctaw Newborn
## Act of 1905    Volume XI

The letters heretofore addressed to you upon this subject to Coalgate, Indian Territory, have been returned "unclaimed."

Respectfully,

Commissioner.

---

7-NB-734

Muskogee, Indian Territory, November 15, 1905.

Joseph C. Harrison,
Bailey, Indian Territory.

Dear Sir:

Receipt is hereby acknowledged of your letter of November 11, 1905, transmitting certified copy of the marriage license and certificate between yourself and Leola Mays in the matter of the enrollment of your child Ruth Juanita Harrison as a citizen by blood of the Choctaw Nation blood of the Choctaw Nation and the same has been filed with the record in this case.

Respectfully,

Commissioner.

---

7-NB-734

Muskogee, Indian Territory, February 2, 1906.

Joseph C. Harrison,
Bailey, Indian Territory.

Dear Sir:

Receipt is hereby acknowledged of your letter of January 29, 1906, in which you ask if Ruth Juanita Harrison has been approved and if land can now be set aside for her allotment.

In reply to your letter you are advised that the name of Ruth Juanita Harrison has been placed upon a schedule of new born citizens of the Choctaw Nation which has been forwarded the Secretary of the Interior and you will be notified when her enrollment is approve by the Department.

Respectfully,

Acting Commissioner.

---

# Applications for Enrollment of Choctaw Newborn
## Act of 1905   Volume XI

7-NB-734

Muskogee, Indian Territory, April 30, 1906.

W. B. Wynns,
    Box 104,
        Marlow, Indian Territory.

Dear Sir:

    Receipt is hereby acknowledged of your letter of April 25, 1906, asking if Juanita Harrison has been approved so that she can now file on land.

    In reply to your letter you are advised that on March 14, 1906, the Secretary of the Interior approved the enrollment of Ruthie Juanita Harrison as a new born citizen of the Choctaw Nation and selection of allotment may now be made in her behalf in accordance with the rules and regulations governing the selection of allotments and the designation of homesteads in the Choctaw and Chickasaw Nations.

                Respectfully,

                        Commissioner.

---

*(The Marriage Certificate, Marriage License and Application below, typed as given.)*

### Certificate of Record of Marriage.

United States of America,
Indian Territory,    (ss.
Southern District.

    I, C.M. Campbell, Clerk of the United States Court, in the Indian Territory and District aforesaid, Do Hereby Certify, that the license for and Certificate of Marriage of Mr. J.C. Harrison and Leola Mays were filed in my Office in said Territory and District the 24th. day of December A.D. 1902, and duly recorded in Book G of Marriage Record, Page 68.

    Witness my hand and seal of said Court, at Ardmore, Indian Territory this 24th. day of December A.D. 1902.

                C.M. Campbell, Clerk

---

MARRIAGE LICENSE.

# Applications for Enrollment of Choctaw Newborn
## Act of 1905   Volume XI

NO. 825.

United States of America,

Indian Territory,      § ss.      To Any Person Authorized by Law to

Southern District.    §           Solemize Marriage, Greeting:

You are hereby commanded to solemize the right and publish the Banns of Matrimony between Mr.J.C.Harrison of Bailey in the Indian Territory, aged 25 years, and Miss Leola Mays of Bailey,in the Indian Territory, aged 22 years, according to law;and do you officially sign and return this license to the parties therin named.

Witness my hand and official seal,this the 19th day of December A.D.1902.

C.M.Campbell,
Clerk of the United States Court.

By J.W.Speake,Deputy.

### Certificate of Marriage.

United States of America,
Indian Territory,    (ss.       I,D.W.Garvin,Minister of the Gospel do
Southern District.

hereby certify that on the 21st.day of December A.D.1902, I did duly and according to law, as commanded in the foregoing license, solemize the right and publish the Banns of Matrimony between the parties therin named.

Witness my hand this 22nd.day of December A.D.1902.

My credentials are recorded in the office of the Clerk of the United States Court,Indian Territory,Southern District,at Ardmore Book C,page 12.

D.W.Garvin.

Southern District,(                              a minister of the Gospel.
Indian Territory.

This is to certify that the above is an exact copy of the Marriage License of J.C.Harrison to Leola Mayes, and said copy is made by me,and I,do so certify.

F.B. Allen
Notary Public, Southern District,I.T.

My commission expires the 10th day of May 1909.

## Applications for Enrollment of Choctaw Newborn
## Act of 1905   Volume XI

IN RE APPLICATION FOR ENROLLMENT, as a citizen of the   Choctaw   Nation of   Ruth Juanita Harrison   born on the   25   day of   March   190 4

Name of Father   Joseph Colbert Harrison   citizen of   Choctaw   Nation
Name of Mother   Leola Harrison   citizen of   "   Nation

Post Office.

### AFFIDAVIT OF MOTHER

United States of America Southern District of the Indian Territory:

I,   Leola Harrison   on oath state that I am   25   years of age and a citizen by intermarriage   of the   Choctaw   Nation that I am the lawful wife of   Joseph Colbert Harrison   who is a citizen by blood   of the Ch octaw   Nation that a   Female   Child was born to me on the   25   day of   March   190 4   that said Child has been named   Ruth Juanita Harrison   and was living March 4, 1905.

Leola Harrison
Subscribed and sworn to before me this the   5   day of   April   A.D. 190 5

J.M. Gibbins
Notary Public.

### AFFIDAVIT OF ATTENDING PHYSICIAN

United States of America Southern District of the Indian Territory:

I,   Edga Lee Harrison   a   midwife   on oath state that I attend on Mrs   Leola Harrison   wife of   Joseph Colbert Harrison   on the   25   day of   March   190 4   and that there was born to her on that date a   Female   child and that said child was living March 4 1905. and is said to have been named   Ruth Juanita Harrison

Edga Lee Harrison
Subscribed and sworn to before me this the       day of   April   1905.

J.M. Gibbins
Notary Public.
My commission
expires 4/24/1907

# Applications for Enrollment of Choctaw Newborn
# Act of 1905   Volume XI

Choc New Born 735
   Ollie Virgie Ireton   b. 2-28-04

---

7-NB-735

Muskogee, Indian Territory, August 4, 1905.

Chief Clerk,
   Chickasaw Land Office,
      Ardmore, Indian Territory.

Dear Sir:

There is inclosed you herewith application for the enrollment of Ollie Virgie Ireton, born February 28, 1904.

J. E. Williams, the Notary before whom the affidavits were executed, failed to affix his notarial seal to the mother's affidavit. Please have the seal of Mr. Williams, affixed to the affidavit, and return to this office.

Respectfully,

*Lm 2/4*

Commissioner.

---

7-NB-735

Muskogee, Indian Territory, August 14, 1905.

Henry Ireton,
   Chickasha, Indian Territory.

Dear Sir:

Receipt is hereby acknowledged of your letter of August 5, 1905, asking if your child Ollie Virgil Ireton is approved.

In reply to your letter you are advised that the name of your child Ollie Virgil Ireton has not yet been placed upon a schedule of citizens by blood of the Choctaw Nation which has been forwarded the Secretary of the Interior and in event further evidence is necessary to determine your right to enrollment you will be duly notified.

Respectfully,

Acting Commissioner.

## Applications for Enrollment of Choctaw Newborn
## Act of 1905   Volume XI

**BIRTH AFFIDAVIT.**

### DEPARTMENT OF THE INTERIOR.
### COMMISSION TO THE FIVE CIVILIZED TRIBES.

IN RE APPLICATION FOR ENROLLMENT, as a citizen of the Choctaw Nation, of Ollie Virgil Ireton, born on the 28 day of February, 1904

Name of Father: Henry Ireton      a citizen of the Choctaw Nation.
Name of Mother: Laura Ireton      a citizen of the Choctaw Nation.

Postoffice   Chickasha I.T.

**AFFIDAVIT OF MOTHER.**

UNITED STATES OF AMERICA, Indian Territory,
Southern DISTRICT.

I, Laura Ireton, on oath state that I am 30 years of age and a citizen by marriage, of the Choctaw Nation; that I am the lawful wife of Henry Ireton, who is a citizen, by blood of the Choctaw Nation; that a female child was born to me on 28$^{th}$ day of February, 1904; that said child has been named Ollie Virgil Ireton, and was living March 4, 1905.

Laura Ireton

Witnesses To Mark:

Subscribed and sworn to before me this 6$^{th}$ day of April, 1905.

JE Williams
Notary Public.

**AFFIDAVIT OF ATTENDING PHYSICIAN OR MID-WIFE.**

UNITED STATES OF AMERICA, Indian Territory,
Southern DISTRICT.

I, Ella C. Portlock, a midwife, on oath state that I attended on Mrs. Laura Ireton, wife of Henry Ireton on the 28 day of February, 1904; that there was born to her on said date a Female child; that said child was living March 4, 1905, and is said to have been named Ollie Virgil

Ella C. Portlock

## Applications for Enrollment of Choctaw Newborn
## Act of 1905 Volume XI

Witnesses To Mark:
{

    Subscribed and sworn to before me this 5 day of April , 1905

                              James B Pilgreen
                              Notary Public.
My Comson[sic] Experes[sic] 18 March
                        1909

---

Choc New Born 736
    Julia Tecumseh b. 1-28-04

7-7870    7-7165
**BIRTH AFFIDAVIT.**
                        DEPARTMENT OF THE INTERIOR.
            **COMMISSION TO THE FIVE CIVILIZED TRIBES.**

      IN RE APPLICATION FOR ENROLLMENT, as a citizen of the    Choctaw   Nation, of
Julia Tecumseh  , born on the  28th  day of  January  , 1904

Name of Father: Houston Tecumseh     a citizen of the  Choctaw  Nation.
Name of Mother: Ida Tecumseh         a citizen of the  Choctaw  Nation.

                  Postoffice    Bokoshe, Ind. Ter.

                  **AFFIDAVIT OF MOTHER.**

UNITED STATES OF AMERICA, Indian Territory,}
    Central         DISTRICT.}

    I, Ida Tecumseh  , on oath state that I am  22  years of age and a citizen by blood  , of the  Choctaw  Nation; that I am the lawful wife of  Houston Tecumseh  , who is a citizen, by blood  of the  Choctaw  Nation; that a female  child was born to me on  28th  day of  January  , 1904; that said child has been named  Julia Tecumseh  , and was living March 4, 1905.

                            Ida Tecumseh

Witnesses To Mark:
{

# Applications for Enrollment of Choctaw Newborn
# Act of 1905 Volume XI

Subscribed and sworn to before me this 5 day of April, 1905

OL Johnson
Notary Public.

---

**AFFIDAVIT OF ATTENDING PHYSICIAN OR MID-WIFE.**

UNITED STATES OF AMERICA, Indian Territory, }
   Central             DISTRICT.

I, Levicey Barnett, a midwife, on oath state that I attended on Mrs. Ida Tecumseh, wife of Houston Tecumseh on the 28th day of January, 1904; that there was born to her on said date a female child; that said child was living March 4, 1905, and is said to have been named Julia Tecumseh

                                    her
                               Levicey x Barnett
Witnesses To Mark:           mark
  { *(Name Illegible)*
     OL Johnson

Subscribed and sworn to before me this 5 day of April, 1905

OL Johnson
Notary Public.

---

## *Affidavit of Attending Physician or Midwife*

UNITED STATES OF AMERICA, }
    INDIAN TERRITORY,
  Central    DISTRICT

I, Wysee Barnett a Midwife on oath state that I attended on Mrs. Ida Tecumseh wife of Houston Tecumseh on the 28 day of January, 1904, that there was born to her on said date a female child, that said child is now living, and is said to have been named Julia Tecumseh

                                  her
                        Wysee Barnett x     M. D.
                                mark

Subscribed and sworn to before me this the 6 day of February 1905

James Bower
Notary Public.

WITNESSETH:
  Must be two witnesses { Loren Cobb
  who are citizens and
  know the child.       Jesse Tecumseh

Applications for Enrollment of Choctaw Newborn
Act of 1905   Volume XI

We hereby certify that we are well acquainted with   Wysee Barnett   a   midwife   and know   her   to be reputable and of good standing in the community.

Must be two citizen witnesses. { Loren Cobb
Jesse Tecumseh

# NEW BORN AFFIDAVIT

No ........

## CHOCTAW ENROLLING COMMISSION

IN THE MATTER OF THE APPLICATION FOR ENROLLMENT as a citizen of the Choctaw Nation, of   Julia Tecumseh   born on the   28   day of   January   190 4

Name of father   Houston Tecumseh   a citizen of   Choctaw   Nation, final enrollment No.   7165

Name of mother   Ida Tecumseh   a citizen of   Choctaw   Nation, final enrollment No.   7870

Bokoshe I.T.   Postoffice.

**AFFIDAVIT OF MOTHER**

UNITED STATES OF AMERICA
INDIAN TERRITORY
DISTRICT   Central

I   Ida Tecumseh   , on oath state that I am   24   years of age and a citizen by   blood   of the   Choctaw   Nation, and as such have been placed upon the final roll of the   Choctaw   Nation, by the Honorable Secretary of the Interior my final enrollment number being   7870   ; that I am the lawful wife of   Houston Tecumseh   , who is a citizen of the   Choctaw   Nation, and as such has been placed upon the final roll of said Nation by the Honorable Secretary of the Interior, his final enrollment number being   7165   and that a   female   child was born to me on the   28   day of   January   190 4; that said child has been named   Julia Tecumseh   , and is now living.

Ida Tecumseh

WITNESSETH:
Must be two witnesses who are citizens { Loren Cobb
Jesse Tecumseh

## Applications for Enrollment of Choctaw Newborn
## Act of 1905   Volume XI

Subscribed and sworn to before me this, the  6   day of    February   , 190 5

James Bower<br>Notary Public.

My Commission Expires:
Sept 23-1907

---

Choc New Born 737
      Oscar Cotten   b.  11-21-04
      Nellie Cotten   b.  11-21-04

7 N B 737

Muskogee, Indian Territory, April 17, 1905.

David Oscar Cotton,
    Lindsey, Indian Territory.

Dear Sir:

    There is inclosed you herewith for execution application for the enrollment of your infant children, Oscar Cotton and Nellie Cotton, born November 21, 1904.

    In having these affidavits executed care should be exercised to see that all names are written in full, as they appear in the body of the affidavit, and in the event that either of the persons signing the affidavit are unable to write, signatures by mark must be attested by two witnesses. Each affidavit must be executed before a Notary Public and the notarial seal and signature of the officer must be attached to each separate affidavit.

Respectfully,

LM 17-100.                                                                              Chairman.

# Applications for Enrollment of Choctaw Newborn
## Act of 1905 Volume XI

**BIRTH AFFIDAVIT.**

## DEPARTMENT OF THE INTERIOR.
## COMMISSION TO THE FIVE CIVILIZED TRIBES.

---

**IN RE APPLICATION FOR ENROLLMENT,** as a citizen of the Choctaw Nation, of Nellie Cotton, born on the 21st day of November, 1904

Name of Father: David Oscar Cotton     a citizen of the Choctaw Nation.
Name of Mother: Cora J Cotton     a citizen of the Choctaw Nation.

Postoffice    Lindsey I.T.

---

**AFFIDAVIT OF MOTHER.**

UNITED STATES OF AMERICA, Indian Territory, }
................................................ DISTRICT. }

I, Cora J Cotton, on oath state that I am 32 years of age and a citizen by intermarriage, of the Choctaw Nation; that I am the lawful wife of David Oscar Cotton, who is a citizen, by blood of the Choctaw Nation; that a female child was born to me on 21st day of November, 1904; that said child has been named Nellie Cotton, and was living March 4, 1905.

Witnesses To Mark:
{

Subscribed and sworn to before me this ............... day of ............., 190....

Notary Public.

---

**AFFIDAVIT OF ATTENDING PHYSICIAN OR MID-WIFE.**

UNITED STATES OF AMERICA, Indian Territory, }
   Southern          DISTRICT. }

I, Robt E Looney MD, a Physician, on oath state that I attended on Mrs. Cora J Cotton, wife of David Oscar Cotton on the 21st day of November, 1904; that there was born to her on said date a female child; that said child was living March 4, 1905, and is said to have been named Nellie Cotton

                         Robt E Looney MD

Witnesses To Mark:
{

## Applications for Enrollment of Choctaw Newborn
## Act of 1905 Volume XI

Subscribed and sworn to before me this 20th day of April , 1905

         Geo. F. Johnson
         Notary Public.

---

**BIRTH AFFIDAVIT.**

### DEPARTMENT OF THE INTERIOR.
### COMMISSION TO THE FIVE CIVILIZED TRIBES.

**IN RE APPLICATION FOR ENROLLMENT,** as a citizen of the Choctaw Nation, of Oscar Cotton & Nellie Cotton (Twins), born on the 21st day of November , 1904

Name of Father: David Oscar Cotton    a citizen of the Choctaw Nation.
Name of Mother: Cora J Cotton    a citizen of the Choctaw Nation.

     Postoffice  Lindsey Ind. Ter.

---

**AFFIDAVIT OF MOTHER.**

UNITED STATES OF AMERICA, Indian Territory,}
 Southern    DISTRICT.

  I, Cora J Cotton , on oath state that I am Thirty two years of age and a citizen by intermarriage , of the Choctaw Nation; that I am the lawful wife of David Oscar Cotton , who is a citizen, by blood of the Choctaw Nation; that a male & female child ~~was~~ *were* born to me on 21st day of November , 1904; that said child has been named *Respectedly*[sic] Oscar Cotton and Nellie Cotton , and was living March 4, 1905.

        Cora J. Cotten
Witnesses To Mark:
 { Robt E Lee

Subscribed and sworn to before me this 6th day of April , 1905
     *Robt E Lee*
     ~~Cora J Cotten~~
        Notary Public.

## Applications for Enrollment of Choctaw Newborn
## Act of 1905   Volume XI

United States of America,
Indian Territory,
Southern District.
      Dr. Robert E. Looney, a licensed and practicing physician at Lindsey in the Southern District of Indian Territory on his oath states that on the 21st day of November, 1904, he attended Mrs. Cora J. Cotten, wife of David Oscar Cotten, and that on that date she gave birth to twins, a boy and a girl, which he understands to have been named Oscar and Nellie Cotten.

                              Robt E Looney MD

Subscribed and sworn to before me this 5gh[sic] day of April, 1905.

                              Claire L. M$^c$Arthur
                              Notary Pub.

BIRTH AFFIDAVIT.

### DEPARTMENT OF THE INTERIOR.
### COMMISSION TO THE FIVE CIVILIZED TRIBES.

IN RE APPLICATION FOR ENROLLMENT, as a citizen of the CHOCTAW Nation, of Oscar Cotten, born on the 21st day of November, 1904

Name of Father: David Oscar Cotten    a citizen of the CHOCTAW Nation.
Name of Mother: Cora J Cotten    a citizen of the CHOCTAW Nation.

                    Postoffice    Lindsey Ind Ter

AFFIDAVIT OF MOTHER.

UNITED STATES OF AMERICA, Indian Territory,
    Southern          DISTRICT.

      I, David Oscar Cotten, on oath state that I am 36 years of age and a citizen by blood, of the Choctaw Nation; that I am the lawful ~~wife~~ *Husband* of Cora J Cotten, *who died 14th day of April, 1905 and*, who is a citizen, by intermarriage of the Choctaw Nation; that a male child was born to ~~me~~ *her* on the 21st day of November, 1904; that said child has been named Oscar Cotten, and was living March 4, 1905.

                              David Oscar Cotten

Witnesses To Mark:

## Applications for Enrollment of Choctaw Newborn
## Act of 1905   Volume XI

Subscribed and sworn to before me this 24th day of April, 1905

H.C. Miller
Notary Public.

**BIRTH AFFIDAVIT.**

### DEPARTMENT OF THE INTERIOR.
### COMMISSION TO THE FIVE CIVILIZED TRIBES.

IN RE APPLICATION FOR ENROLLMENT, as a citizen of the Choctaw Nation, of Oscar Cotton, born on the 21$^{st}$ day of November, 1904

Name of Father: David Oscar Cotton    a citizen of the Choctaw Nation.
Name of Mother: Cora J Cotton    a citizen of the Choctaw Nation.

Postoffice    Lindsey I.T.

**AFFIDAVIT OF MOTHER.**

UNITED STATES OF AMERICA, Indian Territory, } DISTRICT.

I, Cora J Cotton, on oath state that I am 32 years of age and a citizen by intermarriage, of the Choctaw Nation; that I am the lawful wife of David Oscar Cotton, who is a citizen, by blood of the Choctaw Nation; that a male child was born to me on 21$^{st}$ day of November, 1904; that said child has been named Oscar Cotton, and was living March 4, 1905.

Witnesses To Mark:

Subscribed and sworn to before me this ........ day of ........, 190....

Notary Public.

**AFFIDAVIT OF ATTENDING PHYSICIAN OR MID-WIFE.**

UNITED STATES OF AMERICA, Indian Territory, } Southern    DISTRICT.

I, Robt E Looney MD, a Physician, on oath state that I attended on Mrs. Cora J Cotton, wife of David Oscar Cotton on the 21$^{st}$ day of

## Applications for Enrollment of Choctaw Newborn
## Act of 1905   Volume XI

November   , 1904; that there was born to her on said date a   male   child; that said child was living March 4, 1905, and is said to have been named   Oscar Cotton

Robt E Looney MD

Witnesses To Mark:

{

Subscribed and sworn to before me this   20<sup>th</sup>   day of   April   , 1905

Geo. F. Johnson<br>Notary Public.

---

**BIRTH AFFIDAVIT.**

### DEPARTMENT OF THE INTERIOR.
### COMMISSION TO THE FIVE CIVILIZED TRIBES.

---

**IN RE APPLICATION FOR ENROLLMENT,** as a citizen of the   CHOCTAW   Nation, of   Nellie Cotten   , born on the   21st   day of   November   , 1904

Name of Father: David Oscar Cotten     a citizen of the   CHOCTAW   Nation.
Name of Mother: Cora J Cotten          a citizen of the   CHOCTAW   Nation.

Postoffice   Lindsey Ind Ter

---

**AFFIDAVIT OF MOTHER.**

UNITED STATES OF AMERICA, Indian Territory, }
     Southern           DISTRICT.

I,   David Oscar Cotten   , on oath state that I am   36   years of age and a citizen by   blood   , of the   Choctaw   Nation; that I am the lawful ~~wife~~ *Husband* of   Cora J Cotten, *who died April 14, 1905 and*   , who is a citizen, by   Intermarriage   of the   Choctaw   Nation; that a   female   child was born to ~~me~~ *her* on   the 21st   day of   November   , 1904; that said child has been named   Nellie Cotten   , and was living March 4, 1905.

David Oscar Cotten

Witnesses To Mark:

{

Subscribed and sworn to before me this   24th   day of   April   , 1905

H.C. Miller<br>Notary Public.

## Applications for Enrollment of Choctaw Newborn
## Act of 1905   Volume XI

<u>Choc New Born 738</u>
Bennie McFerran b. 10-3-03

*Enroolment*[sic] *No. 8217*

**BIRTH AFFIDAVIT.**

**DEPARTMENT OF THE INTERIOR.**
**COMMISSION TO THE FIVE CIVILIZED TRIBES.**

**IN RE APPLICATION FOR ENROLLMENT,** as a citizen of the   Choctaw   Nation, of Walls I.T.   , born on the 3   day of   October   , 1903

Name of Father:  Walter M<sup>c</sup>Ferran   a citizen of the   Choctaw   Nation.
Name of Mother:  Isabell M<sup>c</sup>Ferran   a citizen of the   Choctaw   Nation.

Postoffice   Walls I.T.

**AFFIDAVIT OF MOTHER.**

**UNITED STATES OF AMERICA, Indian Territory,**
   Central        **DISTRICT.**

   I,   Isabell M<sup>c</sup>Ferran   , on oath state that I am   26   years of age and a citizen by   Blood   , of the   Choctaw   Nation; that I am the lawful wife of   Walter M<sup>c</sup>Ferran   , who is a citizen, by   Intermarriage   of the   Choctaw Nation; that a   Male   child was born to me on   3$^{rd}$   day of   October   , 1903; that said child has been named   Bennie M<sup>c</sup>Ferran   , and was living March 4, 1905.

Isabel[sic] M<sup>c</sup>Ferran
Witnesses To Mark:
{

Subscribed and sworn to before me this 5$^{th}$   day of   April   , 1905

C.L. Stone
Notary Public.

**AFFIDAVIT OF ATTENDING PHYSICIAN OR MID-WIFE.**

**UNITED STATES OF AMERICA, Indian Territory,**
   Central        **DISTRICT.**

   I,   I.C. Talley   , a   Phycian[sic]   , on oath state that I attended on Mrs.   Isabell M<sup>c</sup>Ferran   , wife of   Walter M<sup>c</sup>Ferran   on the 3$^{rd}$   day of

## Applications for Enrollment of Choctaw Newborn
## Act of 1905   Volume XI

October    , 1903; that there was born to her on said date a    Male    child; that said child was living March 4, 1905, and is said to have been named   Bennie M$^c$Ferran

Isham C Talley

Witnesses To Mark:
{

Subscribed and sworn to before me this 5$^{th}$   day of    April    , 1905

C.L. Stone<br>Notary Public.

---

Choc New Born 739
    Daisy M. Thompson  b. 5-11-04

7-5420

Muskogee, Indian Territory, April 11, 1905.

Cyrus R. Thompson,
    Coalgate, Indian Territory.

Dear Sir:

    Receipt is hereby acknowledged of the affidavits of Mrs. Clemmie Thompson and W. M. Hume to the birth of Daisy M. Thompson, daughter of Cyrus R. and Clemmie Thompson, May 11, 1904, and the same have been filed with our records as an application for the enrollment of said child.

Respectfully,

Commissioner in Charge.

## Applications for Enrollment of Choctaw Newborn
## Act of 1905   Volume XI

*Affidavit of Attending Physician or Midwife*

UNITED STATES OF AMERICA,  
   INDIAN TERRITORY,  
Central    DISTRICT

I, W. M. Hume a Physician on oath state that I attended on Mrs. Clemmie Thompson wife of Cyrus R. Thompson on the 11$^{th}$ day of May, 1904, that there was born to her on said date a female child, that said child is now living, and is said to have been named Daisy M. Thompson

                                    W.M. Hume    M. D.

Subscribed and sworn to before me this the 11$^{th}$ day of Feb 1905

                                (Name Illegible)  
                                    Notary Public.

WITNESSETH:

Must be two witnesses who are citizens and know the child.  {  Henry Pebworth  
                           his  
                          Johnson x Ott  
                            mark

We hereby certify that we are well acquainted with D$^r$ W.M. Hume a Physician and know him to be reputable and of good standing in the community.

                      Must be two citizen witnesses.  {  Samuel A Ott  
                                              his  
                                              Lewis x Duncan  
                                                   mark

# NEW BORN AFFIDAVIT

No

### CHOCTAW ENROLLING COMMISSION

IN THE MATTER OF THE APPLICATION FOR ENROLLMENT as a citizen of the Choctaw Nation, of Daisy M Thompson born on the 11$^{th}$ day of May 1904

Name of father Cyrus R. Thompson a citizen of Choctaw Nation, final enrollment No. ~~606~~ 13740

## Applications for Enrollment of Choctaw Newborn
## Act of 1905   Volume XI

Name of mother  Clemmie Thompson  a citizen of  Choctaw  Nation,
final enrollment No. 606
Coalgate I.T.  Postoffice.

### AFFIDAVIT OF MOTHER

UNITED STATES OF AMERICA  
   INDIAN TERRITORY  
DISTRICT  Central

   I  Clemmie Thompson  , on oath state that I am  34  years of age and a citizen by  marriage  of the  Choctaw  Nation, and as such have been placed upon the final roll of the  Choctaw  Nation, by the Honorable Secretary of the Interior my final enrollment number being  606  ; that I am the lawful wife of  Cyrus R Thompson  , who is a citizen of the  Choctaw  Nation, and as such has been placed upon the final roll of said Nation by the Honorable Secretary of the Interior, his final enrollment number being  13740  and that a  female  child was born to me on the  11th  day of  May  1904; that said child has been named  Daisy M. Thompson  , and is now living.

                                        her  
                             Clemmie x Thompson  
WITNESSETH:                      mark

Must be two witnesses { Henry Pebworth  
who are citizens               his  
                       Johnson x Ott  
                       mark

Subscribed and sworn to before me this, the  11th  day of  Febr  , 1905

                                  (Name Illegible)  
                                      Notary Public.

My Commission Expires:  
Feb 8th 1908

---

**BIRTH AFFIDAVIT.**

### DEPARTMENT OF THE INTERIOR.
### COMMISSION TO THE FIVE CIVILIZED TRIBES.

IN RE APPLICATION FOR ENROLLMENT, as a citizen of the  Choctaw  Nation, of  Daisy M Thompson  , born on the  11th  day of  May  , 1904

Name of Father: Cyrus R. Thompson     a citizen of the  Choctaw  Nation.  
Name of Mother: Mrs. Clemmie Thompson     a citizen of the  Choctaw  Nation.

                          Postoffice  Coalgate, Ind. Ter.

## Applications for Enrollment of Choctaw Newborn
## Act of 1905   Volume XI

**AFFIDAVIT OF MOTHER.**

UNITED STATES OF AMERICA, Indian Territory, }
   Central           DISTRICT. }

I,  M$^{rs}$ Clemmie Thompson   , on oath state that I am   34    years of age and a citizen by   marriage   , of the   Choctaw   Nation; that I am the lawful wife of Cyrus R. Thompson   , who is a citizen, by   birth   of the   Choctaw Nation; that a   female   child was born to me on  11$^{th}$   day of   May   , 1904; that said child has been named   Daisy M. Thompson   , and was living March 4, 1905.

her<br>M$^{rs}$ Clemmie x Thompson<br>mark

Witnesses To Mark:
{ E.H. Maddox
{ J S Hume

Subscribed and sworn to before me this   3$^{d}$  day of   April    , 1905

(Name Illegible)<br>Notary Public.

---

**AFFIDAVIT OF ATTENDING PHYSICIAN OR MID-WIFE.**

UNITED STATES OF AMERICA, Indian Territory, }
   Central           DISTRICT. }

I,   W. M. Hume   , a   Physician   , on oath state that I attended on Mrs.   Clemmie Thompson   , wife of   Cyrus R. Thompson   on the  11$^{th}$   day of May   , 1904; that there was born to her on said date a   female   child; that said child was living March 4, 1905, and is said to have been named   Daisy M Thompson

W.M. Hume M.D.

Witnesses To Mark:
{ JS Hume
{ EH Maddox

Subscribed and sworn to before me this   3$^{d}$  day of   April    , 1905

(Name Illegible)<br>Notary Public.

## Applications for Enrollment of Choctaw Newborn
## Act of 1905    Volume XI

Choc New Born 740
            Mary Eunice Moore   b.  9-12-04

                                        7-5848

                        Muskogee, Indian Territory, April 11, 1905.

F. B. Moore,
        Silo, Indian Territory.

Dear Sir:

            Receipt is hereby acknowledged of the affidavits of Ada Bell Moore and W. G. Austin to the birth of Mary Eunice Moore, daughter of F. B. and Ada Bell Moore, September 12, 1904, and the same have been filed with our records as an application for the enrollment of said child.
                        Respectfully,

                                        Commissioner in Charge.

**BIRTH AFFIDAVIT.**
                    **DEPARTMENT OF THE INTERIOR.**
                **COMMISSION TO THE FIVE CIVILIZED TRIBES.**

            **IN RE APPLICATION FOR ENROLLMENT,** as a citizen of the    Choctaw    Nation, of Mary Eunice Moore        , born on the   12   day of   September   , 1904

Name of Father: F.B. Moore            a citizen of the United States ~~Nation~~.
Name of Mother: Ada Bell Moore        a citizen of the    Choctaw    Nation.

                    Postoffice    Silo Ind. Ter.

                    **AFFIDAVIT OF MOTHER.**

UNITED STATES OF AMERICA, Indian Territory, }
        Central             DISTRICT. }

            I,  Ada Bell Moore    , on oath state that I am   20   years of age and a citizen by   blood   , of the   Choctaw    Nation; that I am the lawful wife of   F.B. Moore, who is a citizen, by _____ of the   United States   Nation; that a   female   child was born to me on   12   day of   September   , 1904; that said child has been named   Mary Eunice Moore   , and was living March 4, 1905.

                            Ada Bell Moore

145

## Applications for Enrollment of Choctaw Newborn
## Act of 1905   Volume XI

Witnesses To Mark:
{

Subscribed and sworn to before me this 29 day of March, 1905

Luther D Davis
Notary Public.

#### AFFIDAVIT OF ATTENDING PHYSICIAN OR MID-WIFE.

UNITED STATES OF AMERICA, Indian Territory,
Central     DISTRICT.

I, W.C. Austin, a Medical Doctor, on oath state that I attended on Mrs. Ada Bell Moore, wife of F.B. Moore on the 12th day of September, 1904; that there was born to her on said date a female child; that said child was living March 4, 1905, and is said to have been named W.G. Austin M.D.

Witnesses To Mark:
{

Subscribed and sworn to before me this 6th day of April, 1905

Luther D Davis
Notary Public.

---

Choc New Born 741
Jessie Redmond Carr   b. 9-8-04

BIRTH AFFIDAVIT.
#### DEPARTMENT OF THE INTERIOR.
#### COMMISSION TO THE FIVE CIVILIZED TRIBES.

IN RE APPLICATION FOR ENROLLMENT, as a citizen of the Choctaw Nation, of Jessie Redmond Carr, born on the ........ day of ................................, 1........

Name of Father: Daniel H Carr         a citizen of the Choctaw Nation.
Name of Mother: Lillie M$^c$Clung Carr     a citizen of the Choctaw Nation.

## Applications for Enrollment of Choctaw Newborn
## Act of 1905  Volume XI

Postoffice  Sulphur Indian Territory

**AFFIDAVIT OF MOTHER.**

UNITED STATES OF AMERICA, Indian Territory, }
Southern  DISTRICT.

I, Lillie M$^c$Clung Carr , on oath state that I am 31 years of age and a citizen by Blood , of the Choctaw Nation; that I am the lawful wife of Daniel H Carr , who is a citizen, by Marriage of the Choctaw Nation; that a Male child was born to me on 8th day of Sept , 1904; that said child has been named Jessie Redmond Carr , and was living March 4, 1905.

Lillie McClung Carr

Witnesses To Mark:
{

Subscribed and sworn to before me this 5th day of April , 1905

J M Webster
Notary Public.

**AFFIDAVIT OF ATTENDING PHYSICIAN OR MID-WIFE.**

UNITED STATES OF AMERICA, Indian Territory, }
Southern  DISTRICT.

I, ~~S.E. Boyd~~ E.S. Boyd , a M.D. , on oath state that I attended on Mrs. Lillie M$^c$Clung Carr , wife of Daniel H Carr on the 8$^{th}$ day of Sept , 1904; that there was born to her on said date a male child; that said child was living March 4, 1905, and is said to have been named Jessie Redmond Carr

E S Boyd M.D.

Witnesses To Mark:
{ SS Arnold
  G.M. Rucker

Subscribed and sworn to before me this 1$^{st}$ day of April , 1905

H.G. Campbell J.P. & Ex officio
Notary Public.
Hunt County Texas

# Applications for Enrollment of Choctaw Newborn
## Act of 1905    Volume XI

BIRTH AFFIDAVIT.    #149

**IN RE-APPLICATION FOR ENROLLMENT**, as a citizen of the  Choctaw    Nation, of Jessie Redmon[sic] Carr, born on the  8$^{th}$   day of  Sept  , 190 4

Name of Father:  D.H. Carr              a citizen of the  Choctaw    Nation.
Name of Mother:  Lillie Carr            a citizen of the  Choctaw    Nation.

Postoffice    Sulphur Ind Ter

### AFFIDAVIT OF MOTHER.

UNITED STATES OF AMERICA, INDIAN TERRITORY,  
Southern                District.

I,    Lillie Carr   , on oath state that I am   31   years of age and a citizen by Blood   , of the   Choctaw    Nation; that I am the lawful wife of    D.H. Carr   , who is a citizen, by   Marriage    of the    Choctaw    Nation; that a    male    child was born to me on  8$^{th}$   day of  April   , 1904 , that said child has been named   Jessie Redman[sic] Carr   , and is now living.

Lillie Carr

Witnesses To Mark:

{

Subscribed and sworn to before me this   24$^{th}$   day of  Feby   , 1905.

T.T. Gafford  
Notary Public.

### AFFIDAVIT OF ATTENDING PHYSICIAN OR MID-WIFE.

UNITED STATES OF AMERICA, INDIAN TERRITORY,  
Hunt County, Texas         District.

I,    E.S. Boyd         , a    MD         , on oath state that I attended on Mrs.   Lillie Carr   , wife of  D.H. Carr    on the  8$^{th}$   day of  Sept   , 190 4; that there was born to her on said date a    male    child; that said child is now living and is said to have been named   Jesse Redman Carr

E.S. Boyd M.D.

Witnesses To Mark:

{

## Applications for Enrollment of Choctaw Newborn
## Act of 1905   Volume XI

Subscribed and sworn to before me this   27   day of   Feby   , 1905.

                              MB Mathews
                                  Notary Public.
                              Hunt County Texas

My Commission Expires June 10$^{th}$ 1905

---

Choc New Born 742
      Thelma Morris   b.  11-12-02

                                              7-2734

                    Muskogee, Indian Territory, April 11, 1905.

John N. Morris,
      Shadypoint, Indian Territory.

Dear Sir:

      Receipt is hereby acknowledged of the affidavits of Belle Morris and J. J. Hardy to the birth of Thelma Morris, daughter of John W. and Belle Morris, November 12, 1902, and the same have been filed with our records as an application for the enrollment of said child.

                        Respectfully,

                                            Commissioner in Charge.

**NEW-BORN AFFIDAVIT.**

                Number..................

...Choctaw Enrolling Commission...

      IN THE MATTER OF THE APPLICATION FOR ENROLLMENT, as a citizen of the Choctaw      Nation, of           Thelma Morris

born on the   12   day of ___November___ 190 2

# Applications for Enrollment of Choctaw Newborn
## Act of 1905 Volume XI

Name of father   John N. Morris             a citizen of   United States
Nation final enrollment No............
Name of mother   Belle Morris nee Belle Lewis   a citizen of   Choctaw
Nation final enrollment No.  7987

                        Postoffice   Shady Point I.T.

### AFFIDAVIT OF MOTHER.

UNITED STATES OF AMERICA
INDIAN TERRITORY
  Central    DISTRICT

I  Belle Morris nee Belle Lewis  , on oath state that I am 23 years of age and a citizen by blood of the Choctaw Nation, and as such have been placed upon the final roll of the Choctaw Nation, by the Honorable Secretary of the Interior my final enrollment number being 7987 ; that I am the lawful wife of John N Morris , who is a citizen of the United States ~~Nation~~, and as such has been placed upon the final roll of said Nation by the Honorable Secretary of the Interior, his final enrollment number being ............ and that a Female child was born to me on the 12th day of November 190 2; that said child has been named Thelma Morris , and is now living.

                                      Belle Morris nee Belle Lewis

Witnesseth.
  Must be two } Ben Folsom
  Witnesses who
  are Citizens.   Noel Folsom

Subscribed and sworn to before me this 28  day of  Jan   190 5

                              WH Phillips
                                      Notary Public.

My commission expires:  19 day of Jan 1907

## AFFIDAVIT OF ATTENDING PHYSICIAN OR MIDWIFE

UNITED STATES OF AMERICA
INDIAN TERRITORY
  Central    DISTRICT

I,  J J Hardy   a   Physician
on oath state that I attended on Mrs. Belle Morris nee Belle Lewis wife of  John N Morris on the  12th   day of  November  , 190 2 , that there was born to her on said date a Female  child, that said child is now living, and is said to have been named  Thelma Morris

                              J J Hardy    *M.D.*

## Applications for Enrollment of Choctaw Newborn
## Act of 1905   Volume XI

Subscribed and sworn to before me this, the  28  day of Jan  190 5

W.H. Phillips   Notary Public.

WITNESSETH:
Must be two witnesses who are citizens { Ben Folsom
Noel Folsom

We hereby certify that we are well acquainted with  J J Hardy  a  Physician  and know  him  to be reputable and of good standing in the community.

Noel Folsom

Frank Lewis

BIRTH AFFIDAVIT.

### DEPARTMENT OF THE INTERIOR.
### COMMISSION TO THE FIVE CIVILIZED TRIBES.

IN RE APPLICATION FOR ENROLLMENT, as a citizen of the  Choctaw  Nation, of  Thelma Morris  , born on the 12  day of  November  , 1902

Name of Father: John N Morris      a citizen of the   U. S.   ~~Nation~~.
Name of Mother: Belle Morris nee Lewis      a citizen of the   Choctaw   Nation.

Postoffice   Shady Point I.T.

**AFFIDAVIT OF MOTHER.**

UNITED STATES OF AMERICA, Indian Territory,
Central     DISTRICT.

I,  Belle Morris  , on oath state that I am  23  years of age and a citizen by Blood  , of the  Choctaw  Nation; that I am the lawful wife of  John N Morris  , who is a citizen, by _____ of the  United States  Nation; that a  female  child was born to me on  12  day of  November  , 1902; that said child has been named  Thelma Morris  , and was living March 4, 1905.

Belle Morris nee Lewis

Witnesses To Mark:
{

# Applications for Enrollment of Choctaw Newborn
# Act of 1905   Volume XI

Subscribed and sworn to before me this  6   day of    April        , 1905

                                         W.H. Phillips
                                         Notary Public.

---

**AFFIDAVIT OF ATTENDING PHYSICIAN OR MID-WIFE.**

UNITED STATES OF AMERICA, Indian Territory, }
........................................ DISTRICT. }

    I,   J J Hardy      , a   Physician     , on oath state that I attended on Mrs.   Belle Morris   , wife of  John N Morris    on the  12  day of November    , 1902; that there was born to her on said date a    Female     child; that said child was living March 4, 1905, and is said to have been named Thelma Morris

                                      J. J. Hardy M.D.
Witnesses To Mark:
{

Subscribed and sworn to before me this  6   day of    April        , 1905

                                         W.H. Phillips
                                         Notary Public.

---

Choc New Born 743
    Sophiraan[sic] Everidge  b. 4-9-03

                                              7-1556

                    Muskogee, Indian Territory, April 11, 1905.

Robert T. Everidge,
    Grant, Indian Territory.

Dear Sir:

    Receipt is hereby acknowledged of the affidavits of Lula Everidge and Ida Russell to the birth of Sophiram Everidge, daughter of Robert Thomas and Lula Everidge, April 9, 1903, and the same have been filed with our records as an application for the enrollment of said child.

Applications for Enrollment of Choctaw Newborn
Act of 1905  Volume XI

Respectfully,

Commissioner in Charge.

*Affidavit of Attending Physician or Midwife*

UNITED STATES OF AMERICA,
INDIAN TERRITORY,
Central    DISTRICT

I, Eda[sic] Russell    a    midwife on oath state that I attended on Mrs. Lula Everidge    wife of Robt T Everidge on the 9 day of April, 190 3, that there was born to her on said date a    female    child, that said child is now living, and is said to have been named Sofia Ann Everidge

her
Eda x Russell    M. D.
mark

Subscribed and sworn to before me this the 17 day of Jan 1905

James Bower
Notary Public.

WITNESSETH:

Must be two witnesses who are citizens and know the child.
{ J C Kirkpatrick
  Geo W Oakes

We hereby certify that we are well acquainted with    Eda Russell    a    midwife    and know    her    to be reputable and of good standing in the community.

Must be two citizen witnesses.
{ J C Kirkpatrick
  Geo W Oakes

**NEW-BORN AFFIDAVIT.**

Number

## Choctaw Enrolling Commission.

IN THE MATTER OF THE APPLICATION FOR ENROLLMENT, as a citizen of the Choctaw    Nation, of    Sofia Ann Everidge

born on the 9 day of April    190 3

# Applications for Enrollment of Choctaw Newborn
## Act of 1905   Volume XI

Name of father   Robt T. Everidge            a citizen of   Choctaw
Nation final enrollment No   4365
Name of mother   Lula Everidge              a citizen of   Choctaw
Nation final enrollment No 81

                          Postoffice    Grant I.T.

### AFFIDAVIT OF MOTHER.

UNITED STATES OF AMERICA, }
   INDIAN TERRITORY,       }
  Central      DISTRICT          }

    I    Lula Everidge                          on oath state that I am   37   years of age and a citizen by   marriage      of the   Choctaw      Nation, and as such have been placed upon the final roll of the     Choctaw     Nation, by the Honorable Secretary of the Interior my final enrollment number being    81    ; that I am the lawful wife of   Robt T. Everidge           , who is a citizen of the   Choctaw           Nation, and as such has been placed upon the final roll of said Nation by the Honorable Secretary of the Interior, his final enrollment number being   4365     and that a    female     child was born to me on the   9   day of   April      190 3 ; that said child has been named    Sofia Ann Everidge       , and is now living.
                                                                                                                                    *Lula*  her
                                                                                                                                   ~~Sofia Ann~~ x Everidge
WITNESSETH:                                                                   mark
Must be two   } J C Kirkpatrick
Witnesses who }
are Citizens.  } Geo W Oakes

    Subscribed and sworn to before me this    17    day of    Jan         190 5

                                                                   James Bower
                                                                                 Notary Public.
My commission expires   Sept 23 1905

---

**BIRTH AFFIDAVIT.**
### DEPARTMENT OF THE INTERIOR.
### COMMISSION TO THE FIVE CIVILIZED TRIBES.

---

    IN RE APPLICATION FOR ENROLLMENT, as a citizen of the      Chocktaw[sic]     Nation, of Sophiraan Everidge        , born on the   9th    day of   April   , 1903

Name of Father:  Robert Turner Everidge       a citizen of the    Chocktaw   Nation.
Name of Mother:  Lula Everidge                a citizen of the    Chocktaw   Nation.

                                     Postoffice    Grant IT

# Applications for Enrollment of Choctaw Newborn
## Act of 1905   Volume XI

### AFFIDAVIT OF MOTHER.

UNITED STATES OF AMERICA, Indian Territory,
Grant Central        DISTRICT.

I, Lula Everidge, on oath state that I am 37 years of age and a citizen by marriage, of the Choctaw Nation; that I am the lawful wife of Robert Turner Everidge, who is a citizen, by Blood of the Choctaw Nation; that a Female child was born to me on 9th day of April, 1903; that said child has been named Sophiraan Everidge, and was living March 4, 1905.

                                        her
Witnesses To Mark:         Lula x Everidge
{ S. F. Williams              mark
{ Martin V Everidge

Subscribed and sworn to before me this 6 day of April, 1905

                                C W Hill
                                Notary Public.

---

### AFFIDAVIT OF ATTENDING PHYSICIAN OR MID-WIFE.

UNITED STATES OF AMERICA, Indian Territory,
......................................................... DISTRICT.

I, Eda Russell, a midwife, on oath state that I attended on Mrs. Lula Everidge, wife of Robert Turner Everidge on the 9th day of April, 1903; that there was born to her on said date a Female child; that said child was living March 4, 1905, and is said to have been named Sophiraan Everidge

                                        her
                                Eda x Russell
Witnesses To Mark:          mark
{ S. F. Williams
{ Martin V Everidge

Subscribed and sworn to before me this 6 day of April, 1905

                                C W Hill
                                Notary Public.

# Applications for Enrollment of Choctaw Newborn
## Act of 1905    Volume XI

Choc New Born 744
   Isa May Brashears  b. 11-12-03

Choctaw 2564.

Muskogee, Indian Territory, April 11, 1905.

Benjamin F. Brashears,
   Panama, Indian Territory.

Dear Sir:

Receipt is hereby acknowledged of the affidavits of Myrtle Brashears and Charles H. Mahar to the birth of Isa May Brashears, daughter of Benjamin Franklin Brashears and Myrtle Brashears, November 12, 1903, and the same have been filed with our records as an application for the enrollment of said child.

Respectfully,

[sic]

7- 7450        7- 113
**BIRTH AFFIDAVIT.**
   **DEPARTMENT OF THE INTERIOR.**
   **COMMISSION TO THE FIVE CIVILIZED TRIBES.**

IN RE APPLICATION FOR ENROLLMENT, as a citizen of the    Choctaw    Nation, of Isa May Brashears    , born on the 12   day of November  , 1903

Name of Father: Benjamin ~~Franklin~~ Brashears    a citizen of the   Choctaw    Nation.
                                                  by intermarriage
Name of Mother: Myrtle Brashears        a citizen of the   Choctaw    Nation.

Postoffice    Panama I.T.

**AFFIDAVIT OF MOTHER.**

UNITED STATES OF AMERICA, Indian Territory,
   Central         DISTRICT.

I,  Myrtle Brashears  , on oath state that I am  20   years of age and a citizen by    intermarriage   , of the   Choctaw   Nation; that I am the lawful wife of Benjamin Franklin Brashears     , who is a citizen, by  blood   of the    Choctaw

## Applications for Enrollment of Choctaw Newborn
## Act of 1905   Volume XI

Nation; that a   female   child was born to me on  12   day of   November   , 1903; that said child has been named   Isa May Brashears   , and was living March 4, 1905.

Myrtle Brashears

Witnesses To Mark:
{

Subscribed and sworn to before me this  Fourth  day of  April  , 1905

Frank Lewis<br>Notary Public.

**AFFIDAVIT OF ATTENDING PHYSICIAN OR MID-WIFE.**

UNITED STATES OF AMERICA, Indian Territory, }
Central            DISTRICT.

I,  C. H. Mahar   , a   physician   , on oath state that I attended on Mrs.  Myrtle Brashears   , wife of  Benjamin Franklin Brashears   on the 12$^{th}$ day of   November   , 1903; that there was born to her on said date a   female   child; that said child was living March 4, 1905, and is said to have been named  Isa May Brashears

Charles H Mahar M.D.

Witnesses To Mark:
{

Subscribed and sworn to before me this  6$^{th}$  day of   April   , 1905

Frank Lewis<br>Notary Public.

---

Choc New Born 745
    Ike Williams  b. 3-4-05
    Sarah Williams  b. 5-5-04

## NEW BORN
### CHOCTAW
### ENROLLMENT

IKE WILLIAMS

(BORN March 4, 1905)

SARAH WILLIAMS

(BORN MAY 5, 1904)

As Citizen of the
CHOCTAW NATION
Act of Congress
Approved March 3, 1905

NO. 2 March 4, 1905
NO. 2 REFUSED JUNE 22, 1905
IKE WILLIAMS TRANSFERRED TO N. B. 660
UNDER ACT OF APRIL 26, 1906.
RECORD FORWARDED DEPARTMENT JUNE 22, 1905
ACTION APPROVED BY SECRETARY OF INTERIOR
JULY 22, 1905.

NOTICE OF DEPARTMENTAL ACTION MAILED
APPLICANT'S FATHER AUGUST 1, 1905.

NOTICE OF DEPARTMENTAL ACTION FORWARDED
ATTORNEYS FOR CHOCTAW AND CHICKASAW
NATIONS AUGUST 1, 1905

## Applications for Enrollment of Choctaw Newborn
## Act of 1905   Volume XI

7-4567

**COPY**

Muskogee, Indian Territory, March 6, 1905.

Joseph Williams,
    Muse, Indian Territory.

Dear Sir:

    Receipt is hereby acknowledged of the affidavits of Motsy Williams and Joseph Williams to the birth of Sarah Williams, infant daughter of Joseph and Motsy Williams May 5, 1904. It is stated in the affidavit of the mother that she is a citizen by blood of the Choctaw Nation and the lawful wife of Joseph Williams who is also a citizen by blood of the Choctaw Nation. If this is correct you are requested to state when, where and under what name application was made for the enrollment of yourself and Motsy Williams, the names of your parents and any other information which will enable the Commission to identify you and Motsy Williams upon its records as applicants for enrollment in the Choctaw and Chickasaw Nations.

    If your wife Motsy Williams has other children you are requested to state their names also.

                    Respectfully,

              SIGNED

                    *Tams Bixby*
                    Commissioner in Charge.

---

7-2072

Muskogee, Indian Territory, April 11, 1905.

Joseph Williams,
    Talihina, Indian Territory.

Dear Sir:

    Receipt is hereby acknowledged of the affidavits of Molsy[sic] Williams and Joseph Williams to the birth of Sarah Williams, daughter of Joseph and Molsy Williams, May 5, 1904, and the same have been filed with our records as an application for the enrollment of said child.

                    Respectfully,

                      Commissioner in Charge.

# Applications for Enrollment of Choctaw Newborn
## Act of 1905   Volume XI

7 N B 745

Muskogee, Indian Territory, April 17, 1905.

Joseph Williams,
    Talihina, Indian Territory.

Dear Sir:

    Referring to the affidavits heretofore forwarded, relative to the enrollment of your infant children, Sarah Williams and Ike Williams, it appears therein that you filled out the affidavit of the attending physician or mid-wife. In the event that you were the only one in attendance at the birth of said child, it will be necessary that you secure the affidavits of two persons who have actual knowledge of the fact, that the children were born, the dates of their birth, that they were living on March 4, 1905, and that Motsy Williams is their mother.

Respectfully,

Chairman.

7-N.B. 745.

Muskogee, Indian Territory, May 3, 1905.

Joseph Williams,
    Muse, Indian Territory.

Dear Sir:

    Receipt is hereby acknowledged of the affidavits of Motsy Williams and Joseph Williams, Henry Johnson and Charles Billy to the birth of Sarah Williams, daughter of Joseph and Motsy Williams, May 5, 1904, and the same have been filed with our records in the matter of the enrollment of said child.

    Receipt is also acknowledged of the affidavits of Motsy Williams, Joseph Williams, Benjamin Willis and Scion Beams to the birth of Ike Williams, son of Motsy and Joseph Williams, March 4, 1905.

    You are advised that under the provisions of the act of Congress approved March 3, 1905, the Commission is authorized for period of sixty days from that date to receive application for the enrollment of children born to enrolled citizens by blood of the Choctaw and Chickasaw Nations, between September 25, 1902, and March 4, 1905.

Respectfully,

Chairman.

## Applications for Enrollment of Choctaw Newborn
## Act of 1905   Volume XI

BIRTH AFFIDAVIT.

## DEPARTMENT OF THE INTERIOR,
### COMMISSION TO THE FIVE CIVILIZED TRIBES.

IN RE Application for Enrollment, as a citizen of the Choctaw Nation, of Sarah Williams, born on the 5 day of May, 1904

Name of Father: Joseph Williams   a citizen of the Choctaw Nation.
Name of Mother: Motsy Williams    a citizen of the Choctaw Nation.

Post-Office:  Muse I T

*Joseph Williams Interpreter*

**AFFIDAVIT OF MOTHER.**

UNITED STATES OF AMERICA, }
   INDIAN TERRITORY.
Central     District.

I, Motsy Williams, on oath state that I am 31 years of age and a citizen by Blood, of the Choctaw Nation; that I am the lawful wife of Joseph Williams, who is a citizen, by Blood of the Choctaw Nation; that a Female child was born to me on 5 day of May, 1904, that said child has been named Sarah Williams, and is now living.

Motsy Williams

WITNESSES TO MARK:

Subscribed and sworn to before me this 1 day of March, 1905.

Sam T. Roberts Jr.
NOTARY PUBLIC.

**AFFIDAVIT OF ATTENDING PHYSICIAN OR MID-WIFE.**

UNITED STATES OF AMERICA, }
   INDIAN TERRITORY.
Central     District.

*Motsy Williams*

I, Joseph Williams, a husband of, on oath state that I attended on Mrs. my wife Motsy Williams on the 5 day of May, 1904; that there was

## Applications for Enrollment of Choctaw Newborn
## Act of 1905 Volume XI

born to her on said date a  female  child; that said child is now living and is said to have been named  Sarah Williams

Joseph Williams

**WITNESSES TO MARK:**

{

Subscribed and sworn to before me this 1 day of March , 1905.

Sam T. Roberts Jr.
*NOTARY PUBLIC.*

---

**BIRTH AFFIDAVIT.**

# DEPARTMENT OF THE INTERIOR,
### COMMISSION TO THE FIVE CIVILIZED TRIBES.

---

IN RE *Application for Enrollment,* as a citizen of the  Choctaw  Nation, of  Sarah Williams , born on the  5  day of  May , 1904

Name of Father: Joseph Williams     a citizen of the  Choctaw  Nation.
Name of Mother: Motsy Williams     a citizen of the  Choctaw  Nation.

Post-Office:  Talihina I T

---

*Guslukes*[sic] *Interpreter*

**AFFIDAVIT OF MOTHER.**

---

UNITED STATES OF AMERICA, }
  INDIAN TERRITORY.
Central  District. }

I,  Motsy Williams , on oath state that I am about 32  years of age and a citizen by  Blood , of the  Choctaw  Nation; that I am the lawful wife of  Joseph Williams , who is a citizen, by  Blood  of the  Choctaw  Nation; that a  Female  child was born to me on  5  day of  May , 1904 , that said child has been named  Sarah Williams , and is now living. *now living March 4 - 1905*

Motsy Williams

**WITNESSES TO MARK:**

{

Subscribed and sworn to before me this 6 day of April , 1905.

My commission expires Feb. 4, 1908
Commission from U.S. Court at So. McAlester I.T.    Sam T. Roberts Jr.
MY OFFICE TALIHINA, I. T.            *NOTARY PUBLIC.*

# Applications for Enrollment of Choctaw Newborn
## Act of 1905   Volume XI

**AFFIDAVIT OF ATTENDING PHYSICIAN OR MID-WIFE.**

UNITED STATES OF AMERICA,  
   **INDIAN TERRITORY.**  
Central District.

I, Joseph Williams, a ——————, on oath state that I attended on Mrs. Motsy Williams wife of my wife on the 5 day of May, 1904; that there was born to her on said date a female child; that said child ~~is now~~ living and is said to have been named Sarah Williams *was living March 4-1905*

                                      Joseph Williams

**WITNESSES TO MARK:**

Subscribed and sworn to before me this 6 day of April, 1905.

                                       Sam T. Roberts Jr.
                                            **NOTARY PUBLIC.**

---

United States of America,  
Indian Territoy[sic]          Affidavit,  
Central District.

I Charles Billy on oath state that I am 40 years of age and a citizen of the Choctaw Nation by Blood.

That I know Joseph Williams, and know him to be a citizen by blood of the Choctaw Nation. I also know his wife Motsy Williams and know her to be a Citizen of the Choctaw Nation by blood.

I know that on the 5th day of May 1904, there was born to Motsy Williams wife of Joseph Williams a female child, that she was living on the 4th day of March 1905, and is still living. That she has been named Sarah.

I am in no way related to Joseph or Motsy Williams, I am a disintered[sic] party.

                                        Charles Billy

Witnesses,  
   Thomas Bohanan  
   M F Calhoun

Subscribed and sworn to before me this the 26th day of April 1905.

               My com. expires     F.B. Lunsford  
               Feb. 4 1908            Notary Public.

## Applications for Enrollment of Choctaw Newborn
## Act of 1905  Volume XI

United States of America,
Indian Territoy[sic]  Affidavit,
Central District.

I   Henry Johnson   on oath state that I am  50  years of age and a citizen of the Choctaw Nation by Blood.

That I know Joseph Williams, and know him to be a citizen by blood of the Choctaw Nation. I also know his wife Motsy Williams and know her to be a Citizen of the Choctaw Nation by blood.

I know that on the 5th day of May 1904, there was born to Motsy Williams wife of Joseph Williams a female child, that she was living on the 4th day of March 1905, and is still living. That she has been named Sarah.

I am in no way related to Joseph or Motsy Williams, I am a disintered[sic] party.

                                  Henry Johnson
Witnesses,
  Thomas Bohanan
  M F Calhoun

Subscribed and sworn to before me this the 26th day of April 1905.

                My com. expires   F.B. Lunsford
                Feb. 4 1908   Notary Public.

**BIRTH AFFIDAVIT.**
                      **DEPARTMENT OF THE INTERIOR.**
              **COMMISSION TO THE FIVE CIVILIZED TRIBES.**

**IN RE APPLICATION FOR ENROLLMENT,** as a citizen of the   Choctaw   Nation, of Sarah Williams   , born on the  5th  day of  May  , 1904

Name of Father: Josep[sic] Williams     a citizen of the  Choctaw  Nation.
Name of Mother: Motsy Williams      a citizen of the  Choctaw  Nation.

                      Postoffice   Muse I. T.

# Applications for Enrollment of Choctaw Newborn
## Act of 1905   Volume XI

### AFFIDAVIT OF MOTHER.

UNITED STATES OF AMERICA, Indian Territory, }
Central        DISTRICT.

I, Motsy Williams, on oath state that I am 32 years of age and a citizen by blood, of the Choctaw Nation; that I am the lawful wife of Joseph Williams, who is a citizen, by blood of the Choctaw Nation; that a female child was born to me on the 5th day of May 1904, 1........; that said child has been named Sarah, and was living March 4, 1905.

                                        Motsy Williams
Witnesses To Mark:
 { (Name Illegible)
   C.J. Anderson

Subscribed and sworn to before me this 26 day of April, 1905

My com. expires                    F.B. Lunsford
Feb. 4, 1908                              Notary Public.

---

### AFFIDAVIT OF ATTENDING PHYSICIAN OR MID-WIFE.

UNITED STATES OF AMERICA, Indian Territory, }
Central District        DISTRICT.

I, Joseph Williams husband of Motsy Williams, on oath state that I attended on Mrs. Motsy Williams, wife of Joseph Williams on the 5th day of May 1904, 1........; that there was born to her on said date a ................ child; that said child was living March 4, 1905, and is said to have been named Sarah

                                        Joseph Williams
Witnesses To Mark:
 { (Name Illegible)
   C.J. Anderson

Subscribed and sworn to before me this 26 day of April, 1905

My com. expires                    F.B. Lunsford
Feb. 4, 1908                              Notary Public.

## Applications for Enrollment of Choctaw Newborn
## Act of 1905   Volume XI

<u>Choc New Born 746</u>
Goldie Loma Davis   b. 5-12-04

Choctaw 4428.

Muskogee, Indian Territory, April 11, 1905.

Alonzo M. Davis,
    Byars, Indian Territory.

Dear Sir:

    Receipt is hereby acknowledged of the affidavits of Lorena Davis and W. B. Tackett to the birth of Goldie Loma Davis, daughter of Alonzo and Lorena Davis, May 12, 1904, and the same have been filed with our records as an application for the enrollment of said child.

        Respectfully,

        Commissioner in Charge.

**BIRTH AFFIDAVIT.**

### DEPARTMENT OF THE INTERIOR.
### COMMISSION TO THE FIVE CIVILIZED TRIBES.

**IN RE APPLICATION FOR ENROLLMENT,** as a citizen of the    Choctaw    Nation, of Goldie Loma Davis    , born on the $12^{th}$   day of   May   , 1904

Name of Father: Alonzo M. Davis    a citizen of the   Choctaw   Nation.
Name of Mother: Lorena Davis    a citizen of the   Choctaw   Nation.

        Postoffice    Byars Ind Terr

**AFFIDAVIT OF MOTHER.**

**UNITED STATES OF AMERICA, Indian Territory,**
    Southern    **DISTRICT.**

    I,   Lorena Davis   , on oath state that I am   Thirty seven   years of age and a citizen by   Blood   , of the   Choctaw   Nation; that I am the lawful wife of Alonzo M. Davis   , who is a citizen, by  Intermarriage   of the   Choctaw   Nation; that a   Female   child was born to me on   $12^{th}$   day of   May   , 1904; that said child has been named   Goldie Loma Davis   , and was living March 4, 1905.

        Lorena Davis

## Applications for Enrollment of Choctaw Newborn
## Act of 1905   Volume XI

Witnesses To Mark:
{ W N Gaylord
{ J.T. M<sup>c</sup>Donnell

    Subscribed and sworn to before me this  5   day of     April     , 1905

                                              J.W. Gaylord
                                              Notary Public.

---

**AFFIDAVIT OF ATTENDING PHYSICIAN OR MID-WIFE.**

UNITED STATES OF AMERICA, Indian Territory, }
    Sothern[sic]              DISTRICT. }

    I,    W. B. Jackett       , a      Physon[sic]      , on oath state that I attended on Mrs.  Lorena Davis     , wife of    Alonzo Davis     on the  12   day of    May    , 1904; that there was born to her on said date a      Female      child; that said child was living March 4, 1905, and is said to have been named  Goldie Loma Davis

                                          W.B. Jackett MD
Witnesses To Mark:
{ W L Lee
{ L. Binswanger

    Subscribed and sworn to before me this  5   day of     April     , 1905

                                               J.W. Gaylord
                                            Notary Public.

---

Choc New Born 747
    Lorena Pearl Roach  *(b.)*  12-10-04

# Applications for Enrollment of Choctaw Newborn
## Act of 1905   Volume XI

Choctaw 4437.

Muskogee, Indian Territory, April 11, 1905.

Robert W. Roach,
Wapanucka, Indian Territory.

Dear Sir:

Receipt is hereby acknowledged of the affidavits of Joanna Roach and Dr. R. W. Roach to the birth of Lorena Pearl Roach, daughter of Robert W. and Joanna Roach, December 10, 1904, and the same have been filed with our records as an application for the enrollment of said child.

Respectfully,

Commissioner in Charge.

---

7-NB-747.

Muskogee, Indian Territory, May 29, 1905.

Robert W. Roach,
Wapanucka, Indian Territory.

Dear Sir:

Referring to the application for the enrollment of your infant child, Lorena Pearl Roach, born December 10, 1904, it is noted from the affidavits heretofore filed in this office that you were the physician in attendance upon your wife at the time of the birth of the applicant.

If there was no other physician or no midwife in attendance it will be necessary that you file in this office the affidavits of two persons, who are disinterested and not related to the applicant, who have actual knowledge of the facts that the child was born, the date of her birth; that she was living on March 4, 1905, and that Joanna Roach is her mother.

Respectfully,

Chairman.

---

## Applications for Enrollment of Choctaw Newborn
## Act of 1905   Volume XI

7 NB 747

Muskogee, Indian Territory, June 20, 1905.

Robert W. Roach,
    Wapanucka, Indian Territory.

Dear Sir:

    Receipt is hereby acknowledged of the joint affidavit of Sam Shipley and J. A. Woods to the birth of Lorena Pearl Roach, daughter of Robert W. and Joanna Roach, December 10, 1904, and the same has been filed with our records in the matter of the enrollment of said child.

Respectfully,

Chairman.

---

*(The affidavit below typed as given.)*

Before the Commission to the Five Tribes, Muskogee Ind. Ter.
    In re Enrollment of Lorena Roach.
    Affidavit.

    We J.A.Woods and Sam Shipley each having been first duly sworn on oath state each that we were each acquainted with Robert W.Roach and his wife Joanna Roach, citizens of the Choctaw Nation who reside near Wapanucka, I.T., and just prior to December the tenth 1904., she the said Joana Roach was in an encient condition, and just a few days after the said date we saw her nursing a babe a few days old,

    It was a female child and has been named Lorena Pearl Roach, and was living on the fourth day of March, 1905., and was born on the tenth day of December 1904, Joana Roach is the mother of said child.

We are neither related to the parties named or interested in the matters mentioned herein.

Sam Shipley

J A Woods

Subscribed and sworn to before me this the 16th day of June 1905.

W Richards
Notary Public.

My Commission expires Feby 7th 1909.

---

## Applications for Enrollment of Choctaw Newborn
## Act of 1905 Volume XI

**BIRTH AFFIDAVIT.**

### DEPARTMENT OF THE INTERIOR.
### COMMISSION TO THE FIVE CIVILIZED TRIBES.

IN RE APPLICATION FOR ENROLLMENT, as a citizen of the Choctaw Nation, of Lorena Pearl Roach, born on the 10$^{th}$ day of Dec, 1904

Name of Father: Robert W Roach     a citizen of the Choctaw Nation.
Name of Mother: Joanna Roach     a citizen of the Choctaw Nation.

Postoffice    Wapanucka Ind. Ty.

**AFFIDAVIT OF MOTHER.**

UNITED STATES OF AMERICA, Indian Territory,
Southern DISTRICT.

I, Joanna Roach, on oath state that I am Thirty three years of age and a citizen by blood, of the Choctaw Nation; that I am the lawful wife of Robert W. Roach, who is a citizen, by Marriage of the Choctaw Nation; that a Female child was born to me on 10$^{th}$ day of December, 1904; that said child has been named Lorena Pearl Roach, and was living March 4, 1905.

Joanna Roach

Witnesses To Mark:

Subscribed and sworn to before me this 4 day of April, 1905

A A Faulk
Notary Public.

**AFFIDAVIT OF ATTENDING PHYSICIAN OR MID-WIFE.**

UNITED STATES OF AMERICA, Indian Territory,
Southern DISTRICT.

I, Dr. Robert W. Roach, on oath state that I attended on Mrs. Joanna Roach, wife of Robert W Roach on the 10$^{th}$ day of Dec, 1904; that there was born to her on said date a Female child; that said child was living March 4, 1905, and is said to have been named Lorena Pearl Roach

Dr. R.W. Roach

Witnesses To Mark:

## Applications for Enrollment of Choctaw Newborn
## Act of 1905   Volume XI

Subscribed and sworn to before me this   4   day of     April    , 1905

                                                  A A Faulk
                                                  Notary Public.

---

<u>Choc New Born 748</u>
    Edmon Ree Cleaveland   b.  11-16-04

**BIRTH AFFIDAVIT.**

*No 7810*

**DEPARTMENT OF THE INTERIOR.**
**COMMISSION TO THE FIVE CIVILIZED TRIBES.**

    IN RE APPLICATION FOR ENROLLMENT, as a citizen of the    Choctaw    Nation, of    Edmon Ree Cleveland    , born on the   16th   day of   November   , 1904

Name of Father:  Edward Cleveland        a citizen of the United States ~~Nation~~.
Name of Mother:  Mollie Cleveland         a citizen of the   Choctaw   Nation.

                Postoffice    Cowlington, Ind. Ter.

**AFFIDAVIT OF MOTHER.**

UNITED STATES OF AMERICA, Indian Territory, }
   Central             DISTRICT.

    I,   Mollie Cleveland   , on oath state that I am   22   years of age and a citizen by    blood    , of the   Choctaw   Nation; that I am the lawful wife of   Edward Cleveland        , who is a citizen, ~~by~~ ................. of the    United States   Nation; that a    male    child was born to me on  16th    day of   November  , 1904; that said child has been named   Edmon Ree Cleveland    , and was living March 4, 1905.

                                  Mollie Cleaveland[sic]
Witnesses To Mark:
  {

    Subscribed and sworn to before me this   4th   day of    April    , 1905

                                    OL Johnson
                                    Notary Public.

## Applications for Enrollment of Choctaw Newborn
## Act of 1905   Volume XI

**AFFIDAVIT OF ATTENDING PHYSICIAN OR MID-WIFE.**

UNITED STATES OF AMERICA, Indian Territory, }
   Central              DISTRICT.

    I,   Jas. B. Beckett   , a   physician   , on oath state that I attended on Mrs.   Mollie Cleveland   , wife of   Edward Cleveland   on the   16th day of November   , 1904; that there was born to her on said date a   male   child; that said child was living March 4, 1905, and is said to have been named   Edmon Ree Cleveland

                                    J B Beckett MD

Witnesses To Mark:
{

    Subscribed and sworn to before me this  4  day of   April   , 1905

                                   A.H. Crouthamel
                                   Notary Public.

---

Choc New Born 749
    Alfred Earl Brown  b. 8-20-03

                                      Choctaw 5710.

                      Muskogee, Indian Territory, April 12, 1905.

Elum Brown,
    Indianola, Indian Territory.

Dear Sir:

    Receipt is hereby acknowledged of the affidavits of Ida F. Brown and Pheby C. Staton to the birth of Alfred Earl Brown, son of Elum and Ida F. Brown, August 20th, 1903, and the same have been filed with our records as an application for the enrollment of said child.

                              Respectfully,

                                      Commissioner in Charge.

## Applications for Enrollment of Choctaw Newborn
## Act of 1905   Volume XI

**NEW-BORN AFFIDAVIT.**

Number..............

...Choctaw Enrolling Commission...

IN THE MATTER OF THE APPLICATION FOR ENROLLMENT, as a citizen of the Choctaw Nation, of   Alfred Earl Brown

born on the   20   day of ___August___ 190 3

Name of father   Elum Brown             a ^non citizen of   Choctaw
Nation final enrollment No. ———
Name of mother   Ida F Brown            a citizen of   Choctaw
Nation final enrollment No.  15513

                                        Postoffice   Indianola IT

**AFFIDAVIT OF MOTHER.**

UNITED STATES OF AMERICA
INDIAN TERRITORY
   Western   DISTRICT

I   Ida F Brown                         , on oath state that I am 23   years of age and a citizen by   Blood   of the   Choctaw   Nation, and as such have been placed upon the final roll of the   Choctaw   Nation, by the Honorable Secretary of the Interior my final enrollment number being   15513  ; that I am the lawful wife of   Elum Brown          , who is a *non* citizen of the   Choctaw   Nation, and as such has been placed upon the final roll of said Nation by the Honorable Secretary of the Interior, his final enrollment number being ———and that a   Male   child was born to me on the   20   day of   August       190 3; that said child has been named   Alfred Earl Brown   , and is now living.

                                           her
                                    Ida  x  F Brown
Witnesseth.                             mark
   Must be two     ⎫  Will T. Walker
   Witnesses who   ⎬
   are Citizens.   ⎭  John J Beams

      Subscribed and sworn to before me this   25<sup>th</sup>   day of   Feb    190 5

                           S.M. Gold
                                        Notary Public.
My commission expires: 2/19-1908

## Applications for Enrollment of Choctaw Newborn
## Act of 1905   Volume XI

## AFFIDAVIT OF ATTENDING PHYSICIAN OR MIDWIFE

UNITED STATES OF AMERICA
INDIAN TERRITORY
Western   DISTRICT

I, Phoeby[sic] C Staton   a   Midwife on oath state that I attended on Mrs. Ida F Brown wife of   Elum Brown on the 20$^{th}$ day of August, 190 3, that there was born to her on said date a male child, that said child is now living, and is said to have been named   Alfred Earl Brown

                                 her
                          Phoeby C x Staton   *M.D.*

Subscribed and sworn to before me this, the   mark   25$^{th}$   day of February   190 5

WITNESSETH:                      SM Gold      Notary Public.
Must be two witnesses { Will T Walker
who are citizens        John J Beams

We hereby certify that we are well acquainted with   Phoby[sic] C Staton a   Midwife   and know   her   to be reputable and of good standing in the community.

_____      Will T Walker

_____      John J Beams

**BIRTH AFFIDAVIT.**

## DEPARTMENT OF THE INTERIOR.
## COMMISSION TO THE FIVE CIVILIZED TRIBES.

**IN RE APPLICATION FOR ENROLLMENT,** as a citizen of the   Choctaw   Nation, of Alfred Earl Brown   , born on the   20   day of   Aug   , 1903

Name of Father: Elum Brown      a citizen of the United States Nation.
Name of Mother: Ida F Brown      a citizen of the   Choctaw   Nation.

                        Postoffice   Indianola I.T.

## Applications for Enrollment of Choctaw Newborn
## Act of 1905  Volume XI

**AFFIDAVIT OF MOTHER.**

UNITED STATES OF AMERICA, Indian Territory, ⎫
Western  DISTRICT. ⎭

I, Ida F. Brown, on oath state that I am 23 years of age and a citizen by Blood, of the Choctaw Nation; that I am the lawful wife of Elum Brown, who is a citizen, by ✗ of the United States Nation; that a male child was born to me on 20 day of August, 1903; that said child has been named Alfred Earl Brown, and was living March 4, 1905.

Ida F Brown

Witnesses To Mark:
⎰ Christopher C Choate
⎱ Daniel Davis

Subscribed and sworn to before me this 8 day of April, 1905

T.J. Rice
Notary Public.

---

**AFFIDAVIT OF ATTENDING PHYSICIAN OR MID-WIFE.**

UNITED STATES OF AMERICA, Indian Territory, ⎫
Western  DISTRICT. ⎭

I, Pheby C Staton, a mid wife, on oath state that I attended on Mrs. Ida F Brown, wife of Elum Brown on the 20 day of August, 1903; that there was born to her on said date a male child; that said child was living March 4, 1905, and is said to have been named Alfred Earl Brown

her
Pheby C x Staton
mark

Witnesses To Mark:
⎰ Christopher C Choate
⎱ Daniel Davis

Subscribed and sworn to before me this 8 day of April, 1905

T.J. Rice
Notary Public.

# Applications for Enrollment of Choctaw Newborn
## Act of 1905 Volume XI

Choc New Born 750
    Henry Harrison Belvin b. 7-27-03

---

                                                            Choctaw 3436.

                      Muskogee, Indian Territory, April 11, 1905.

Watson Belvin,
    Boswell, Indian Territory.

Dear Sir:

    Receipt is hereby acknowledged of the affidavits of Mabel Belvin and Irene Dudly[sic] to the birth of Henry Harrison J. Belvin, son of Watson and Mabel Belvin, July 27, 1903, and the same have been filed with our records as an application for the enrollment of said child.

                    Respectfully,

                                        Commissioner in Charge.

---

*Sub*

                                                         7-NB-750.

                    Muskogee, Indian Territory, May 31, 1905.

Watson Belvin,
    Boswell, Indian Territory.

Dear Sir:

    There is returned herewith application for the enrollment of your infant child, Henry Harrison J. Belvin, born July 27, 1903, in which the Notary Public failed to affix his seal to the affidavits of the mother and the midwife.

    Please have the Notary, before whom they were made, to attach his seal, which must be an impression and not a scroll, to these affidavits and then return them to this office.

                    Respectfully,

VR 29-1.                                                [sic]

Applications for Enrollment of Choctaw Newborn
Act of 1905   Volume XI

7-NB-750

Muskogee, Indian Territory, June 7, 1905.

Watson Belvin,
~~Watson~~ Boswell, Indian Territory.

Dear Sir:

Receipt is hereby acknowledged of the application for the enrollment of Henry Harrison J. Belvin corrected by having the Notary Public before whom the affidavits were acknowledged affix his seal to the affidavits of the mother and the midwife.

Respectfully,

Chairman.

**NEW-BORN AFFIDAVIT.**

Number............

## Choctaw Enrolling Commission.

IN THE MATTER OF THE APPLICATION FOR ENROLLMENT, as a citizen of the Choctaw   Nation, of   Henry Harrison Jones Belvin

born on the  27$^{th}$  day of   July   190 3

Name of father   Watson Belvin     a citizen of   Choctaw
Nation final enrollment No   9793
Name of mother   Mabel Belvin     a citizen of   Choctaw
Nation final enrollment No   326

Postoffice   Boswell I.T.

**AFFIDAVIT OF MOTHER.**

UNITED STATES OF AMERICA,
INDIAN TERRITORY,
Central   DISTRICT

I   Mabel Belvin   on oath state that I am   22   years of age and a citizen by   intermarriage   of the   Choctaw   Nation, and as such have been placed upon the final roll of the   Choctaw   Nation, by the Honorable Secretary of the Interior my final enrollment number being   326   ; that I am the lawful wife of Watson Belvin   , who is a citizen of the   Choctaw   Nation, and as such

## Applications for Enrollment of Choctaw Newborn
## Act of 1905   Volume XI

has been placed upon the final roll of said Nation by the Honorable Secretary of the Interior, his final enrollment number being  9793  and that a  male  child was born to me on the  27  day of  July  190 3; that said child has been named  Henry Harrison Jones Belvin , and is now living.

Mabel Belvin

WITNESSETH:
Must be two Witnesses who are Citizens.  } Sampson Scott
Daniel F Wade

Subscribed and sworn to before me this  30  day of  January  190 5

S H Downing
Notary Public.

My commission expires  March 14th 1908

---

*Affidavit of Attending Physician or Midwife*

UNITED STATES OF AMERICA,
INDIAN TERRITORY,
Central  DISTRICT

I,  Irene Dudley  a  midwife  on oath state that I attended on Mrs. Mabel Belvin  wife of  Watson Belvin  on the  27th  day of  July  , 190 3, that there was born to her on said date a  male  child, that said child is now living, and is said to have been named  Henry Harrison Jones Belvin

her
Irene x Dudley   Midwife
mark

Subscribed and sworn to before me this the  30  day of  January  1905

SH Downing
Notary Public.

WITNESSETH:
Must be two witnesses who are citizens and know the child.  { Sampson Scott
Daniel F Wade

We hereby certify that we are well acquainted with  Irene Dudley  a  midwife  and know  her  to be reputable and of good standing in the community.

Must be two citizen witnesses.  { Sampson Scott
Daniel F Wade

## Applications for Enrollment of Choctaw Newborn
## Act of 1905   Volume XI

**BIRTH AFFIDAVIT.**

### DEPARTMENT OF THE INTERIOR.
### COMMISSION TO THE FIVE CIVILIZED TRIBES.

**IN RE APPLICATION FOR ENROLLMENT,** as a citizen of the   Choctaw   Nation, of Henry Harrison J. Belvin   , born on the   27th   day of   July   , 1903

Name of Father: Watson Belvin   a citizen of the   Choctaw   Nation.
Name of Mother: Mabel Belvin   a citizen of the   Choctaw   Nation.

Postoffice   Boswell, Indian Territory

**AFFIDAVIT OF MOTHER.**

UNITED STATES OF AMERICA, Indian Territory, }
Central   DISTRICT. }

I,   Mabel Belvin   , on oath state that I am   22   years of age and a citizen by intermarriage   , of the   Choctaw   Nation; that I am the lawful wife of   Watson Belvin   , who is a citizen, by blood   of the   Choctaw   Nation; that a male   child was born to me on   27th   day of   July,1903   , 1........; that said child has been named   Henry Harrison J. Belvin   , and was living March 4, 1905.

Mabel Belvin

Witnesses To Mark:
{

Subscribed and sworn to before me this  6th   day of   April, 1905   , 190....

JR Armstrong
Notary Public.

**AFFIDAVIT OF ATTENDING PHYSICIAN OR MID-WIFE.**

UNITED STATES OF AMERICA, Indian Territory, }
Central   DISTRICT. }

I,   Irene Dudley   , a   midwife   , on oath state that I attended on Mrs.   Mabel Belvin   , wife of   Watson Belvin   on the   27th   day of   July, 1903   , 1......; that there was born to her on said date a   male   child; that said child was living March 4, 1905, and is said to have been named   Henry Harrison J. Belvin

her
Irene x Dudley
mark

# Applications for Enrollment of Choctaw Newborn
## Act of 1905  Volume XI

Witnesses To Mark:
{ OA Simmons
  Jos R Armstrong

Subscribed and sworn to before me this 6th day of   April, 1905 , 190....

JR Armstrong
Notary Public.

---

Choc New Born 751
   David A. Brackett  b. 11-15-03

Choctaw 3842.

Muskogee, Indian Territory, April 11, 1905.

Henry A. Brackett,
   Bennington, Indian Territory.

Dear Sir:

Receipt is hereby acknowledged of the affidavits of Laura A. Brackett and R. M. Parish to the birth of David A. Brackett, son of Henry A. and Laura A. Brackett, November 15, 1903, and the same have been filed with our records as an application for the enrollment of said child.

Respectfully,

Commissioner in Charge.

**BIRTH AFFIDAVIT.**

**DEPARTMENT OF THE INTERIOR.**
**COMMISSION TO THE FIVE CIVILIZED TRIBES.**

**IN RE APPLICATION FOR ENROLLMENT,** as a citizen of the   Choctaw   Nation, of David A Brackett  , born on the 15$^{th}$ day of Nov , 1903

Name of Father: Henry A Brackett      a citizen of the   Choctaw   Nation.
Name of Mother: Laura A Brackett      a citizen of the   Choctaw   Nation.

Postoffice   Bennington I.T.

# Applications for Enrollment of Choctaw Newborn
# Act of 1905   Volume XI

**AFFIDAVIT OF MOTHER.**

UNITED STATES OF AMERICA, Indian Territory, }
Cent                DISTRICT.

I,   Laura A Brackett   , on oath state that I am   29   years of age and a citizen by   blood   , of the   Choctaw   Nation; that I am the lawful wife of Henry A Brackett   , who is a citizen, by Intermarriage   of the   Choctaw Nation; that a   male   child was born to me on   15$^{th}$   day of   November   , 1903; that said child has been named   David A Brackett   , and was living March 4, 1905.

Laura A Brackett

Witnesses To Mark:
{

Subscribed and sworn to before me this   6$^{th}$   day of   April   , 1905

BW Williams
Notary Public.

**AFFIDAVIT OF ATTENDING PHYSICIAN OR MID-WIFE.**

UNITED STATES OF AMERICA, Indian Territory, }
Cent                DISTRICT.

I,   R.M. Parish   , a   Physician   , on oath state that I attended on Mrs.   Laura A Brackett   , wife of   Henry A Brackett   on the   15$^{th}$   day of Nov   , 1903; that there was born to her on said date a   male   child; that said child was living March 4, 1905, and is said to have been named David A Brackett

R M Parish

Witnesses To Mark:
{

Subscribed and sworn to before me this   6$^{th}$   day of   April   , 1905

BW Williams
Notary Public.

## Applications for Enrollment of Choctaw Newborn
## Act of 1905   Volume XI

Choc New Born 752
    Mary Catherine Culberson   b. 11-15-04

---

                                            Choctaw 2324.

                    Muskogee, Indian Territory, April 11, 1905.

James Culberson,
    Durant, Indian Territory.

Dear Sir:

    Receipt is hereby acknowledged of the affidavits of Martha V. Culberson and Elizabeth C. Harris to the birth of Mary Catherine Culberson, daughter of James and Martha V. Culberson, November 15, 1904, and the same have been filed with our records as an application for the enrollment of said child.

                    Respectfully,

                                  Commissioner in Charge.

---

**BIRTH AFFIDAVIT.**
                    **DEPARTMENT OF THE INTERIOR.**
              **COMMISSION TO THE FIVE CIVILIZED TRIBES.**

    **IN RE APPLICATION FOR ENROLLMENT,** as a citizen of the   Choctaw   Nation, of Mary Catherine   , born on the 15   day of November   , 1904

Name of Father: James Culberson        a citizen of the   Choctaw   Nation.
Name of Mother: Martha V. Culberson      a citizen of the   Choctaw   Nation.

                        Postoffice   Durant I.T.

---

                        **AFFIDAVIT OF MOTHER.**

**UNITED STATES OF AMERICA, Indian Territory,** }
    Central           **DISTRICT.**

    I,   Martha V. Culberson   , on oath state that I am   31   years of age and a citizen by   Marriage   , of the   Choctaw   Nation; that I am the lawful wife of James Culberson   , who is a citizen, by Blood   of the   Choctaw   Nation; that a   Female   child was born to me on   15"   day of November   , 1904; that said child has been named   Mary Catherine   , and was living March 4, 1905.

# Applications for Enrollment of Choctaw Newborn
## Act of 1905   Volume XI

              Martha V Culberson

Witnesses To Mark:
{

  Subscribed and sworn to before me this   6<sup>th</sup>   day of   April   , 1905
  My commission
  expires Nov 27" 1908    J H Downing
              Notary Public.

---

**AFFIDAVIT OF ATTENDING PHYSICIAN OR MID-WIFE.**

UNITED STATES OF AMERICA, Indian Territory, }
................................................. DISTRICT. }

  I,   Elizabeth C Harris   , a   nurse   , on oath state that I attended on Mrs.   Martha V Culberson   , wife of   James Culberson   on the   15"   day of   November   , 1904; that there was born to her on said date a   Female   child; that said child was living March 4, 1905, and is said to have been named   Mary Catherine

             Elizabeth C Harris

Witnesses To Mark:
{ R.P. Harris
  J.B. Wier

  Subscribed and sworn to before me this   1<sup>st</sup>   day of   April   , 1905

             H B Wier
             Notary Public.
     *My commission expires May 27, 19(illegible)*

---

Choc New Born 753
  Benjamin F. Henderson   b. 12-16-04

# Applications for Enrollment of Choctaw Newborn
## Act of 1905   Volume XI

7-NB-753

Muskogee, Indian Territory, March 14, 1906.

E. E. Henderson,
    Bailey, Indian Territory.

Dear Madam:

    Receipt is hereby acknowledged of your letter of March 5, 1906, asking the date of the approval of the enrollment of your child Benjamin F. Henderson.

    In reply to your letter you are advised that the enrollment of this child as a new born citizen of the Choctaw Nation was approved by the Secretary of the Interior July 22, 1905.

                  Respectfully,

                              Acting Commissioner.

---

Choctaw 4422.

Muskogee, Indian Territory, April 11, 1905.

J. H. Henderson,
    Bailey, Indian Territory.

Dear Sir:

    Receipt is hereby acknowledged of the affidavits of Edna E. Henderson and P. J. Hampton to the birth of Benjaman[sic] F. Henderson, son of J. H. and Edna E. Henderson, December 16, 1904, and the same have been filed with our records as an application for the enrollment of said child.

                  Respectfully,

                              Commissioner in Charge.

## Applications for Enrollment of Choctaw Newborn
## Act of 1905 Volume XI

BIRTH AFFIDAVIT.

### DEPARTMENT OF THE INTERIOR.
### COMMISSION TO THE FIVE CIVILIZED TRIBES.

IN RE APPLICATION FOR ENROLLMENT, as a citizen of the Choctaw Nation, of Benjaman Franklin Henderson , born on the 16 day of Dec , 1904

Name of Father: J H Henderson a citizen of the U S Nation.
Name of Mother: Edner[sic] E Henderson a citizen of the Choctaw Nation.

Postoffice  Bailey Ind Ter

**AFFIDAVIT OF MOTHER.**

UNITED STATES OF AMERICA, Indian Territory,
Southern DISTRICT.

I, Edner E Henderson , on oath state that I am 34 years of age and a citizen by Blood , of the Choctaw Nation; that I am the lawful wife of J H Henderson , who is a citizen, by —— of the ——— Nation; that a Male child was born to me on 16 day of Dec , 1904; that said child has been named Benjamin F Henderson , and was living March 4, 1905.

Edna E Henderson

Witnesses To Mark:

Subscribed and sworn to before me this 5 day of April , 1905

C W Harper
Notary Public.

**AFFIDAVIT OF ATTENDING PHYSICIAN OR MID-WIFE.**

UNITED STATES OF AMERICA, Indian Territory,
Southern DISTRICT.

I, PJ Hampton M D , a Physician , on oath state that I attended on Mrs. Edna E Henderson , wife of J H Henderson on the 16 day of December , 1904; that there was born to her on said date a male child; that said child was living March 4, 1905, and is said to have been named Benjamin F Henderson

P J Hampton MD

## Applications for Enrollment of Choctaw Newborn
## Act of 1905   Volume XI

Witnesses To Mark:

{

Subscribed and sworn to before me this 5 day of April, 1905

C W Harper
Notary Public.

---

Choc New Born 754
    Montie J. Rockman b. 10-15-03

Choctaw 2747.

Muskogee, Indian Territory, April 11, 1905.

Lizzie Rockman,
    Garland, Indian Territory.

Dear Madam:

    Receipt is hereby acknowledged of your letter of April 5, enclosing the affidavits of Lizzie Rockman and J. M. Cook to the birth of Montie J. Rockman, son of Joseph E. and Lizzie Rockman, October 15, 1903, and the same have been filed with our records as an application for the enrollment of said child.

    Respectfully,

Commissioner in Charge.

**COPY**

7 NB 754

Muskogee, Indian Territory, April 21, 1905.

J. E. Rockman,
    Garland, Indian Territory.

Dear Sir:

    Receipt is hereby acknowledged of your letter of April 14, 1905, asking if birth affidavit for the enrollment of Montie J. Rockman has been received.

## Applications for Enrollment of Choctaw Newborn
### Act of 1905   Volume XI

In reply to your letter you are informed that the affidavits of Lizzie Rockman and J. M. Cook to the birth of your child Montie J. Rockman, October 15, 1903, have been filed with our records as an application for the enrollment of said child.

Respectfully,

SIGNED  *Tams Bixby*
Chairman.

---

### AFFIDAVIT OF ATTENDING PHYSICIAN OR MIDWIFE

UNITED STATES OF AMERICA
INDIAN TERRITORY
Central     DISTRICT

I, J M Cook    a    physician on oath state that I attended on Mrs. Lizzie Rockman    wife of  J E Rockman on the  15  day of  October  , 190 3 , that there was born to her on said date a  male child, that said child is now living, and is said to have been named    Montie J Rockman

J.M. Cook MD

Subscribed and sworn to before me this, the ................................. day of Jan 24   190 5

WITNESSETH:                              CC Jones        Notary Public.

Must be two witnesses { WG Garland
who are citizens      { Joseph Garland

We hereby certify that we are well acquainted with    J M Cook MD   a   Physician    and know   him    to be reputable and of good standing in the community.

W G Garland

Joseph Garland

## Applications for Enrollment of Choctaw Newborn
## Act of 1905   Volume XI

**NEW-BORN AFFIDAVIT.**

Number ..........

...Choctaw Enrolling Commission...

IN THE MATTER OF THE APPLICATION FOR ENROLLMENT, as a citizen of the Choctaw Nation, of Montie J Rockman

born on the 15 day of __October__ 190 3

| | | |
|---|---|---|
| Name of father  J E Rockman | a citizen of | white |
| Nation final enrollment No. .......... | | |
| Name of mother  Lizzie Rockman | a citizen of | Choctaw |
| Nation final enrollment No. 8046 | | |

Postoffice   Garland I.T.

**AFFIDAVIT OF MOTHER.**

UNITED STATES OF AMERICA
INDIAN TERRITORY
  Central   DISTRICT

I   Lizzie Rockman   , on oath state that I am 29 years of age and a citizen by blood of the Choctaw Nation, and as such have been placed upon the final roll of the Choctaw Nation, by the Honorable Secretary of the Interior my final enrollment number being 8046 ; that I am the lawful wife of  J E Rockman  , who is a citizen of the Choctaw Nation, and as such has been placed upon the final roll of said Nation by the Honorable Secretary of the Interior, his final enrollment number being .......... and that a Male child was born to me on the 15 day of October 190 3; that said child has been named Montie J Rockman , and is now living.

Lizzie Rockman

Witnesseth.
  Must be two ⎫   *(Name Illegible)*
  Witnesses who ⎬
  are Citizens. ⎭   Elliot Cooper

Subscribed and sworn to before me this 2 day of Jan 190 5

James Bower
Notary Public.

My commission expires:
  Sept 23 - 1907

## Applications for Enrollment of Choctaw Newborn
## Act of 1905 Volume XI

**BIRTH AFFIDAVIT.**

### DEPARTMENT OF THE INTERIOR.
### COMMISSION TO THE FIVE CIVILIZED TRIBES.

IN RE APPLICATION FOR ENROLLMENT, as a citizen of the Choctaw Nation, of Montie J Rockman, born on the 15 day of October, 1903

Name of Father: Joseph E Rockman    a citizen of the ~~Choctaw~~ *white* Nation.
Name of Mother: Lizzie Rockman    a citizen of the Choctaw Nation.

Postoffice   Garland I.T.

**AFFIDAVIT OF MOTHER.**

UNITED STATES OF AMERICA, Indian Territory, }
Central    DISTRICT.

I, Lizzie Rockman, on oath state that I am Thirty years of age and a citizen by Blood, of the Choctaw Nation; that I am the lawful wife of Joseph E Rockman, who is a citizen, by Intermarriage of the Choctaw Nation; that a male child was born to me on 15 day of October, 1903; that said child has been named Montie J Rockman, and was living March 4, 1905.

                 Lizzie Rockman

Witnesses To Mark:
{

Subscribed and sworn to before me this 31 day of march, 1905

                 C C Jones
                 Notary Public.

**AFFIDAVIT OF ATTENDING PHYSICIAN OR MID-WIFE.**

UNITED STATES OF AMERICA, Indian Territory, }
Central    DISTRICT.

I, J M Cook, a Physician, on oath state that I attended on Mrs. Lizzie Rockman, wife of Joseph E Rockman on the 15 day of October, 1903; that there was born to her on said date a male child; that said child was living March 4, 1905, and is said to have been named Montie J Rockman

                 J M Cook M.D.

Witnesses To Mark:
{

Applications for Enrollment of Choctaw Newborn
Act of 1905 Volume XI

Subscribed and sworn to before me this 31 day of March , 1905

C C Jones
Notary Public.

---

Choc New Born 755
Harry Edward Curtis b. 1-6-04

Choctaw 2283.

Muskogee, Indian Territory, April 11, 1905.

Marion C. Curtis,
Reichert, Indian Territory.

Dear Sir:

Receipt is hereby acknowledged of affidavits of Luvicy Curtis and Nancy H. Curtis to the birth of Harry Edward Curtis, January 6, 1904, and the same have been filed with our records as an application for the enrollment of said child.

Respectfully,

Commissioner in Charge.

## NEW BORN AFFIDAVIT

No

### CHOCTAW ENROLLING COMMISSION

IN THE MATTER OF THE APPLICATION FOR ENROLLMENT as a citizen of the Choctaw Nation, of Harry Edward Curtis born on the 6 day of January 190 4

Name of father M. C. Curtis a citizen of non Nation,
final enrollment No. ———
Name of mother Luvicey Curtis a citizen of Choctaw Nation,
final enrollment No. 6617

## Applications for Enrollment of Choctaw Newborn
## Act of 1905   Volume XI

Reichert I.T.                   Postoffice.

**AFFIDAVIT OF MOTHER**

UNITED STATES OF AMERICA  
    INDIAN TERRITORY  
DISTRICT    Central

    I    Luvicey[sic] Curtis           , on oath state that I am   30    years of age and a citizen by    blood    of the    Choctaw    Nation, and as such have been placed upon the final roll of the   Choctaw    Nation, by the Honorable Secretary of the Interior my final enrollment number being   6617   ; that I am the lawful wife of    M.C. Curtis    , who is a citizen of the    non         Nation, and as such has been placed upon the final roll of said Nation by the Honorable Secretary of the Interior, his final enrollment number being ———   and that a    male    child was born to me on the    6 day of   January     190 4; that said child has been named    Harry Edward Curtis   , and is now living.

WITNESSETH:                                  Luvicy Curtis  
  Must be two witnesses { David Ward  
    who are citizens      John Folsom

    Subscribed and sworn to before me this, the   16   day of   February   , 190 5

                                    James Bower  
                                       Notary Public.

My Commission Expires:  
Sept 23-1907

## *Affidavit of Attending Physician or Midwife*

UNITED STATES OF AMERICA,  
    INDIAN TERRITORY,  
  Central     DISTRICT

    I,    Nancy Curtis      a      midwife on oath state that I attended on Mrs.  Luvicy Curtis    wife of   M.C. Curtis on the    6   day of   January   , 190 4, that there was born to her on said date a    male    child, that said child is now living, and is said to have been named    Harry Edward Curtis

                                Nancy H Curtis

    Subscribed and sworn to before me this the    17   day of   Feb     1905

                                James Bower  
                                     Notary Public.

# Applications for Enrollment of Choctaw Newborn
## Act of 1905   Volume XI

WITNESSETH:
Must be two witnesses who are citizens and know the child. { David Ward
John Folsom

We hereby certify that we are well acquainted with Nancy Curtis a midwife and know her to be reputable and of good standing in the community.

Must be two citizen witnesses. { David Ward
John Folsom

BIRTH AFFIDAVIT.

### DEPARTMENT OF THE INTERIOR.
### COMMISSION TO THE FIVE CIVILIZED TRIBES.

IN RE APPLICATION FOR ENROLLMENT, as a citizen of the Choctaw Nation, of Harry Edward Curtis, born on the 6th day of January, 1904

Name of Father: Marion C Curtis — a citizen of the United States Nation.
Name of Mother: Luvicy Curtis — a citizen of the Choctaw Nation.

Postoffice   Richard[sic], Ind Ter
*Reichert*

### AFFIDAVIT OF MOTHER.

UNITED STATES OF AMERICA, Indian Territory,
Central DISTRICT.

I, Luvicy Curtis, on oath state that I am 31 years of age and a citizen by blood, of the Choctaw Nation; that I am the lawful wife of Marion C Curtis, who is a citizen, ~~by~~ _____ of the United States ~~Nation~~; that a male child was born to me on 6th day of January, 1904; that said child has been named Harry Edward Curtis, and was living March 4, 1905.

Luvicy Curtis

Witnesses To Mark:
{

Subscribed and sworn to before me this 30th day of March, 1905

Wirt Franklin
Notary Public.

## Applications for Enrollment of Choctaw Newborn
## Act of 1905   Volume XI

AFFIDAVIT OF ATTENDING PHYSICIAN OR MID-WIFE.

UNITED STATES OF AMERICA, Indian Territory,
Central            DISTRICT.

I, Nancy H Curtis, a midwife, on oath state that I attended on Mrs. Luvicy Curtis, wife of Marion C Curtis on the 6 day of Jan, 1904; that there was born to her on said date a male child; that said child was living March 4, 1905, and is said to have been named Harry Edward Curtis

Nancy H Curtis

Witnesses To Mark:
{

Subscribed and sworn to before me this 7 day of April, 1905

J.J. Riggs
Notary Public.

---

Choc New Born 756
  Claude Gibson   b. 8-5-04

Choctaw 5565.

Muskogee, Indian Territory, April 11, 1905.

W. T. Gibson,
  Foster, Indian Territory.

Dear Sir:

Receipt is hereby acknowledged of the affidavits of Laura Gibson and John B. Morgan to the birth of Claude Gibson, August 5, 1904, and the same have been filed with our records as an application for the enrollment of said child.

Respectfully,

Commissioner in Charge.

Applications for Enrollment of Choctaw Newborn
Act of 1905   Volume XI

# NEW BORN AFFIDAVIT

No ........

## CHOCTAW ENROLLING COMMISSION

IN THE MATTER OF THE APPLICATION FOR ENROLLMENT as a citizen of the Choctaw Nation, of   Claude Gibson   born on the   5   day of   August   190 4

Name of father   W.T. Gibson   a citizen of   Choctaw   Nation, final enrollment No.   14078
Name of mother   Laura Gibson   a citizen of   Choctaw   Nation, final enrollment No...................

Foster IT   Postoffice.

### AFFIDAVIT OF MOTHER

UNITED STATES OF AMERICA  
   INDIAN TERRITORY  
DISTRICT   Southern

I   Laura Gibson   , on oath state that I am   26   years of age and a citizen by   Entermarriage[sic]   of the   Choctaw   Nation, and as such have been placed upon the final roll of the   Choctaw   Nation, by the Honorable Secretary of the Interior my final enrollment number being ............... ; that I am the lawful wife of   W.T. Gibson   , who is a citizen of the   Choctaw   Nation, and as such has been placed upon the final roll of said Nation by the Honorable Secretary of the Interior, his final enrollment number being   14078   and that a   Male   child was born to me on the   5   day of   August   190 4; that said child has been named   Claude Gibson   , and is now living.

WITNESSETH:                                              Laura Gibson
   Must be two witnesses ⎰ Mitchell Gibson
   who are citizens      ⎱ Werley Loomer

Subscribed and sworn to before me this, the   15   day of   March   , 190 5

WW Howerton
Notary Public.

My Commission Expires:   Feb 15 1906

## Applications for Enrollment of Choctaw Newborn
## Act of 1905   Volume XI

### *Affidavit of Attending Physician or Midwife*

UNITED STATES OF AMERICA,  
   INDIAN TERRITORY,  
Southern     DISTRICT

I, Jno B Morgan a Physician on oath state that I attended on Mrs. Laura Gibson wife of W.T. Gibson on the 5 day of August, 1904, that there was born to her on said date a Male child, that said child is now living, and is said to have been named Claude Gibson

                          Jno B Morgan     M. D.

Subscribed and sworn to before me this the 16 day of March 1905

                          WW Howerton
                                Notary Public.

WITNESSETH:  
Must be two witnesses who are citizens and know the child. { Mitchell Gibson  
Werley Loomer

We hereby certify that we are well acquainted with Jno B Morgan a Physician and know him to be reputable and of good standing in the community.

                  Must be two citizen witnesses. { Mitchell Gibson  
                                       Werley Loomer

---

Choc New Born 757  
    Elizabeth Williams  b. 12-9-03

## Applications for Enrollment of Choctaw Newborn
## Act of 1905  Volume XI

Choctaw 4709.

Muskogee, Indian Territory, April 11, 1905.

Robert Williams,
McAlester, Indian Territory.

Dear Sir:

Receipt is hereby acknowledged of the affidavits of Julia A. Williams and W. E. Abbott to the birth of Elizabeth Williams, December 9, 1903, and the same have been filed with our records as an application for the enrollment of said child.

Respectfully,

Commissioner in Charge.

**BIRTH AFFIDAVIT.**

**DEPARTMENT OF THE INTERIOR.**
**COMMISSION TO THE FIVE CIVILIZED TRIBES.**

IN RE APPLICATION FOR ENROLLMENT, as a citizen of the    Choctaw    Nation, of Elizabeth Williams    , born on the $9^{th}$ day of December    , 1903

Name of Father: Robert Williams         a citizen of the United States Nation.
Name of Mother: Julia Williams          a citizen of the   Choctaw    Nation.

Postoffice    M$^c$Alester I.T.

**AFFIDAVIT OF MOTHER.**

UNITED STATES OF AMERICA, Indian Territory,
Central                DISTRICT.

I,  Julia A Williams  , on oath state that I am  19  years of age and a citizen by  Blood  , of the  Choctaw  Nation; that I am the lawful wife of  Robert Williams  , who is a citizen, by ............... of the  United States  Nation; that a  Female  child was born to me on $9^{th}$ day of  December  , 1903; that said child has been named  Elizabeth Williams  , and was living March 4, 1905.

Julia A Williams

Witnesses To Mark:

## Applications for Enrollment of Choctaw Newborn
## Act of 1905  Volume XI

Subscribed and sworn to before me this 8 day of   April   , 1905

*(Name Illegible)*
Notary Public.

---

**AFFIDAVIT OF ATTENDING PHYSICIAN OR MID-WIFE.**

UNITED STATES OF AMERICA, Indian Territory, ⎱
  Central    DISTRICT. ⎰

I,   W.E. Abbott   , a   Physician   , on oath state that I attended on Mrs.   Julia A. Williams   , wife of   Robert Williams   on the 9$^{th}$ day of December   , 1903; that there was born to her on said date a   Female   child; that said child was living March 4, 1905, and is said to have been named   Elizabeth Williams

W E Abbott MD

Witnesses To Mark:
{

Subscribed and sworn to before me this 8 day of   April   , 1905

*(Name Illegible)*
Notary Public.

---

Choc New Born 758
  Joseph Carpenter  b. 10-20-04

**BIRTH AFFIDAVIT.**

DEPARTMENT OF THE INTERIOR.
## COMMISSION TO THE FIVE CIVILIZED TRIBES.

IN RE APPLICATION FOR ENROLLMENT, as a citizen of the   Choctaw   Nation, of Joseph Carpenter   , born on the  20 day of Oct.  , 1904

Name of Father: Soloman Carpenter        a citizen of the  Choctaw  Nation.
Name of Mother: Kitsy Carpenter           a citizen of the  Choctaw  Nation.

Postoffice   Guertie I.T.

# Applications for Enrollment of Choctaw Newborn
## Act of 1905   Volume XI

### AFFIDAVIT OF MOTHER.

UNITED STATES OF AMERICA, Indian Territory, }
Central            DISTRICT.

I, Kitsy Carpenter, on oath state that I am 39 years of age and a citizen by Blood, of the Choctaw Nation; that I am the lawful wife of Soloman Carpenter, who is a citizen, by Blood of the Choctaw Nation; that a Male child was born to me on 20$^{th}$ day of October, 1904; that said child has been named Joseph Carpenter, and was living March 4, 1905.

          her
        Kitsy x Carpenter
Witnesses To Mark:   mark
{ Nannie Pusley
{ *(Name Illegible)*

Subscribed and sworn to before me this 6 day of April, 1905

        J.I. Givens
        Notary Public.

---

### AFFIDAVIT OF ATTENDING PHYSICIAN OR MID-WIFE.

UNITED STATES OF AMERICA, Indian Territory, }
Central            DISTRICT.

I, Nancy Walton, a Midwife, on oath state that I attended on Mrs. Kitsy Carpenter, wife of Soloman Carpenter on the 20$^{th}$ day of Oct, 1904; that there was born to her on said date a male child; that said child was living March 4, 1905, and is said to have been named Joseph Carpenter

         her
      Nancy x Walton (midwife)
Witnesses To Mark:   mark
{ Nannie Pusley
{ *(Name Illegible)*

Subscribed and sworn to before me this 6 day of April, 1905

        J.I. Givens
        Notary Public.

## Applications for Enrollment of Choctaw Newborn
## Act of 1905   Volume XI

Choctaw 3289.

Muskogee, Indian Territory, April 11, 1905.

Solomon[sic] Carpenter,
    Guertie, Indian Territory.

Dear Sir:

    Receipt is hereby acknowledged of the affidavits of Kitsy Carpenter and Nancy Walton to the birth of Joseph Carpenter, October 20th, 1904, and the same have been filed with our records as an application for the enrollment of said child.

Respectfully,

Commissioner in Charge.

**NEW-BORN AFFIDAVIT.**

Number..................

...Choctaw Enrolling Commission...

    IN THE MATTER OF THE APPLICATION FOR ENROLLMENT, as a citizen of the Choctaw Nation, of Joseph Carpenter

born on the 20 day of __October__ 190 4

| | | |
|---|---|---|
| Name of father   Soloman Carpenter | a citizen of | Choctaw |
| Nation final enrollment No. 9480 | | |
| Name of mother   Kitsy Carpenter | a citizen of | Choctaw |
| Nation final enrollment No. 9481 | | |

Postoffice   Guertie I.T.

**AFFIDAVIT OF MOTHER.**

UNITED STATES OF AMERICA
INDIAN TERRITORY
    Central    DISTRICT

    I   Kitsy Carpenter                    , on oath state that I am 39   years of age and a citizen by   Blood   of the   Choctaw   Nation, and as such have been placed upon the final roll of the   Choctaw   Nation, by the Honorable Secretary of the Interior my final enrollment number being   9481  ; that I am the lawful wife of   Soloman Carpenter        , who is a citizen of the   Choctaw   Nation, and as such

## Applications for Enrollment of Choctaw Newborn
## Act of 1905   Volume XI

has been placed upon the final roll of said Nation by the Honorable Secretary of the Interior, his final enrollment number being 9480 and that a Male child was born to me on the 20 day of October 190 4; that said child has been named Joseph Carpenter, and is now living.

                          her
                          Kitsy x Carpenter
Witnesseth.                    mark

Must be two Witnesses who are Citizens. } Osborn Pusley
                John B Pusley

Subscribed and sworn to before me this 17 day of Jan 190 5

                    J.I. Givens
                              Notary Public.

My commission expires: Feb 1$^{st}$ 1908

---

## AFFIDAVIT OF ATTENDING PHYSICIAN OR MIDWIFE

UNITED STATES OF AMERICA
INDIAN TERRITORY
   Central      DISTRICT

    I, Nancy Walton a Mid Wife on oath state that I attended on Mrs. Kitsy Carpenter wife of Soloman Carpenter on the 20 day of October , 190 4 , that there was born to her on said date a male child, that said child is now living, and is said to have been named Joseph Carpenter

                        her
                    Nancy x Walton (midwife *M.D.*
                        mark

Subscribed and sworn to before me this, the 17 day of Jan 190 5

                    J.I. Givens     Notary Public.

WITNESSETH:
Must be two witnesses who are citizens { Osborn Pusley
                        John B Pusley

    We hereby certify that we are well acquainted with Nancy Walton a Mid Wife and know her to be reputable and of good standing in the community.

                                John B Pusley

                                Osbon Pusley

## Applications for Enrollment of Choctaw Newborn
## Act of 1905  Volume XI

Choc New Born 759
    Maud Mahalie Brown  b. 10-22-03

Choctaw 2601.

Muskogee, Indian Territory, April 11, 1905.

Charles Brown,
    Milton, Indian Territory.

Dear Sir:

    Receipt is hereby acknowledged of the affidavits of Annie E. Brown and M. E. Talbert to the birth of Maud Mahalie Brown, October 22nd, 1903, and the same have been filed with our records as an application for the enrollment of said child.

Respectfully,

Commissioner in Charge.

**NEW-BORN AFFIDAVIT.**

Number............

...Choctaw Enrolling Commission...

    IN THE MATTER OF THE APPLICATION FOR ENROLLMENT, as a citizen of the Choctaw  Nation, of  Maud Mahalie Brown

born on the  22  day of ___October___ 190 3

Name of father  Charles Brown       a citizen of  Choctaw
Nation final enrollment No. ——
Name of mother  Annie E Brown     a citizen of  Choctaw
Nation final enrollment No.  7536

                      Postoffice  Milton, I.T.

# Applications for Enrollment of Choctaw Newborn
## Act of 1905 Volume XI

### AFFIDAVIT OF MOTHER.

UNITED STATES OF AMERICA
INDIAN TERRITORY
Central DISTRICT

I Annie E. Brown , on oath state that I am 22 years of age and a citizen by blood of the ................ Nation, and as such have been placed upon the final roll of the Choctaw Nation, by the Honorable Secretary of the Interior my final enrollment number being 7536 ; that I am the lawful wife of Charles Brown , who is a citizen of the Choctaw Nation, and as such has been placed upon the final roll of said Nation by the Honorable Secretary of the Interior, his final enrollment number being —— and that a girl child was born to me on the 22 day of Oct 190 3; that said child has been named Maud Mahalie Brown , and is now living. her

Annie E x Brown
Witnesseth. mark

Must be two Witnesses who are Citizens. } J W Leflore
Ruth Blaylock

Subscribed and sworn to before me this 23 day of M$^c$h 190 5

Jas. L. Lewis
Notary Public.

My commission expires:
3/11/09

---

## AFFIDAVIT OF ATTENDING PHYSICIAN OR MIDWIFE

UNITED STATES OF AMERICA
INDIAN TERRITORY
Central DISTRICT

I, M.E. Talburt a Midwife on oath state that I attended on Mrs. Annie E Brown wife of Charles Brown on the 22 day of October , 190 3 , that there was born to her on said date a girl child, that said child is now living, and is said to have been named Maud Mahalie Brown

J.W. Leflore { Witnesses

M.E. Talburt (her mark) M.D.

Subscribed and sworn to before me this, the 23 day of March 190 5

WITNESSETH:
Must be two witnesses who are citizens { J.W. Leflore
Ruth Blaylock

Jas. L. Lewis Notary Public.

## Applications for Enrollment of Choctaw Newborn
## Act of 1905   Volume XI

We hereby certify that we are well acquainted with     M.E. Talburt a   Midwife   and know   her   to be reputable and of good standing in the community.

_____     J.W. Leflore

_____     Ruth Blaylock

_____

**BIRTH AFFIDAVIT.**

## DEPARTMENT OF THE INTERIOR,
### COMMISSION TO THE FIVE CIVILIZED TRIBES.

_____

IN RE Application for Enrollment, as a citizen of the   Choctaw   Nation, of   Maud Mahalie Brown   , born on the   22   day of   October   , 1903

*by marriage*

Name of Father: Charles Brown     a citizen of the   Choctaw   Nation.
Name of Mother: Annie E. Brown     a citizen of the   Choctaw   Nation.

Post-Office:   Milton, Ind. Ter.

_____

**AFFIDAVIT OF MOTHER.**

UNITED STATES OF AMERICA, ⎫
    INDIAN TERRITORY.   ⎬
  Central   District. ⎭

I,   Annie E. Brown   , on oath state that I am   22   years of age and a citizen by   blood   , of the   Choctaw   Nation; that I am the lawful wife of   Charles Brown   , who is a citizen, by   Marriage   of the   Choctaw   Nation; that a   girl   child was born to me on   22   day of   October   , 1903 , that said child has been named   Maud Mahalie Brown   , and is now living.

          her
Annie E. x Brown
          mark

**WITNESSES TO MARK:**
   { J.W. Leflore
   { V.V. Cruz

*Subscribed and sworn to before me this*   23   *day of*   March   , 1905.

James L. Lewis
*NOTARY PUBLIC.*

# Applications for Enrollment of Choctaw Newborn
## Act of 1905   Volume XI

### AFFIDAVIT OF ATTENDING PHYSICIAN OR MID-WIFE.

UNITED STATES OF AMERICA,  
    INDIAN TERRITORY.  
Central   District.

I,   M.E. Talburt  , a   midwife  , on oath state that I attended on Mrs. Annie Brown  , wife of   Charles Brown   on the   22   day of   October  , 1903 ; that there was born to her on said date a   girl   child; that said child is now living and is said to have been named   Maud Mahalie Brown

                         her  
                     M.E. x Talburt

**WITNESSES TO MARK:**           mark  
{ J.W. LeFlore  
  V.V. Cruz

*Subscribed and sworn to before me this*   23   *day of*   March  , *1905.*

                    Jas. L. Lewis  
My commission expires Mar. 11, 1906       **NOTARY PUBLIC.**

---

<u>Choc New Born 760</u>  
    Nealy Clarence Curtis  b. 5-29-03

                                    7-2334

Muskogee, Indian Territory, April 11, 1905.

Thomas A. Curtis,  
    Richard, Indian Territory.

Dear Sir:

    Receipt is hereby acknowledged of the affidavits of Ella Curtis and E. E. Shippey to the birth of Nealy Clarence Curtis, son of Thomas A. and Ella Curtis, May 29, 1903, and the same have been filed with our records as an application for the enrollment of said child.

                    Respectfully,

                             Commissioner in Charge.

## Applications for Enrollment of Choctaw Newborn
## Act of 1905   Volume XI

BIRTH AFFIDAVIT.

**DEPARTMENT OF THE INTERIOR.**
**COMMISSION TO THE FIVE CIVILIZED TRIBES.**

IN RE APPLICATION FOR ENROLLMENT, as a citizen of the   Choctaw   Nation, of Nealy Clarence Curtis   , born on the 29th   day of May   , 1903

Name of Father: Thomas A. Curtis         a citizen of the United States Nation.
Name of Mother: Ella Curtis              a citizen of the   Choctaw   Nation.

Postoffice   Richard, Ind. Ter.
(Reichert)

**AFFIDAVIT OF MOTHER.**

UNITED STATES OF AMERICA, Indian Territory,
Central                DISTRICT.

I,   Ella Curtis   , on oath state that I am   25   years of age and a citizen by blood , of the   Choctaw   Nation; that I am the lawful wife of   Thomas A Curtis   , who is a citizen, ~~by~~ ............... of the   United States   Nation; that a   male   child was born to me on   29th   day of   May   , 1903; that said child has been named   Nealy Clarence Curtis   , and was living March 4, 1905.

Ella Curtis

Witnesses To Mark:

Subscribed and sworn to before me this   30th   day of   March   , 1905

Wirt Franklin
Notary Public.

**AFFIDAVIT OF ATTENDING PHYSICIAN OR MID-WIFE.**

UNITED STATES OF AMERICA, Indian Territory,
Central                DISTRICT.

I,   Dr E E Shippey   , a   MD   , on oath state that I attended on Mrs.   Ella Curtis   , wife of   Thomas A Curtis   on the   29   day of   May   , 1903; that there was born to her on said date a   male   child; that said child was living March 4, 1905, and is said to have been named   Nealy Clarence Curtis

# Applications for Enrollment of Choctaw Newborn
## Act of 1905 Volume XI

Dr E.E. Shippey

Witnesses To Mark:
{

Subscribed and sworn to before me this   7   day of   Apr   , 1905

J.J. Riggs
Notary Public.

---

## *Affidavit of Attending Physician or Midwife*

UNITED STATES OF AMERICA, ⎫
   INDIAN TERRITORY, ⎬
  Central    DISTRICT ⎭

I,   E.E. Shippey   a   Practicing Physician on oath state that I attended on Mrs.   Ella Curtis   wife of   Thomas Curtis   on the   29   day of   May   , 190 3, that there was born to her on said date a   male   child, that said child is now living, and is said to have been named   Nealy Clarence Curtis

E.E. Shippey            M. D.

Subscribed and sworn to before me this the   17   day of   February   1905

James Bower
Notary Public.

WITNESSETH:

Must be two witnesses ⎰ John Folsom
who are citizens and  ⎱
know the child.         David Ward

We hereby certify that we are well acquainted with   E.E. Shippey   a   Practicing Physician   and know ............... to be reputable and of good standing in the community.

Must be two citizen ⎰ *(Name Illegible)*
witnesses.                  ⎱ Fannie Free

Applications for Enrollment of Choctaw Newborn
Act of 1905  Volume XI

# NEW BORN AFFIDAVIT

No ........

## CHOCTAW ENROLLING COMMISSION

IN THE MATTER OF THE APPLICATION FOR ENROLLMENT as a citizen of the Choctaw Nation, of  Nealy Clarence Curtis  born on the 29 day of May  190 3

Name of father  Thomas Curtis  a citizen of  non  Nation, final enrollment No. ——
Name of mother  Ella Curtis  a citizen of  Choctaw  Nation, final enrollment No. 6757

Reichert, I.T.  Postoffice.

### AFFIDAVIT OF MOTHER

UNITED STATES OF AMERICA
INDIAN TERRITORY
DISTRICT  Central

I  Ella Curtis  , on oath state that I am  25  years of age and a citizen by  blood  of the  Choctaw  Nation, and as such have been placed upon the final roll of the  Choctaw  Nation, by the Honorable Secretary of the Interior my final enrollment number being  6757  ; that I am the lawful wife of  Thomas Curtis  , who is a citizen of the  non  Nation, and as such has been placed upon the final roll of said Nation by the Honorable Secretary of the Interior, his final enrollment number being  ——  and that a  male  child was born to me on the  29  day of  May  190 3; that said child has been named  Nealy Clarence Curtis  , and is now living.

WITNESSETH:  Ella Curtis
Must be two witnesses ⎧ John Folsom
who are citizens      ⎩ David Ward

Subscribed and sworn to before me this, the  16  day of  February  , 190 5

James Bower
Notary Public.

My Commission Expires:
Sept 23 - 1907

# Applications for Enrollment of Choctaw Newborn
## Act of 1905   Volume XI

<u>Choc New Born 761</u>
Jimmie Nero  b. 2-20-03

Granted 12-24-06

DEPARTMENT OF THE INTERIOR,
COMMISSIONER TO THE FIVE CIVILIZED TRIBES.
-----

In the matter of the application for the enrollment as a citizen by blood of the Choctaw Nation . . . . . . . . .

JIMMY NERO..............7-NB-761.

**NEW-BORN AFFIDAVIT.**

Number............

...Choctaw Enrolling Commission...

IN THE MATTER OF THE APPLICATION FOR ENROLLMENT, as a citizen of the Choctaw       Nation, of        Jimmie Nero

born on the ........ day of    February      190 3

Name of father   Joseph Nero            a citizen of   Creek
Nation final enrollment No. ........................
Name of mother   Jane Nero             a citizen of   Choctaw
Nation final enrollment No.  13308

Postoffice     Eufaula I.T.

**AFFIDAVIT OF MOTHER.**

UNITED STATES OF AMERICA
INDIAN TERRITORY
    Central     DISTRICT

I      Jane Nero           , on oath state that I am 32     years of age and a citizen by  blood   of the   Choctaw        Nation, and as such have been placed upon the final roll of the     Choctaw   Nation, by the Honorable Secretary of the Interior my final enrollment number being     13308  ; that I am the lawful wife of    Joseph Nero     , who is a citizen of the    Creek      Nation, and as such has been placed upon the final roll of said Nation by the Honorable Secretary of the Interior, his final enrollment number being    — — -  and that a     Male     child was born to me on the

## Applications for Enrollment of Choctaw Newborn
## Act of 1905 Volume XI

_____ day of February 190 3; that said child has been named Jimmie Nero, and is now living.

Witnesseth.
 Must be two
 Witnesses who
 are Citizens.

Subscribed and sworn to before me this _____ day of _____ 190__.

_____
Notary Public.

My commission expires:

## AFFIDAVIT OF ATTENDING PHYSICIAN OR MIDWIFE

UNITED STATES OF AMERICA
INDIAN TERRITORY
 Central DISTRICT

I, Nancy Nero a Mid wife on oath state that I attended on Mrs. Jane Nero wife of Joseph Nero on the _____ day of February, 190 3, that there was born to her on said date a male child, that said child is now living, and is said to have been named Jimmie Nero

_____ *midwife*
~~M.D~~.

WITNESSETH:
 Must be two witnesses
 who are citizens and
 know the child.

Subscribed and sworn to before me this, the _____ day of _____ 190__.

_____ Notary Public.

We hereby certify that we are well acquainted with Nancy Nero a Mid wife and know her to be reputable and of good standing in the community.

## Applications for Enrollment of Choctaw Newborn
## Act of 1905 Volume XI

United States of America, #
                                      #
Indian Territory,         #
                                      #    ss.
Western District.       #
                                      #

    Tokee Riddle, being by me first duly sworn, on her oath deposes and says:I am acquainted with Jane Nero, and that the said Jane Nero is the wife of Joseph Nero; that on February 20th., 1903, a male child was born to the said Jane Nero, and that said child is said to have been named Jimmy Nero; that the said child is now living with his father, Joseph Nero, and that I am not acquainted with the present residence of the mother of said child.

Witnesses / WH Echelkamp                  her
to mark { (Name Illegible)            Tokee x Riddle
                                     mark

    Subscribed and sworn to before me this 21st. day of April, 1905.

                                    (Name Illegible)
                                       Notary Public.
My commission expires July 8-1906

---

United States of America, #
                                      #
Indian Territory,         #    ss.
                                      #
Western District.       #

    Steward Riddle, being by me first duly sworn, on his oath deposes and says:I am acquainted with Jane Nero, and I know her to be the wife of Joseph Nero; that on Feb. 20th.,1903, a male child was born to the said Jane Nero, and said child is said to have been named Jimmy Nero; that said child is now living with his father,Joseph Nero, and that the present whereabouts of the said Jane Nero are to me unknown.

Witnesses / (Name Illegible)                his
to mark { WH Echelkamp           Steward x Riddle
                                     mark

    Subscribed and sworn to before me this 21st. day of April, 1905.

                                    (Name Illegible)
                                       Notary Public.
My commission expires July 8-1906

Applications for Enrollment of Choctaw Newborn
Act of 1905 Volume XI

BIRTH AFFIDAVIT.

DEPARTMENT OF THE INTERIOR.
## COMMISSION TO THE FIVE CIVILIZED TRIBES.

IN RE APPLICATION FOR ENROLLMENT, as a citizen of the Choctaw Nation, of Jimmie Nero, born on the 20$^{th}$ day of Feb, 1903

Name of Father: Joseph Nero     a citizen of the Creek Nation.
Name of Mother: Jane Nero     a citizen of the Choctaw Nation.

Postoffice    Eufaula, Indian Ter.

*Father*
AFFIDAVIT OF ~~MOTHER~~.

UNITED STATES OF AMERICA, Indian Territory, ⎫
    Western            DISTRICT. ⎭

I, Joseph Nero, on oath state that I am forty-five years of age and a citizen by freedman, of the Creek Nation; that I am the lawful ~~wife~~ *husband* of Jane Nero, who is a citizen, by blood of the Choctaw Nation; that a male child was born to ~~me~~ *her* on 20$^{th}$ day of February, 1903; that said child has been named Jimmy Nero, and was living March 4, 1905, *that said child is living with me*

                        Joseph Nero
Witnesses To Mark:
⎰
⎱

Subscribed and sworn to before me this 21st day of April, 1905

              *(Name Illegible)*
My Commission expires July 8-1906     Notary Public.

AFFIDAVIT OF ATTENDING PHYSICIAN OR MID-WIFE.

UNITED STATES OF AMERICA, Indian Territory, ⎫
    Western            DISTRICT. ⎭

I, Nancy Nero, a midwife, on oath state that I attended on Mrs. Jane Nero, wife of Joseph Nero on the 20$^{th}$ day of February, 1903; that there was born to her on said date a male child; that said child was living March 4, 1905, and is said to have been named Jimmy Nero

                           her
                  Nancy Nero x
                           mark

# Applications for Enrollment of Choctaw Newborn
## Act of 1905   Volume XI

Witnesses To Mark:
{ W.H.Eckelkamp
{ *(Name Illegible)*

Subscribed and sworn to before me this 21$^{st}$ day of   April   , 1905

My Commission expires July 8-1906

*(Name Illegible)*
Notary Public.

---

DEPARTMENT OF THE INTERIOR,
COMMISSIONER TO THE FIVE CIVILIZED TRIBES.

So. McAlester, Indian Territory, November 6, 1906.

------------------------------------

In the matter of the application for the enrollment, as a New Born citizen of the Choctaw Nation, of Jimmy Nero, Choctaw Care Number 761.

Testimony taken at Eufaula, Indian Territory, October 18, 1906.

JOSEPH NERO, being duly sworn, by James T. PRIMROSE, Notary Public in and for the Western District of Indian Territory, testified as follows:

BY THE COMMISSIONER:

Q What is your name?  A Joseph Nero.
Q How old are you?  A I am about 49.
Q What is your post office address?  A Eufaula, I. T.
Q Are you a member of any Indian Tribe, if so state your connection with said Tribe.
A I am a Creek by blood.
Q Are you on the Creek roll of citizens by blood?
A Yes, I am on the by blood roll.
Q What is your purpose in appearing before this party to-day?
A To make application for the enrollment of Jimmy nero[sic].
Q Who is the mother of this child you wish to enroll?
A Jane Nero.
Q Is Jane Nero your lawful wife?  A Yes, sir.
Q Is she a member of any Indian Tribe?
A She is a member of the Choctaw Tribe, a Choctaw by blood.
Q Have you children on the approved roll by Jane Nero other than the one you make application for?  A Yes, sir
Q Upon what roll do their names appear?
A On the Choctaw roll by blood.
Q Mention the names of the children of yourself and Jane Nero?
A Henry, Delia, Hallie and Jimmy.

## Applications for Enrollment of Choctaw Newborn
## Act of 1905   Volume XI

Q  Do the names of Henry, Delia and Hallie appear upon the approved roll of citizens by blood of the Choctaw Nation?
A  Yes, sir.
Q  When was Jimmy Nero born?  A  February 20, 1903.
Q  Is the child living?  A  Yes, sir, here he is (indicating small child).
Q  Does the mother of this child now reside with you?
A  No, sir.
Q  Do you know her whereabouts?  A  No, sir.
Q  How old was the child Jimmy Nero when you last knew the whereabouts of the mother?  A  He was about 22 months old.
Q  Who acted in the capacity of midwife at the birth of your lawful son, Jimmy Nero?
A  My mother, Nancy Nero?[sic]

Witness Excused.

NANCY NERO, being duly sworn, by James T. Primrose, Notary Public in and for the Western District of Indian Territory, testified as follows:

BY THE COMMISSIONER:

Q  What is your name?  A  Nancy Nero.
Q  What is your age?  A  I do not know, I am very old.
Q  What is your post office?  A  Eufaula, I. T.
Q  Are you a member of any Indian Tribe, if so what tribe and how connected?  A  I am a Creek by blood.
Q  Are you the mother of Joseph Nero?  A  Yes, sir.
Q  Who was Joseph Nero's wife?  A  Jane Nero.
Q  Was she an Indian, if so to what Tribe did she belong?
A  She was an Indian, a Choctaw.
Q  Has she children?  A  Yes, sir, these are Jane's children: Henry, Delia, Hallie and Jimmie (indicating children present).
Q  How many of these children are on the Indian roll, and on what roll do their names appear?
A  They are all on the Choctaw roll except Jimmy.
Q  When was Jimmy born?  A  I do not know, he is more than two years old.
Q  Did you attend Jane Nero at the time she gave birth to Jimmy?
A  Yes, sir.
Q  Was any one else present save yourself?  A  No, sir, I was just alone.
Q  With whom does this child now reside?
A  He lives with me and Joseph Nero.
Q  Is Jane Nero at the present time making her home with your son Joseph Nero?
A  No, she left Joseph just after Jimmie was weaned.
Q  Do you know the present whereabouts of Jane Nero?
A  No, sir.
Q  Is Jimmy Nero living at the present time?
A  Yes, sir, he is here.

## Applications for Enrollment of Choctaw Newborn
## Act of 1905   Volume XI

Witness Excused.

-------------  --------------------  ---------------

JANE PARO, being duly sworn, by James T. Primrose, Notary Public in and for the Central District of Indian Territory, testified as follows:

BY THE COMMISSIONER:

Q State your name? A Jane Paro.
Q What is your age? A About 50 years old.
Q What is your post office address? A Eufaula, I. T.
Q Are you acquainted with Joseph Nero? A Yes, sir.
Q Is he a man of family? A Yes, sir, he has some little children.
Q Who is the mother of these children? A Jane Nero.
Q Is Jane Nero an Indian, if so to what Tribe does she belong?
A Yes, sir, she is a Choctaw by blood.
Q It appears that application has been made for the enrollment of Jimmy Nero; Do you know this child?
A Yes, sir, I know when he was born.
Q When was he born? A I can not tell exactly but I know.
Q What is his present age, judging from his size?
A I do not know, I know he is more than a year old.
Q Who is the mother of this child? A Jane Nero.
Q You have actual and personal knowledge that Jane Nero is the mother of this child?
A Yes, sir.
Q Did you ever see the child in its mother's arms?
A Yes, sir.
Q How near did you live to the mother of this child?
A I guess it is about six miles.
Q Did you frequently visit her? A Yes, sir
Q Is the child living at the present time? A He is living and is here to-day.
Q From the records of the Commission to the Five Civilized Tribes the names Henry, Delia and Hallie Nero appear as the children of Joseph Nero: Do you know these children? A Yes, sir.
Q Do you know the Jimmy Nero to be a full brother or to have the same father and mother as these children?
A Yes, sir, that's what she said.
Q State why you know Jane Nero to be the mother of Jimmy Nero?
A Well I know when the child was born and she has come to my house and brought Jimmy with het[sic] and the other children.
Q Have you any interest directly or indirectly in any allotment to which Jimmy Nero may be entitled by virtue of his enrollment as a citizen by blood of the Choctaw Nation?
A No, sir, I am no kin to him.

Witness Excused.

-------------------------------------------------

## Applications for Enrollment of Choctaw Newborn
## Act of 1905    Volume XI

T. L. Boone, being duly sworn, testified as follows:

Oath administered by James T. Primrose, Notary Public in and for the Western District of Indian Territory.

BY THE COMMISSIONER:

Q  What is your name?  A  T. L. Boone.
Q  How old are you?  A  I do not know exactly my age, I am about 45 or 46.
Q  What is your post office address?  A  Eufaula, I. T?[sic]
Q  Are you acquainted with Joseph Nero?  A  Yes, sir.
Q  State the extent of your acquaintance with Joseph Nero?
A  I have been knowing Joseph ever since he was a young boy, I have lived in three or four miles of him.
Q  Is he a man of family?  A  Well, he has children and he did have a woman, but his woman left.
Q  What was the name of his woman that you mention?
A  Her name was Jane Nero.
Q  Was she generally known as Joseph Nero's lawful wife?
A  Yes, sir.
Q  Was she an Indian, if so to what Tribe did she belong?
A  She was said to be a Choctaw by blood.
Q  How many children did she have by Joseph Nero?
A  She had four to my knowing.
Q  What are their names?  A  Henry, Delia, Hallie and Jimmy the youngest.
Q  When was Jimmy born?  A  I do not know the exact time I would think he was about two years old going on three.
Q  How old was the child when you first saw him?
A  I saw him when he was a small bit of a baby; his mother was nursing him, I do not know exactly how old he was, I might have seen him as young as two months old.
Q  Have you actual and positive knowledge that Jane Nero is the mother of this child?
A  Yes, I have seen her nursing it.
Q  Do you know Jane Nero's present whereabouts?  A  No, sir.
Q  You state that she deserted Joseph Nero:  How old was Jimmy Nero at the time of her desertion?
A  He could not have been but a little over a year old, when she left, I believe it has been a little over a year since she left.
Q  It is a matter of common knowledge in the vicinity of when you live that Jane Nero is the mother of Jimmy Nero?  A  Yes, sir.
Q  Is this child now living?  A  Yes, sir.
Q  Have you any interest any any[sic] lands to which Jimmy Nero may be entitled by virtue of his enrollment as a member by blood of the Choctaw Tribe of Indians?
A  None at all.

Witness Excused.

---

# Applications for Enrollment of Choctaw Newborn
## Act of 1905   Volume XI

W. P. Covington, being duly sworn, states that the above and foregoing is a full and correct transcript of his stenographic notes taken in said case on said date mentioned.

W. P. Covington

Subscribed and sworn to before me this   8"  day of   Nov   1906.

Lacey P. Bobo
Notary Public.

7 nB 761

UNITED STATES OF AMERICA,   )
                            )
WESTERN DISTRICT,           )  SS:
                            )
INDIAN TERRITORY.           )

Personally appeared before me, the undersigned Notary Public in and for the Western District of the Indian Territory, Joseph Nero, who being first duly sworn, upon oath makes answer to the following interrogatories:

Q What is your name, age and post office address:

[sic]   **Joseph Nero, Eufaula, Indian Territory. Age, 49 or 50 yrs.**

Q Are you the father of Jimmy Nero, an applicant for enrollment as a citizen by blood of the Choctaw Nation?

A   **Yes**

Q Who is the mother of Jimmy Nero?

A   **Jane Nero**

Q Is she a citizen by blood of the Choctaw Nation?

A   **Yes**

Q Are you a citizen by blood of the Creek Nation?

A   **Yes**

Q In case it should be determined that your son, Jimmy Nero, is entitled to enrollment as a citizen by blood of either the Choctaw or Creek Nation, in which nation do you desire to have him take his allotment of lands?

A   **In the Choctaw Nation.**

Joseph Nero

## Applications for Enrollment of Choctaw Newborn
## Act of 1905   Volume XI

Subscribed and sworn to before me this **10th** day of **December**, 1906.

*(Name Illegible)*
Notary Public.

My Commission Expires: **Aug. 20, 1909**
Post Office Address: **Eufaula, I. T.**

---

7-NB-761.
O.L.J.

### DEPARTMENT OF THE INTERIOR,
### COMMISSIONER TO THE FIVE CIVILIZED TRIBES.

-----

In the matter of the application for the enrollment of Jimmy Nero as a citizen by blood of the Choctaw Nation.

### DECISION.

It appears from the record herein that on April 13, 1905, application was made to the Commission to the Five Civilized Tribes for the enrollment of Jimmy Nero as a citizen by blood of the Choctaw Nation under the provisions of the Act of Congress approved March 3, 1905 (33 Stats., 1070).

It further appears from the record herein that said applicant was born February 20, 1903, and is the child of Jane Nero, whose name appears as number 13308 upon the final roll of citizens by blood of the Choctaw Nation approved by the Secretary of the Interior March 19, 1903, and Joseph Nero, whose name appears as number 7020 upon the final roll of citizens by blood of the Creek Nation approved by the Secretary of the Interior March 28, 1902; and that said applicant was living on March 4, 1905.

Under the provisions of Section 21 of the Act of Congress approved June 28, 1898 (30 Stats., 495), Joseph Nero, the father of said applicant, appeared before the Commissioner to the Five Civilized Tribes at Eufaula, Indian Territory, on November 6, 1906, and elected that said applicant take his allotment of lands as a citizen of the Choctaw Nation.

I am, therefore, of the opinion that Jimmy Nero should be enrolled as a citizen by blood of the Choctaw Nation under the provisions of the Act of Congress approved March 3, 1905 (33 Stats., 1070), and it is so ordered.

Tams Bixby   Commissioner.

Muskogee, Indian Territory.
DEC 24 1906

# Applications for Enrollment of Choctaw Newborn
## Act of 1905   Volume XI

7-NB-761

**COPY**

Muskogee, Indian Territory, December 24, 1906.

Joseph Nero,
    Eufaula, Indian Territory.

Dear Sir :--

    Inclosed herewith you will find a copy of the decision of the Commissioner to the Five Civilized Tribes, rendered December 24, 1906, granting the application for the enrollment of Jimmy Nero as a citizen by blood of the Choctaw Nation.

    The attorneys for the Choctaw and Chickasaw Nations have been furnished a copy of this decision and have been allowed fifteen days from the date of this notice with which to file protest against his enrollment. If at the expiration of that time no protest has been filed, the name of Jimmy Nero will be placed upon the final roll of citizens by blood of the Choctaw Nation to be submitted to the Secretary of the Interior for his approval.

Respectfully,

Signed   Wm. O. Beall
Acting Commissioner.

Registered.
Incl. 7-NB-761.

---

7-NB-761

**COPY**

Muskogee, Indian Territory, December 24, 1906.

Mansfield, McMurray & Cornish,
    Attorneys for Choctaw and Chickasaw Nations,
        South McAlester, Indian Territory.

Gentlemen :--

    Inclosed herewith you will find a copy of the decision of the Commissioner to the Five Civilized Tribes, rendered December 24, 1906, granting the application for the enrollment of Jimmy Nero as a citizen by blood of the Choctaw Nation.

    You are hereby advised that you will be allowed fifteen days from the date of this notice within which to file protest against his enrollment. If at the expiration of that time no protest has been filed, the name of Jimmy Nero will be placed upon the final roll of citizens by blood of the Choctaw Nation to be submitted to the Secretary of the Interior for his approval.

## Applications for Enrollment of Choctaw Newborn
## Act of 1905 Volume XI

Respectfully,

Signed Wm. O. Beall
Acting Commissioner.

Registered.
Incl. 7-NB-761.

---

No. 761.

APPLICATION FOR ENROLLMENT OF

Jimmie Nero

Born February 20, 1903,

as a citizen of the Choctaw

Nation under Act of Congress

approved March 3, 1905.

Father------------------Joseph Nero

Mother----------------Jane Nero

Postoffice-------Eufaula, I. T.
It appears from the records
that said child is living with
his father, Joseph Nero.

---

7- N B 761.

Muskogee, Indian Territory, April 17, 1905.

Joseph Nero,
    Eufaula, Indian Territory.

Dear Sir:

There is inclosed you herewith for execution application for the enrollment of your infant child, Jimmie Nero, born in February 1903.

# Applications for Enrollment of Choctaw Newborn
## Act of 1905   Volume XI

In the affidavits heretofore filed with the Commission, the date of the birth of said child was not given, neither were they signed by the mother or mid-wife, nor acknowledged before a Notary Public.

In having said affidavits executed care should be exercised to see that all names are written in full, as they appear in the body of the affidavit, and in the event that either of the persons signing the affidavit are unable to write, signatures by mark must be attested by two witnesses. Each affidavit must be executed before a Notary Public and the notarial seal and signature of the officer must be attached to each separate affidavit.

Respectfully,

Chairman.

LM 17-115.

---

Muskogee, Indian Territory, July 29, 1905.

Clerk in Charge,
Creek Enrollment Division.

Dear Sir:

Application has been made for the enrollment of Jimmy Nero, infant child of Joseph Nero, a freedman of the Creek Nation, and Jane Nero, a citizen by blood of the Choctaw Nation, born February 20, 1903.

You are requested to advise the Choctaw-Chickasaw Enrollment Division, whether any application has been made for his enrollment as a freedman of the Creek Nation. If application has been made, advise date when made and card number of same.

Respectfully,

Commissioner.

## Applications for Enrollment of Choctaw Newborn
## Act of 1905   Volume XI

7-4822

Muskogee, Indian Territory, May 1, 1905.

Joseph Nero,
    Eufaula, Indian Territory.

Dear Sir:

    Receipt is hereby acknowledged of your letter of April 21, 1905 enclosing the affidavits of Joseph Nero, Nancy Nero, Tokee Riddle and Steward Riddle to the birth of Jimmie Nero son of Joseph and Jane Nero, February 20, 1903, and the same have been filed with our records as an application for the enrollment of said child.

                    Respectfully,

                                Chairman.

---

REFER IN REPLY TO THE FOLLOWING:

**DEPARTMENT OF THE INTERIOR,**
**COMMISSIONER TO THE FIVE CIVILIZED TRIBES.**

Muskogee, Indian Territory, August 1, 1905.

Clerk in Charge,
    Choctaw-Chickasaw Enrollment Division.

Dear Sir:

    Receipt is acknowledged of your letter of July 29, 1905, in which you ask if application has been made for the enrollment of Jimmy Nero, infant child of Joseph Nero, a freedman of the Creek Nation and Jane Nero, a citizen by blood of the Chickasaw[sic] Nation; born February 20, 1903, as a freedman of the Creek Nation.

    In reply, you are advised that it does not appear from the records of this office that application has ever been made for the enrollment of said Jimmy Nero as a freedman of the Creek Nation.

                    Respectfully,
                                Tams Bixby
                                Commissioner.

---

*(The above letter given again, without letterhead.)*

# Applications for Enrollment of Choctaw Newborn
## Act of 1905  Volume XI

7-NB-761.

Muskogee, Indian Territory, August 18, 1905.

Jane Nero,
    Eufaula, Indian Territory.

Dear Madam:

An application was made to the Commission to the Five Civilized Tribes by Joseph Nero, your husband, for the enrollment of Jimmy Nero, born February 30[sic], 1903, as a citizen by blood of the Choctaw Nation. It is stated in said application that you are the mother of said child and that Joseph Nero is his father.

If this is correct you are requested to have the inclosed affidavit executed and return it to this office in the inclosed envelope.

Respectfully,

Acting Commissioner.

CTD-1.

*(The above letter given again.)*

7-NB-761.

Muskogee, Indian Territory, September 8, 1905.

Joseph Nero,
    Eufaula, Indian Territory.

Dear Sir:

Receipt is hereby acknowledged of your letter of the 4th instant in reference to the enrollment of your minor child, Jimmie Nero, as a citizen of the Choctaw Nation and in which you state that your wife, Jane Nero, has mysteriously disappeared and that it will be impossible for you to secure her affidavit to the birth of the child.

In the absence of the affidavit of the mother of Jimmie Nero, as to his birth, this office will require the most conclusive testimony of disinterested parties, that Jimmie Nero was born to Jane Nero, a citizen by blood of the Choctaw Nation. It is suggested that if you can produce witnesses who have actual knowledge of this fact, that you secure their personal attendance before the Commissioner at Muskogee, Indian Territory, at the earliest practicable date, as otherwise disposition cannot be made of the pending application for the enrollment of your child.

## Applications for Enrollment of Choctaw Newborn
## Act of 1905 Volume XI

Respectfully,

Acting Commissioner.

---

REFER IN REPLY TO THE FOLLOWING:
23-761

**DEPARTMENT OF THE INTERIOR,
COMMISSIONER TO THE FIVE CIVILIZED TRIBES.**

Muskogee, Indian Territory, August 1, 1906.

Lacey P. Bobo,
    Bokoshe, Indian Territory.

Dear Sir[sic]:-

    There is enclosed you herewith copy of the record in the case of Jimmy Nero, and you are requested to investigate this matter and secure additional evidence as to the birth of this child and if he is now living, or if dead the date of his death.

Respectfully,

Encl. 1/2

Commissioner.

---

*(The above letter given again, without letterhead.)*

---

McAlester, Indian Territory, September 19, 1906

Joseph Nero,
    Eufaula, Indian Territory.

Dear Sir:

    Regarding the enrollment of your new born child, Jimmie Nero, you are advised that this case has been referred to this field party for proper investigation. Write this party at once in the enclosed envelope where you live and the distance and direction from Eufaula, Indian Territory, that you and others in your neighborhood may be seen in this enrollment matter. Also state if you know the present whereabouts of Jane Nero, a Choctaw by blood, the mother of this new born child, and if you know write us her post office address that we may see her. Get all the facts in this case and the witnesses ready to give testimony, as this party expects to see you within 30 days.

Respectfully,

[sic]

# Applications for Enrollment of Choctaw Newborn
## Act of 1905  Volume XI

---

J. W. ROBERTSON, EUFAULA      HAZEN GREEN, EUFAULA      W. G. ROBERTSON, MUSKOGEE

ROBERTSON, GREEN & ROBERTSON<br>
ATTORNEYS-AT-LAW<br>
MORHART BLDG<br>
ROOM 7

EUFAULA, INDIAN TERRITORY, Sept. 24, 1906.

Lacy P. Bobo, Esq.,
   Muskogee, I. T.

Dear Sir:- I have your letter of the 19th inst. In reply beg to advise that I live 12 miles West and 3/4 mile North of Eufaula, I. T. I don't know as to the whereabouts of Jane Nero, the mother of Jimmie Nero, I have expected her to be located by her drawing her Choctaw townsite money, but the parties who have the payment of this money in hand have never notified me as to her whereabouts. Let me know a few days ahead of time as to what day you will be at my place, that I may have the witnesses present. If you will instruct me by mail as to what proof you require I will make a strong effort to have the witnesses ready.

    It might be that if you would correspond with the party that should have paid her Choctaw townsite money that he could advise you a[sic] as to Jane Nero's location.
    Awaiting your further instructions in the matter, I am,

Yours very truly,<br><br>Joseph Nero

*Letter to Bobo*

---

McAlester, Indian Territory, October 12, 1906.

Joseph Nero,
   Eufaula, Indian Territory.
      C/o Robinson, Green and Robinson, Attorneys.

Dear Sir :

    In the matter of the enrollment of your new born child, Jimmy Nero, you are advised that this party expects to be in Eufaula, Indian Territory, on the ~~evening~~ afternoon of Thursday, October 18, 1906, for the purpose of securing the most conclusive testimony of disinterested parties that Jimmy Nero was born to Jane Nero, a citizen by blood of the Choctaw Nation, and also wish to establish definitely the date of the child's birth and whether or not said child was living March 4, 1905.

## Applications for Enrollment of Choctaw Newborn
## Act of 1905   Volume XI

It is expected that you secure the personal attendance at Eufaula, Indian Territory, of any witnesses you wish this party to examine on date aforesaid, and if the child is still living that it be brought before this party.

This party has been advised by the United States Indian Agent at the Union Agency, Muskogee, Indian Territory, that Jane Nero has not, on October 9, 1906, appeared before the Choctaw Townsite paying party and secured her $35.00 per capita payment.

Very respectfully,

In Charge Choctaw -Chickasaw Field Party No. 1.

---

7-NB-761.

Muskogee, Indian Territory, December 8, 1906.

Joseph Nero,
    Eufaula, Indian Territory.

Dear Sir:

In the matter of the application for the enrollment of your minor son, Jimmy Nero, as a citizen by blood of the Choctaw Nation, it will be necessary that you furnish this office with certain information relative thereto, and for this purpose there is inclosed you herewith a blank affidavit in interrogatory form, which you are requested to take before some Notary Public and answer under oath the questions therein propounded, returning the same to this office at the earliest possible date.

An envelope requiring no postage is inclosed herewith for reply.

Respectfully,

Acting Commissioner.

Encl. Env.
LBA 8-1.

## Applications for Enrollment of Choctaw Newborn
## Act of 1905    Volume XI

7NB761

Muskogee, Indian Territory, December 15, 1906.

Joseph Nero,
Eufaula, Indian Territory.

Dear Sir:

Receipt is hereby acknowledged of your letter of December 10, enclosing affidavit relative to your child, Jimmie Nero, as a citizen of the Choctaw Nation and the same has been filed with the record in the matter of the enrollment of said child.

Respectfully,

Commissioner.

7 NB 761

UNITED STATES OF AMERICA, )
) 
WESTERN DISTRICT, ) SS:
)
INDIAN TERRITORY. )

Personally appeared before me, the undersigned Notary Public in and for the Western District of the Indian Territory, Joseph Nero, who being first duly sworn, upon oath makes answer to the following interrogatories:

Q What is your name, age and post office address:

A

Q Are you the father of Jimmy Nero, an applicant for enrollment as a citizen by blood of the Choctaw Nation?

A

Q Who is the mother of Jimmy Nero?

A

Q Is she a citizen by blood of the Choctaw Nation?

A

# Applications for Enrollment of Choctaw Newborn
## Act of 1905   Volume XI

Q  Are you a citizen by blood of the Creek Nation?

A

Q  In case it should be determined that your son, Jimmy Nero, is entitled to enrollment as a citizen by blood of either the Choctaw or Creek Nation, in which nation do you desire to have him take his allotment of lands?

A

_____

Subscribed and sworn to before me this ____ day of _____, 190__.

_____
Notary Public.

My Commission Expires: _____.
Post Office Address: _____.

NEW-BORN AFFIDAVIT
    Number. - - - - - - - - - - - - -

. . . CHOCTAW  ENROLLING  COMMISSION. . .

IN THE MATTER OF THE APPLICATION FOR ENROLLMENT, as a citizen of the Choctaw   Nation, of Jimmie Nero born on the ____ day of February 1903

Name of father  Joseph Nero   a citizen of  Creek
Nation, final enrollment No. _____

Name of mother  Jane Nero   a citizen of Choctaw
Nation, final enrollment No.  13308_____

                              Postoffice  Eufaula I. T.

### AFFIDAVIT OF MOTHER

UNITED STATES OF AMERICA
INDIAN TERRITORY
Central   DISTRICT.

    I Jane Nero, on oath state that I am 32 years of age and a citizen by blood, of the Choctaw Nation, and as such have been placed upon the final roll of the Choctaw Nation, by the Honorable Secretary of the Interior my final enrollment No. being 13308; that I am the lawful wife of Joseph Nero, who is a citizen of the Creek Nation, and as such has been placed upon the final roll of said Nation by the Honorable Secretary of the Interior, his final enrollment No. being _____ and that a Male child was born to me on

## Applications for Enrollment of Choctaw Newborn
## Act of 1905   Volume XI

the ___ day of February 1903; that said child has been named Jimmie Nero, and is now living.

Witnesseth.

Must be two                )  _____
witnesses who are
Citizens.                       )  _____
                                    )

Subscribed and sworn to before me this sworn to before me this ___ day of _____ 190__

_____
Notary Public

My Commission Expires:

AFFIDAVIT OF ATTENDING PHYSICIAN OR MIDWIFE

UNITED STATES OF AMERICA
INDIAN TERRITORY
Central    DISTRICT

I, Nancy Nero a Mid Wife on oath state that I attended on Mrs. Jane Nero, wife of Joseph Nero, on the ___ day of February 1903, that there was born to her on said date a Male child, that said child is now living, and is said to have been named Jimmie Nero.

_____Midwife

Witnesseth:

Must be two witnesses        )  _____
who are Citizens and know  )
the child                                  )  _____

Subscribed and sworn to before me this, the _____ of _____ 190__

_____ Notary Public.

We hereby certify that we are well acquainted with Nancy Nero, a Mid Wife and know her to be reputable and of good standing in the community.

( _____
( _____

## Applications for Enrollment of Choctaw Newborn
## Act of 1905 Volume XI

United States of America, )
Indian Territory, ) ss.
Western Territory. )

Tokee Riddle, being be[sic] me first duly sworn, on her oath deposes and says: I am acquainted with Jane Nero, and that the said Jane Nero is the wife of Joseph Nero, and that on February 20th., 1903, a male child was born ot[sic] the said Jane Nero, and that said child is said to have been named Jimmy Nero; that the said child is now living with his father, Joseph Nero, and that I am not acquainted with the present residence of the mother of said child.

her
Tokee Riddle
mark

Witness )
to          (Signed)
mark    )

W H Eckelkamp

Wm C Leedtke

Subscribed and sworn to before me this sworn to before me this 21st. Day of April, 1905.

(Signed) R. L. Simpson
Notary Public.

(Seal) My commission expires July 8-1906.
Western

---

United States of America, )
Indian Territory, ) ss.
Western Territory. )

Steward Riddle, being be[sic] me first duly sworn, on his oath deposes and says: I am acquainted with Jane Nero, and I know her to be the wife of Joseph Nero; that on Feb. 20th., 1903, a male child was born to the said Jane Nero, and said child is said to have been named Jimmy Nero; that said child is now living with his father, Joseph Nero, and that the present whereabouts of the said Jane Nero are to me unknown.

Witness ( Wm C Leedtke
to mark    W H Eckelkamp
              (

his
Steward x Riddle
mark

Subscribed and sworn to before me this 21st. day of April, 1905.

(Signed) R. L Simpson
Notary Public.

My commission expires July 8, 1906.
(Seal)
Western.

## Applications for Enrollment of Choctaw Newborn
## Act of 1905 Volume XI

*(The above affidavit given again.)*

BIRTH AFFIDAVIT.

### DEPARTMENT OF THE INTERIOR,
### COMMISSIONER TO THE FIVE CIVILIZED TRIBES.

ENROLLMENT OF MINORS. ACT OF CONGRESS, APPROVED APRIL 26, 1906.

IN RE APPLICATION FOR ENROLLMENT, as a citizen of the Choctaw Nation, of Jimmy Nero, born on the 20 day of Feb., 1903

Name of Father: Joseph Nero    a citizen of the Creek Nation.
Name of Mother: Jane Nero    a citizen of the Choctaw Nation.

Tribal enrollment of father ............................ Tribal enrollment of mother ............................

Postoffice    Eufaula, Indian Ter.

#### AFFIDAVIT OF MOTHER.

UNITED STATES OF AMERICA, Indian Territory, }
     Western      District.

I, Joseph Nero, on oath state that I am forty-five years of age and a citizen by freedman, of the Creek Nation; that I am the lawful xxxx husband of Jane Nero, who is a citizen, by blood of the Choctaw Nation; that a male child was born to me on 20th day of February, 1903, that said child has been named Jimmy Nero, and was living March 4, 1906. that said child is living with me.

                                         Joseph Nero
WITNESSES TO MARK:
{

Subscribed and sworn to before me this 21st day of April, 1905.

                                       R. L. Simpson
My Commission expires July 8, 1906.          Notary Public.

## Applications for Enrollment of Choctaw Newborn
## Act of 1905   Volume XI

AFFIDAVIT OF ATTENDING PHYSICIAN OR MID-WIFE.

UNITED STATES OF AMERICA, Indian Territory, }
Western  District.

I, Nancy Nero , a mid-wife , on oath state that I attended on Jane Nero , wife of Joseph Nero on the 20th day of February , 1903 ; that there was born to her on said date a male child; that said child was living March 4, 1906, and is said to have been named Jimmy Nero

                                her
                      Nancy Nero x
WITNESSES TO MARK:                mark
{ W. H. Eckelkamp
{ Wm. C. Leedtke

Subscribed and sworn to before me this 21st day of April , 1905.

                        R. L. Simpson
My Commission expires July 8, 1906.      Notary Public.

---

*(The affidavits dated November 6, 1906 with testimony taken October 18, 1906, of Joseph Nero, Nancy Nero, Jane Paro, and T. L. Boone, given again.)*

---

*(The affidavit of Joseph Nero, taken December 10, 1906, given again.)*

---

*(The Decision given by the Commissioner to the Five Civilized Tribes, Dec. 24, 1906, given again.)*

---

*(The letter of December 24, 1906, to Joseph Nero, given again.)*

---

*(The letter of December 24, 1906, to Mansfield, McMurray & Cornish, given again.)*

---

Choc New Born 762
    Ina Beal   b. 3-3-04

# Applications for Enrollment of Choctaw Newborn
## Act of 1905    Volume XI

7-NB-762.

Muskogee, Indian Territory, June 6, 1905.

Reuben Beal,
    Durant, Indian Territory.

Dear Sir:

    Referring to the application for the enrollment of your infant child, Ina Beal, born March 3, 1904, it is noted from the affidavits heretofore filed in this office that the applicant claims through you.

    In this event it will be necessary that you file with the Commission either the original or a certified copy of the license and certificate of your marriage to the applicant's mother, Minnie Beal.

    Respectfully,

[sic]

---

7-NB-762

Muskogee, Indian Territory, July 29, 1905.

Reuben Beal,
    c/o John W. Hampton,
        Durant, Indian Territory.

Dear Sir:

    Your attention is called to a communication addressed to you by the Commission to the Five Civilized Tribes, under date of June 6, 1905, in which you were requested to furnish either the original or a certified copy of the license and certificate of your marriage to your wife, Minnie Beal, in the matter of the enrollment of your infant child, Ina Beal, born March 3, 1904. No reply to this letter has been received.

    The matter should receive your immediate attention as no further action can be taken relative to the enrollment of your said child until the evidence requested is supplied.

    Respectfully,

Commissioner.

## Applications for Enrollment of Choctaw Newborn
## Act of 1905  Volume XI

7-NB-762

Muskogee, Indian Territory, August 10, 1905.

Reuben Beal,
    Durant, Indian Territory.

Dear Sir:

    Receipt is hereby acknowledged of your letter of August 7, 1905, enclosing certified copy of the marriage license and certificate between Reuben Beal and Minnie Halloway[sic] which you offer in support of the application of Ina Beal for enrollment as a citizen by blood of the Choctaw Nation, and the same has been filed with the record in this case.

                  Respectfully,

                              Acting Commissioner.

No. 1103

## MARRIAGE LICENSE.

UNITED STATES OF AMERICA          THE INDIAN TERRITORY,
                                                CENTRAL DISTRICT, SS.

TO ANY PERSON AUTHORIZED BY LAW TO SOLEMNIZE MARRIAGE, GREETING:

    You are hereby commanded to Solemnize the Rite and publish the Banns of Matrimony between Mr. R. B. Beal of Durant in the Indian Territory, aged 40 years, and Miss Minnie Holloway of Durant in the Indian Territory, aged 18 years according to law, and do you officially sign and return this License to the parties therein named.

                      WITNESS my hand and official seal, this 27th
                      day of April A. D. 1903,

                      E. J. Fannin
                          Clerk of the United States Court

(SEAL)

                      W. B. Stone
                          Deputy.

## Applications for Enrollment of Choctaw Newborn
## Act of 1905 Volume XI

UNITED STATES OF AMERICA, )
   THE INDIAN TERRITORY, ) ss.    CERTIFICATE OF MARRIAGE.
CENTRAL DISTRICT. )

I,_____G. F. Deck_____
a Mayor do hereby certify, that on the 29th day of April A.D. 1903, I did, duly and according to law, as commanded in the foregoing License, solemnize the Rite and publish the Banns of Matrimony between the parties therein named.

Witness my hand, this 29th day of April A. D. 1903

My credentials are recorded in the )    G. F. Deck
office of the Clerk of the United )    a Mayor, Silo, I. T.
States Court in the Indian Territory, )
Central District, Book ___, Page ___ )

NOTE.- This License and Certificate of Marriage must be returned to the office of the Clerk of the United States Court of the Indian Territory from whence it was issued, within sexty[sic] days from the date thereof, or the party to whom the License was issued will be liable in the amount of One Hundred Dollars ($100.00).

No. 234

### CERTIFICATE OF RECORD OF MARRIAGES.

UNITED STATES OF AMERICA, )
   THE INDIAN TERRITORY. )SCT.
CENTRAL DISTRICT. )

   I, E. J. Fannin Clerk of the United States Court in the Indian Territory and District aforesaid, do hereby CERTIFY that the License for and Certificate of the Marriage of Mr. R. B. Beal and Miss Minnie Holloway was filed in my office in said Territory and District the 30 day of April A. D. 1903, and duly recorded in Book 1 of Marriage Record, Page 117

   WITNESS my hand and seal of said Court, at Durant this 30 day of April A. D. 1905

                E. J. Fannin
                     Clerk.
      By    W. B. Stone
                Deputy.

P. O. _____

## Applications for Enrollment of Choctaw Newborn
## Act of 1905 Volume XI

DEPARTMENT OF THE INTERIOR,
COMMISSION TO THE FIVE CIVILIZED TRIBES.
FILED Aug. 8, 1905.

BIRTH AFFIDAVIT.

### DEPARTMENT OF THE INTERIOR.
### COMMISSION TO THE FIVE CIVILIZED TRIBES.

IN RE APPLICATION FOR ENROLLMENT, as a citizen of the Choctaw Nation, of Ina Beal , born on the 3rd. day of march , 1904

Name of Father: Reuben Beal     a citizen of the Choctaw Nation.
Name of Mother: Minnie Beal     a citizen of the Choctaw Nation.

Postoffice    Durant, Indian Territory.

**AFFIDAVIT OF MOTHER.**

UNITED STATES OF AMERICA, Indian Territory, }
    Central            DISTRICT.

    I, Minnie Beal , on oath state that I am 19 years of age and a citizen by intermarriage , of the Choctaw Nation; that I am the lawful wife of Reuben Beal , who is a citizen, by blood of the Choctaw Nation; that a female child was born to me on 3rd. day of March , 1904; that said child has been named Ina Beal , and was living March 4, 1905.

                       Minnie Beal

Witnesses To Mark:

    Subscribed and sworn to before me this 5$^{th}$ day of April , 1905

                       John W. Hampton
                       Notary Public.

**AFFIDAVIT OF ATTENDING PHYSICIAN OR MID-WIFE.**

UNITED STATES OF AMERICA, Indian Territory, }
    Central            DISTRICT.

    I, James L. Shuler , a physician , on oath state that I attended on Mrs. Minnie Beal , wife of Reuben Beal on the 3rd. day of March ,

## Applications for Enrollment of Choctaw Newborn
## Act of 1905   Volume XI

1904; that there was born to her on said date a   female   child; that said child was living March 4, 1905, and is said to have been named Ina Beal

James L. Shuler

Witnesses To Mark:
{

Subscribed and sworn to before me this 5<sup>th</sup>   day of   April   , 1905

John W. Hampton
Notary Public.

---

Choc New Born 763
    Mable Fitzgerald   b. 7-11-04

7- 8132
**BIRTH AFFIDAVIT.**
### DEPARTMENT OF THE INTERIOR.
### COMMISSION TO THE FIVE CIVILIZED TRIBES.

**IN RE APPLICATION FOR ENROLLMENT,** as a citizen of the   Choctaw   Nation, of Mable Fitzgerald   , born on the 11   day of   July   , 1904

Name of Father: Thomas A Fitzgerald     a citizen of the   U S    ~~Nation~~.
Name of Mother: Maud Fitzgerald (nee Allen)   a citizen of the   Choctaw   Nation.

Postoffice   Keota Ind. Ter.

---

**AFFIDAVIT OF MOTHER.**

UNITED STATES OF AMERICA, Indian Territory, }
    Central        DISTRICT.   }

I,   Maud Fitzgerald   , on oath state that I am   19   years of age and a citizen by   blood   , of the   Choctaw   Nation; that I am the lawful wife of   Thomas A Fitzgerald   , who is a citizen, ~~by~~ — of the   United States   Nation; that a   female   child was born to me on   11   day of   July   , 1904; that said child has been named   Mable Fitzgerald   , and was living March 4, 1905.

Maud Fitzgerald

## Applications for Enrollment of Choctaw Newborn
## Act of 1905   Volume XI

Witnesses To Mark:

{

    Subscribed and sworn to before me this  3<sup>rd</sup>  day of   April   , 1905

OL Johnson
Notary Public.

---

**AFFIDAVIT OF ATTENDING PHYSICIAN OR MID-WIFE.**

UNITED STATES OF AMERICA, Indian Territory, }
................................................................. DISTRICT. }

    I,................................................, a ........................., on oath state that I attended on Mrs.  Maud Fitzgerald  , wife of   Thomas A Fitzgerald    on the  11<sup>th</sup>  day of  July  , 1904; that there was born to her on said date a    female    child; that said child was living March 4, 1905, and is said to have been named  Mable

L.J. Smith M.D.

Witnesses To Mark:

{

    Subscribed and sworn to before me this  5 day of    April    , 1905

EF Jeffries
Notary Public.
Com Expires Sept 18 1906

---

**NEW-BORN AFFIDAVIT.**

Number..................

### ...Choctaw Enrolling Commission...

---

    IN THE MATTER OF THE APPLICATION FOR ENROLLMENT, as a citizen of the Choctaw    Nation, of        Mable Fitzgerald

born on the   11  day of ____July____ 190 4

Name of father   Thos A Fitzgerald              a citizen of    United States
Nation final enrollment No..................
Name of mother   Maud Fitzgerald             a citizen of    Choctaw
Nation final enrollment No.  8132    *Nee Maud Allen*

# Applications for Enrollment of Choctaw Newborn
## Act of 1905 Volume XI

Postoffice    Star Ind Ter

**AFFIDAVIT OF MOTHER.**

UNITED STATES OF AMERICA
INDIAN TERRITORY
Central    DISTRICT

I    Maud Fitzgerald    nee Maud Allen    , on oath state that I am 18    years of age and a citizen by    Blood    of the    Choctaw    Nation, and as such have been placed upon the final roll of the    Choctaw    Nation, by the Honorable Secretary of the Interior my final enrollment number being    8132  ; that I am the lawful wife of    Thos A Fitzgerald    , who is a citizen of the    United States    Nation, and as such has been placed upon the final roll of said Nation by the Honorable Secretary of the Interior, his final enrollment number being    8132    and that a    Girl    child was born to me on the    11 day of July    190 4; that said child has been named    Mable Fitzgerald    , and is now living.

Maud Fitzgerald nee Maud Allen

Witnesseth.
Must be two Witnesses who are Citizens. } Eugene A Hickman
Laura L Moore

Subscribed and sworn to before me this    21    day of    Jan    190 5

EF Jeffries
Com Expires Sep 18 1906
Notary Public.

My commission expires:

## AFFIDAVIT OF ATTENDING PHYSICIAN OR MIDWIFE

UNITED STATES OF AMERICA
INDIAN TERRITORY
Central    DISTRICT

I,    L J Smith    a    Physician on oath state that I attended on Mrs.    Mrs Maud Fitzgerald    wife of    T.A. Fitzgerald on the    11 day of July    , 190 4 , that there was born to her on said date a    Girl    child, that said child is now living, and is said to have been named    Mable Fitzgerald

Subscribed and sworn to before me this, the    20    day of January    190 5

Lee J Smith MD

WITNESSETH:
Must be two witnesses who are citizens { Eugene A Hickman
Laura L Moore

EF Jeffries    Notary Public.
Com Expires Sep 18 1906

## Applications for Enrollment of Choctaw Newborn
## Act of 1905   Volume XI

We hereby certify that we are well acquainted with     Lee J Smith a     Physician     and know     him     to be reputable and of good standing in the community.

Eugene A Hickman                         _____

Laura L Moore                            _____

---

Choc New Born 764
    Willis Owen McBride   b. 5-15-03

                                    7-N.B. 764.

                    Muskogee, Indian Territory, May 25, 1905.

Mrs. Winnie McBride,
    Calloway, Indian Territory.

Dear Madam:

Receipt is hereby acknowledged of your letter of May 20, asking if Clayton & Brainard of Muskogee, Indian Territory presented the application for the enrollment of your child, Willis Owen McBride.

In reply to your letter you are advised that the affidavits heretofore forwarded to the birth of your child, Willis Owen McBride, have been filed with our records as an application for his enrollment, and in the event further evidence is necessary to enable us to determine the right to enrollment of said child, you will be duly notified.

                    Respectfully,

                                    Chairman.

## Applications for Enrollment of Choctaw Newborn
## Act of 1905   Volume XI

**BIRTH AFFIDAVIT.**

**DEPARTMENT OF THE INTERIOR.**
**COMMISSION TO THE FIVE CIVILIZED TRIBES.**

---

IN RE APPLICATION FOR ENROLLMENT, as a citizen of the   Choctow[sic]   Nation, of   Willis Owen McBride   , born on the   15th   day of   May   , 1903

Name of Father: Emmett C. McBride      a citizen of the   Choctow   Nation.
Name of Mother: Winnie McBride           a citizen of the   Choctow   Nation.

Postoffice   Calloway, Indian Territory

---

**AFFIDAVIT OF MOTHER.**

UNITED STATES OF AMERICA, Indian Territory, }
Central Judicial     DISTRICT.

I,   Winnie McBride   , on oath state that I am   28   years of age and a citizen by blood   , of the   Choctow   Nation; that I am the lawful wife of   Emmett C. McBride   , who is a citizen, by   blood   of the   Choctow   Nation; that a male   child was born to me on   15th   day of   May   , 1903, that said child has been named   Willis Owen McBride   , and is now living.

Winnie J McBride

Witnesses To Mark:
{

Subscribed and sworn to before me this   28   day of   March   , 1905.

I. A. Franklin
Notary Public.

---

**AFFIDAVIT OF ATTENDING PHYSICIAN OR MID-WIFE.**

UNITED STATES OF AMERICA, Indian Territory, }
Central Judicial     DISTRICT.

I,   Mary Jackson   , a   mid-wife   , on oath state that I attended on Mrs.   Winnie McBride   , wife of   Emmett C. McBride   on the   15th   day of   May   , 1903; that there was born to her on said date a   male   child; that said child is now living and is said to have been named   Willis Owen McBride

her
Mary x Jackson
mark

## Applications for Enrollment of Choctaw Newborn
## Act of 1905  Volume XI

Witnesses To Mark:
{ Edmon Jackson
{ E C McBride

Subscribed and sworn to before me this 29 day of March , 1905.

                                            I. A. Franklin
                                            Notary Public.

---

Choc New Born 765
    Selina Bohanan  b. 12-9-04

                                                  7-NB-765.

                           Muskogee, Indian Territory, June 2, 1905.

Levi W. Bohanan,
    Talihina, Indian Territory.

Dear Sir:

    Referring to the application for the enrollment of your infant child, Selina Bohanan, born December 9, 1904, it is noted that the midwife's signature to her affidavit, which is made by mark, is attested by only one witness, while two are required.

    It will, therefore, be necessary that the enclosed application be executed and returned to this office.

    In having the affidavit executed care should be exercised to see that all names are written in full, as they appear in the body of the affidavit. Signatures by mark must be attested by two witnesses. Each affidavit must be executed before a Notary Public and the notarial seal and signature of the officer must be attached to each separate affidavit.

                                              Respectfully,

VR 31-1.                                                          [sic]

## Applications for Enrollment of Choctaw Newborn
## Act of 1905   Volume XI

7 NB 765

Muskogee, Indian Territory, June 19, 1905.

Levi W. Bohanan,
Talihina, Indian Territory.

Dear Sir:

    Receipt is hereby acknowledged of the affidavits of Harriett Bohanan and Eliza Horn to the birth of Selina Bohanan, daughter of Levi W. and Harriett Bohanan, December 9, 1904, and the same have been filed with our records in the matter of the enrollment of said child.

Respectfully,

Chairman.

---

7-NB-765.

Muskogee, Indian Territory, May 31, 1905.

Levi W. Bohanan,
Talihina, Indian Territory.

Dear Sir:

    Referring to the application for the enrollment of your infant child, Selina Bohanan, born December 9, 1904, it is noted that the midwife's signature to her affidavit, which is made by mark, is attested by only one witness, while two are required.

    It will, therefore, be necessary that the enclosed application be executed and returned to this office.

    In having these affidavits executed care should be exercised to see that all names are written in full, as they appear in the body of the affidavit, and in the event that either of the persons signing the affidavit are unable to write, signatures by mark must be attested by two witnesses. Each affidavit must be executed before a Notary Public and the notarial seal and signature of the officer must be attached to each separate affidavit.

Respectfully,

Chairman.

VR 31-1.

## Applications for Enrollment of Choctaw Newborn
## Act of 1905   Volume XI

7-2150

Muskogee, Indian Territory, April 12, 1905.

Harriet Bohanan,
    Talihina, Indian Territory.

Dear Madam:

    Receipt is hereby acknowledged of the affidavits of Harriet Bohanan and Phebe Benton to the birth of Selina Bohanan daughter of Levi and Harriett Bohanan, December 9, 1904, and the same have been filed with our records as an application for the enrollment of said child.

    Receipt is also acknowledged of your affidavit and the affidavit of Nelson Benton to the death of your husband Levi Benton[sic], a citizen by blood of the Choctaw Nation which occurred March 4, 1905, and the same have been filed with our records as evidence of the death of the above named person.

                      Respectfully,

                      Commissioner in Charge.

---

**BIRTH AFFIDAVIT.**

### DEPARTMENT OF THE INTERIOR.
### COMMISSION TO THE FIVE CIVILIZED TRIBES.

**IN RE APPLICATION FOR ENROLLMENT,** as a citizen of the   Choctaw   Nation, of Selina Bohannon[sic]   , born on the  9  day of  December  , 1904

Name of Father: Levi Bohannon[sic]   a citizen of the  Choctaw  Nation.
Name of Mother: Harriett Bohannon   a citizen of the  Choctaw  Nation.

                    Postoffice   Talihina I.T.

**AFFIDAVIT OF MOTHER.**

UNITED STATES OF AMERICA, Indian Territory, }
   Central             DISTRICT.

    I,   Harriett Bohannon   , on oath state that I am  25   years of age and a citizen by   Blood   , of the   Choctaw   Nation; that I am the lawful wife of  Levi Bohannon   , who is a citizen, by Blood   of the   Choctaw   Nation; that a Female   child was born to me on  9   day of   December   , 1904; that said child has been named   Selina Bohannon   , and was living March 4, 1905.

## Applications for Enrollment of Choctaw Newborn
## Act of 1905  Volume XI

Harriett Bohanan

Witnesses To Mark:

Subscribed and sworn to before me this  6  day of    April    , 1905

My commission expires Feb. 4, 1908
Commission from U.S. Court at So. McAlester I.T.
MY OFFICE TALIHINA, I. T.

Sam T Roberts Jr
Notary Public.

---

### AFFIDAVIT OF ATTENDING PHYSICIAN OR MID-WIFE.

*Harriett Bohannon Interpreter*

UNITED STATES OF AMERICA, Indian Territory,
Central    DISTRICT.

I,  Phebe Benton  , a  Midwife  , on oath state that I attended on Mrs.  Harriett Bohannon  , wife of  Levi Bohannon  on the  9  day of  December  , 1904; that there was born to her on said date a  Female  child; that said child was living March 4, 1905, and is said to have been named Selina Bohannon

Witnesses To Mark:
Nelson Benton

Phebe x Benton
her   mark

Subscribed and sworn to before me this  6  day of    April    , 1905

Sam T Roberts Jr
Notary Public.

---

**BIRTH AFFIDAVIT.**

### DEPARTMENT OF THE INTERIOR.
### COMMISSION TO THE FIVE CIVILIZED TRIBES.

**IN RE APPLICATION FOR ENROLLMENT,** as a citizen of the  Choctaw  Nation, of  Selina Bohanan  , born on the  9  day of  December  , 1904

Name of Father: Levi W Bohanan        a citizen of the  Choctaw  Nation.
Name of Mother: Harriet Bohanan        a citizen of the  Choctaw  Nation.

Postoffice    Talihina Ind. Ter.

# Applications for Enrollment of Choctaw Newborn
## Act of 1905   Volume XI

### AFFIDAVIT OF MOTHER.

UNITED STATES OF AMERICA, Indian Territory, }
Central                    DISTRICT.

I, Harriet Bohanon[sic], on oath state that I am 25 years of age and a citizen by Blood, of the Choctaw Nation; that I am the lawful wife of Levi W Bohanon, who is a citizen, by Blood of the Choctaw Nation; that a Female child was born to me on 9 day of December, 1904; that said child has been named Selina Bohanon, and was living March 4, 1905.

Harriett Bohanan

Witnesses To Mark:
{

Subscribed and sworn to before me this 15 day of June, 1905

Sam T Roberts Jr
Notary Public.

---

### AFFIDAVIT OF ATTENDING PHYSICIAN OR MID-WIFE.

UNITED STATES OF AMERICA, Indian Territory, }
Central                    DISTRICT.

I, Eliza Horn, a Midwife, on oath state that I attended on Mrs. Harriet Bohanan, wife of Levi W Bohanan on the 9 day of December, 1904; that there was born to her on said date a female child; that said child was living March 4, 1905, and is said to have been named Selina Bohanan

Eliza Horn

Witnesses To Mark:
{

Subscribed and sworn to before me this 15 day of June, 1905

Sam T Roberts Jr
Notary Public.

# Applications for Enrollment of Choctaw Newborn
## Act of 1905   Volume XI

Choc New Born 766
    Abe Meashintubby   b. 12-1-02
    Andrew Meashintubby   b. 2-6-05

---

7-2094

Muskogee, Indian Territory, April 12, 1905.

Jackson Mieashintubby[sic],
    Talihina, Indian Territory.

Dear Sir:

    Receipt is hereby acknowledged of the affidavits of Lizzie Mischintubbi[sic] and Jackson Mischintubbi to the birth of Andrew Mischintubbi, son of Jackson and Lizzie Mischintubbi, February 6, 1905, also affidavits of Lizzie Mischintubbi and Francis McIntosh to the birth of Abe Mischintubbi, son of Jackson and Lizzie Mischintubbi, December 1, 1902, and the same have been filed with our records as applications for the enrollment of said children.

                Respectfully,

                Commissioner in Charge.

---

7-NB-766.

Muskogee, Indian Territory, May 31, 1905.

Jackson Meashintubby,
    Talihina, Indian Territory.

Dear Sir:

    Referring to the application for the enrollment of your infant child, Andrew Meashintubby, born February 6, 1905, it is noted that you attended upon your wife at the time of birth of the applicant.

    If there was no physician or midwife in attendance it will be necessary for you to file in this office the affidavits of two persons, who are disinterested and not related to the applicant, who have actual knowledge of the facts that the child was born, the date of his birth; that he was living on March 4, 1905, and that Lizzie Meashintubby is his mother.

                Respectfully,

                    Chairman.

## Applications for Enrollment of Choctaw Newborn
## Act of 1905 Volume XI

7 NB 766

Muskogee, Indian Territory, June 8, 1905.

Welch & Welch,
    Attorneys at Law,
        Talihina, Indian Territory.

Gentlemen:

Receipt is hereby acknowledged of your letter of June 3, 1905, enclosing affidavits of Lyman Harrison and Susan Pitchlyn to the birth of Andrew Meashintubby, February 7, 1905, and the same have been filed with our records in the matter of the enrollment of said child.

Respectfully,

Chairman.

---

7-NB-766

Muskogee, Indian Territory, September 26, 1905.

Jno. J. Thomas,
    Talihina, Indian Territory.

Dear Sir:

Replying to your letter of the 21st instant you are advised that on July 22, 1905, the Secretary of the Interior approved the enrollment of Abe Meashintubby as a citizen by blood of the Choctaw Nation and the name of the child appears upon the final roll of new-born citizens of the Choctaw Nation opposite number 729. The child appears upon the records of this office as the minor son of Jackson and Lizzie Meashintubby, both citizens by blood of the Choctaw Nation.

Jackson Meashintubby was early in the month of August of the present year notified of the approval of the enrollment of his minor son, Abe Meashintubby, by the Secretary of the Interior.

Respectfully,

Commissioner.

## Applications for Enrollment of Choctaw Newborn
## Act of 1905   Volume XI

BIRTH AFFIDAVIT.

### DEPARTMENT OF THE INTERIOR.
### COMMISSION TO THE FIVE CIVILIZED TRIBES.

IN RE APPLICATION FOR ENROLLMENT, as a citizen of the   Choctaw   Nation, of Abe Mischentubbi   , born on the 1 day of December , 1902

Name of Father: Jackson Mischentubbi   a citizen of the Choctaw Nation.
Name of Mother: Lizzie Mischentubbi   a citizen of the Choctaw Nation.

Postoffice   Talihina I.T.

Interpreter Austin Billy

### AFFIDAVIT OF MOTHER.

UNITED STATES OF AMERICA, Indian Territory, }
Central   DISTRICT.

I, Lizzie Mischentubbi , on oath state that I am about 30 years of age and a citizen by Blood , of the Choctaw Nation; that I am the lawful wife of Jackson Mischentubbi , who is a citizen, by Blood of the Choctaw Nation; that a male child was born to me on 1st day of December , 1902; that said child has been named Abe Mischentubbi , and was living March 4, 1905.

her
Lizzie x Mischentubbi
mark

Witnesses To Mark:
{ Austin Billy
{ D. Thomas

Subscribed and sworn to before me this 6 day of April , 1905

My commission expires Feb. 4, 1908
Commission from U.S. Court at So. McAlester I.T.
MY OFFICE TALIHINA, I. T.

Sam T. Roberts Jr
Notary Public.

### AFFIDAVIT OF ATTENDING PHYSICIAN OR MID-WIFE.

UNITED STATES OF AMERICA, Indian Territory, }
Central   DISTRICT.

I, Francis M$^c$Intosh , a Midwife , on oath state that I attended on Mrs. Lizzie Mischentubbi , wife of Jackson Mischentubbi on the 1 day of December , 1902; that there was born to her on said date a male child; that said child was living March 4, 1905, and is said to have been named Abe Mischentubbi

her
Francis x M$^c$Intosh
mark

## Applications for Enrollment of Choctaw Newborn
## Act of 1905   Volume XI

Witnesses To Mark:
{ Austin Billy
{ D. Thomas

Subscribed and sworn to before me this  6  day of   April   , 1905

                                      Sam T Roberts Jr
                                      Notary Public.

---

*(The affidavit below typed as given.)*

In re the application for the enrollment of Andrew Meashintubby as a citizen by blood of the Choctaw Nation.

Affidavit of Lyman Harrison,

Before me a notary public within and for the Central District of the Indian Territory duly commissioned and acting, appeared in person, Lyman Harrison, who being by me duly sworn, on his oath says:   I am a Choctaw citizen by blood, my age is 32 years, my post office address is Talihina I.T.  I live in the same neighborhood with Jackson and Lizzie Meashintubby, and within one mile their home.

WELCH & WELCH
Talihina, I. T.

I was at the home of Jackson Meashintubby, on about the 7th day of February 1905, at which time I saw the child of Lizzie Meashintubby, nursing its mother Lizzie Meashintubby, and she Lizzie told me the child was borned the day before.

I know that said Lizzie Meashintubby was pregnant for some time before the date upon which I was at her home, to wit the 7th day of February 1905.

The said child has been named Andrew, and is now living.  I am not related to Jackson or Lizzie Meashintubby, either by blood or marriage.

                                        Lyman Harrison

Sworn to before me this  3$^{rd}$  day of   June   1905.

                                        CA Welch
                                        Notary Public.
                                        My commission expires Jan. 4, 1908
                                        Commission from U.S. Court, So. McAlester I.T.
                                        MY OFFICE TALIHINA, I.T.

# Applications for Enrollment of Choctaw Newborn
## Act of 1905   Volume XI

*(The affidavit below typed as given.)*

In re the application for the enrollment of Andrew Meashintubby as a citizen by blood of the Choctaw Nation.

Affidavit of Susan Pitchlyn,

On this day before me a notary public within and for the Central District of the Indian Territory duly commissioned and acting, Susan Pitchlyn, who being first duly sworn, says:   I am a Choctaw Nation by blood, my post office address is Talihina Indian Territory,   I am personally acquainted with Jackson. Meashintubby, and Lizzie Meashintubby his wife, and lived with them at their home near Talihina for about a year last past before the birth of her said son Andrew. On about the 1st day of February 1905, the home of said Jackson Meashintubby, and went to visit the family of Thomas McDaniel, and when I returned to Jackson Meashintubby's home, the child of said Lizzie Meashintubby had been borned, I returned from McDaniels to Meashintubby's on about the 12th of February, I know that said child was borned between the 1st, and the 12th of February 1905. *And is now living*

WELCH & WELCH
Talihina, I. T.

I am not related to said Lizzie Meashintubby by blood or marriage. I do not know what my age is, but think I am about 60 years old.

*Witnesses to Mark*  
*C A Welch*  
*D. S. Nash*  

Sworn to before me this 3rd day of   June   1905.

her<br>
Susan x Pitchlyn<br>
mark

CA Welch  
Notary Public.  
My commission expires Jan. 4, 1908  
Commission from U.S. Court, So. McAlester I.T.  
MY OFFICE TALIHINA, I.T.

---

**BIRTH AFFIDAVIT.**

## DEPARTMENT OF THE INTERIOR.
## COMMISSION TO THE FIVE CIVILIZED TRIBES.

---

**IN RE APPLICATION FOR ENROLLMENT,** as a citizen of the     Choctaw     Nation, of Andrew Mischentubbi     , born on the   6   day of   Feby   , 1905

Name of Father: Jackson Mischentubbi     a citizen of the   Choctaw   Nation.  
Name of Mother: Lizzie Mischentubbi     a citizen of the   Choctaw   Nation.

Postoffice   Talihina I.T.

# Applications for Enrollment of Choctaw Newborn
## Act of 1905   Volume XI

*Interpreter Austin Billy*

**AFFIDAVIT OF MOTHER.**

UNITED STATES OF AMERICA, Indian Territory, }
Central           DISTRICT.

I, Lizzie Mischentubbi , on oath state that I am about 30 years of age and a citizen by Blood , of the Choctaw Nation; that I am the lawful wife of Jackson Mischentubbi , who is a citizen, by Blood of the Choctaw Nation; that a male child was born to me on 6 day of February , 1905; that said child has been named Andrew Mischentubbi , and was living March 4, 1905.

                              her
                      Lizzie x Mischentubbi

Witnesses To Mark:                 mark
{ Austin Billy
  D. Thomas

Subscribed and sworn to before me this   6  day of    April   , 1905

My commission expires Feb. 4, 1908
Commission from U.S. Court at So. McAlester I.T.     Sam T. Roberts Jr
MY OFFICE TALIHINA, I. T.                    Notary Public.

---

**AFFIDAVIT OF ATTENDING PHYSICIAN OR MID-WIFE.**

UNITED STATES OF AMERICA, Indian Territory, }
Central           DISTRICT.

I, Jackson Mischentubbi , a ———— , on oath state that I attended on Mrs. Lizzie Mischentubbi , wife of My Wife on the 6 day of February , 1905; that there was born to her on said date a male child; that said child was living March 4, 1905, and is said to have been named Andrew Mischentubbi

                        Jackson Mischentubbi

Witnesses To Mark:

{

Subscribed and sworn to before me this   6  day of    April   , 1905

                      Sam T Roberts Jr
                    Notary Public.

## Applications for Enrollment of Choctaw Newborn
## Act of 1905 Volume XI

Choc New Born 767
    Francis Benton   b. 7-13-03

---

7-2126

Muskogee, Indian Territory, April 12, 1905.

Sam T. Roberts,
    Talihina, Indian Territory.

Dear Sir:

    Receipt is hereby acknowledged of your letter of April 6, 1905, enclosing affidavits of Eliza Benton and Eliza Benton, to the birth of Frances Benton, daughter of George and Eliza Benton, July 13, 1903, and the same have been filed with our records as an application for the enrollment of said child.

Respectfully,

Commissioner in Charge.

---

7-NB-767.

Muskogee, Indian Territory, May 29, 1905.

George Benton,
    Talihina, Indian Territory.

Dear Sir:

    Referring to the application for the enrollment of your infant child, Francis Benton, born July 13, 1903, it is noted from the affidavits heretofore filed in this office that Eliza Benton, your wife, attended upon your wife at the time of birth of the applicant.

    If there was no physician or mid-wife, other than Eliza Benton, in attendance upon your wife it will be necessary for you to file in this office the affidavits of two persons, who are disinterested and not related to the applicant, who have actual knowledge of the facts that the child was born, the date of her birth; that she was living on March 4, 1905, and that Eliza Benton is her mother.

Respectfully,

Chairman.

## Applications for Enrollment of Choctaw Newborn
## Act of 1905   Volume XI

Choctaw N B 767

Muskogee, Indian Territory, June 8, 1905.

George Benton,
    Talihina, Indian Territory.

Dear Sir:

    Receipt is hereby acknowledged of your letter of June 3, inclosing affidavits of Harrison Hitcher and Alex McIntosh, to the birth of Francis Benton, child of George and Eliza Benton, and the same are herewith returned to you for the reason that the date of the birth of the child is given therein as July 13 "180e". Please forward corrected affidavits showing the date of the birth of Francis Benton.

                    Respectfully,

                                      Commissioner in Charge.

AB 1-8

---

7-NB-767.

Muskogee, Indian Territory, August 18, 1905.

George Benton,
    Talihina, Indian Territory.

Dear Sir:

    Your attention is called to the letter of the Commission to the Five Civilized Tribes of June 8, 1905, with which there was returned to you for correction the affidavits of Harrison Hitcher and Alex McIntosh relative to the birth of your daughter Francis Benton. You were requested to have the affidavits corrected showing the date of birth of said Francis Benton and return same to this office. To said letter of June 8, 1905, no response has been received.

    You are again advised that until this office is furnished with the affidavits of two disinterested persons as to the birth of your said daughter Francis Benton nothing further can be done in the matter of the enrollment of said child as a citizen by blood of the Choctaw Nation. Said affidavits must set forth said child's name, the date of her birth, the names of her parents and whether or not she was living on March 4, 1905.

                    Respectfully,

                                      Acting Commissioner.

## Applications for Enrollment of Choctaw Newborn
## Act of 1905   Volume XI

7- N B 767

Muskogee, Indian Territory, August 30, 1905.

George Benton,
    Talihina, Indian Territory.

Dear Sir:

    Receipt is hereby acknowledged of your letter of the 26th instant, enclosing affidavits of Thomas H. Frazier and Harrison Hitcher, of August 26, 1905, relative to the birth of Francis Benton.

    These affidavits have been filed with the records of this office and will receive consideration in the disposition of the application for the enrollment of Francis Benton as a new-born citizen by blood of the Choctaw Nation.

                  Respectfully,

                          Commissioner.

7-NB-767

Muskogee, Indian Territory, December 22, 1905.

George Benton,
    Talihina, Indian Territory.

Dear Sir:

    Receipt is hereby acknowledged of your letter of December 18, 1905, asking if your child Francis Benton has been approved as a citizen of the Choctaw Nation.

    In reply to your letter you are advised that the name of Francis Benton has not yet been placed upon a schedule of new born citizens of the Choctaw Nation prepared for forwarding to the Secretary of the Interior, but you will be notified when her enrollment is approved.

                  Respectfully,

                          Commissioner.

# Applications for Enrollment of Choctaw Newborn
## Act of 1905   Volume XI

*(The affidavit below typed as given.)*

United States of America,

Indian Territory

Central District,

Affidavit in matter of irolement of

Francis Benton, child of George & Eliza Benton.

 Now comes   Harrison Hitcher   , who being duly sworn deposes and says my name is   Harrison Hitcher   , my age is   40   years, my post office is Talihina, I. T.

 I know George Benton, and his wife Eliza Benton, I know them both to be citizens of the Choctaw Nation by blood. I am not kin or in any way related to them. *and am a disinterested party*  I know that on July 13th 1903 there was born to Eliza Benton, wife of George Benton a female child, that it is said to have been named Francis Benton. I know that on the 4th day of March 1905 it was living and is still alive. I am a citizen of the Choctaw Nation by Blood.

 Witnessed by,
 E P Pitchlynn
 Henry Johnson

      his
Harrison x Hitcher
     mark

Subscribed and sworn to before me this the 26th day of August 1905.

My Com expires
Feb. 4, 1908

F.B. Lunsford
Notary Public.

---

*(The affidavit below typed as given.)*

United States of America,

Indian Territory

Central District,

Affidavit in matter of irolement of

Francis Benton, child of George & Eliza Benton.

 Now comes   Thomas H Frazier   , who being duly sworn deposes and says my name is   Thomas H Frazier   , my age is   24   years, my post office is Talihina, I. T.

 I know George Benton, and his wife Eliza Benton, I know them both to be citizens of the Choctaw Nation by blood. I am not kin or in any way related to them. *and am a disinterested party*  I know that on July 13th 1903 there was born to Eliza Benton, wife of George Benton a female child, that it is said to have been named Francis Benton. I know that on the 4th day of March 1905 it was living and is still alive. I am a citizen of the Choctaw Nation by Blood.

            Thomas H Frazier

# Applications for Enrollment of Choctaw Newborn
## Act of 1905 Volume XI

Witnessed by,
E P Pitchlynn
Henry Johnson

Subscribed and sworn to before me this the 26th day of August 1905.

My Com expires                F.B. Lunsford
Feb. 4, 1908                  Notary Public.

---

**BIRTH AFFIDAVIT.**

## DEPARTMENT OF THE INTERIOR.
## COMMISSION TO THE FIVE CIVILIZED TRIBES.

**IN RE APPLICATION FOR ENROLLMENT,** as a citizen of the Choctaw Nation, of Francis Benton, born on the 13 day of July, 1903

Name of Father: Geo Benton        a citizen of the Choctaw Nation.
Name of Mother: Eliza Benton      a citizen of the Choctaw Nation.

Postoffice    Talihina I.T.

---

**AFFIDAVIT OF MOTHER.**

UNITED STATES OF AMERICA, Indian Territory, }
   Central            DISTRICT.              }

I, Eliza Benton, on oath state that I am 25 years of age and a citizen by Blood, of the Choctaw Nation; that I am the lawful wife of George Benton, who is a citizen, by Blood of the Choctaw Nation; that a Female child was born to me on 13 day of July, 1903; that said child has been named Francis Benton, and was living March 4, 1905.

                                Eliza Benton
Witnesses To Mark:

Subscribed and sworn to before me this 6 day of April, 1905

My commission expires Feb. 4, 1908
Commission from U.S. Court at So. McAlester I.T.      Sam T. Roberts Jr
MY OFFICE TALIHINA, I. T.                              Notary Public.

# Applications for Enrollment of Choctaw Newborn
## Act of 1905   Volume XI

*Geo Benton Interpreter*

### AFFIDAVIT OF ATTENDING PHYSICIAN OR MID-WIFE.

UNITED STATES OF AMERICA, Indian Territory, }
Central                             DISTRICT. }

*Eliza Benton wife of Geo Benton was*

I,   Eliza Benton   , a *Mother in law of* , on oath state that I attended on *present at the Birth of Francis Benton - to* Mrs.   Eliza Benton   , wife of   George Benton   on the  13  day of  July  , 1903; that there was born to her on said date a  Female  child; that said child was living March 4, 1905, and is said to have been named  Francis Benton

                                                         her
Witnesses To Mark:                  Eliza x Benton
   { George Benton                       mark
   { *(Name Illegible)*

Subscribed and sworn to before me this  6  day of   April   , 1905

                                          Sam T Roberts Jr
                                          Notary Public.

---

<u>Choc New Born 768</u>
      Nelson Bryant  b.  12-31-03

                                                          7-2159

                    Muskogee, Indian Territory, April 12, 1905.

Lillie Barton[sic],
      Talihina, Indian Territory.

Dear Madam:

      Receipt is hereby acknowledged of the affidavits of Lillie Benton and Harrison Hitcher to the birth of Nelson Bryant son of Raymond Bryant and Lillie Benton, December 31, 1903, and the same have been filed with our records as an application for the enrollment of said child.

                                Respectfully,

                                                  Commissioner in Charge.

# Applications for Enrollment of Choctaw Newborn
## Act of 1905    Volume XI

7-NB-768.

Muskogee, Indian Territory, May 29, 1905.

Lillie Benton,
    Talihina, Indian Territory.

Dear Madam:

    Refering to the application for the enrollment of your infant child, Nelson Benton, born December 31, 1903, it appears from the affidavits heretofore filed in this office that the applicant is dead.

    If this is correct you will please execute the enclosed proof of death and return it to this office, in order that this fact may be made a matter of record.

    In having these affidavits executed care should be exercised to see that all names are written in full, as they appear in the body of the affidavit, and in the event that either of the persons signing the affidavit are unable to write, signatures by mark must be attested by two witnesses. Each affidavit must be executed before a Notary Public and the notarial seal and signature of the officer must be attached to each separate affidavit.

                Respectfully,

Enclose D-C.                                                 Chairman.

---

7 NB 768

Muskogee, Indian Territory, July 1, 1905.

Lillie Benton Bryant,
    Care of John J. Thomas,
        Talihina, Indian Territory.

Dear Madam:

    Receipt is hereby acknowledged of your letter of June 24, 1905, stating that if further evidence is necessary to show that your child Nelson Bryant is still living you will forward the same.

    In reply to your letter you are advised that it is not believed further evidence will be necessary in the matter of the application for the enrollment of Nelson Bryant but it additional evidence is required you will be duly notified.

                  Respectfully,

                                            Commissioner.

## Applications for Enrollment of Choctaw Newborn
## Act of 1905  Volume XI

*(The letter below typed as given.)*

Talihina, I. T.<br>June 12, 1905.

The Commission to the Five Civilized Tribes,
          Muscogee, Ind Ter

Gentlemen:

    I have received your letter of May 29 7-NB-768 from which it appears that my application for enrollment of my child Nelson Benton shows that child is dead, if the birth proof shows he is dead it is an error, as the child Nelson Benton is now liveing and was liveing March 4, 1905  Hopeing this will correct the error I remain

Yours truly<br>Lillie Benton

Witness
Dan Bryant
  Interpreter.

---

7 NB 768

Muskogee, Indian Territory, June 16, 1905.

Lillie Benton,
    Talihina, Indian Territory.

Dear Madam:

    Receipt is hereby acknowledged of your letter of June 12, 1905, in which you state that if the application for the enrollment of your child Nelson Benton shows that this child is dead it is an error as he was living March 4, 1905 and is now living.

    This information has been made a matter of record.

Respectfully,<br><br>Chairman.

# Applications for Enrollment of Choctaw Newborn
## Act of 1905   Volume XI

**BIRTH AFFIDAVIT.**

**DEPARTMENT OF THE INTERIOR.**
## COMMISSION TO THE FIVE CIVILIZED TRIBES.

IN RE APPLICATION FOR ENROLLMENT, as a citizen of the Choctaw Nation, of Nelson Bryant, born on the 31 day of December, 1903

Name of Father: Raymond Bryant  a citizen of the Choctaw Nation.
Name of Mother: Lillie Benton  a citizen of the Choctaw Nation.

Postoffice   Talihina I.T.

Interpreter Harriet Bohannon

**AFFIDAVIT OF MOTHER.**

UNITED STATES OF AMERICA, Indian Territory,
Central  DISTRICT.

I, Lillie Benton, on oath state that I am 19 years of age and a citizen by Blood, of the Choctaw Nation; that I ~~am~~ *was* the lawful wife of Raymon Bryant *and from whom I was divorced*, who is a citizen, by Blood of the Choctaw Nation; that a male child was born to me on 31 day of December, 1903, that said child has been named Nelson Bryant, and ~~is now living~~. *was living March 4, 1905*

Lillie Benton

Witnesses To Mark:

Subscribed and sworn to before me this 6 day of April, 1905

My commission expires Feb. 4, 1908
Commission from U.S. Court at So. McAlester I.T.
MY OFFICE TALIHINA, I. T.

Sam T. Roberts Jr
Notary Public.

**AFFIDAVIT OF ATTENDING PHYSICIAN OR MID-WIFE.**

UNITED STATES OF AMERICA, Indian Territory,
Central  DISTRICT.

I, Harrison Hitcher, a ———, on oath state that I attended on Mrs. Lillie Benton, wife of Raymond Bryant on the 31 day of December, 1903; that there was born to her on said date a Male child; that said child ~~is now~~ *was living March 4, 1905* living and is said to have been named Nelson Bryant

his
Harrison x Hitcher
mark

## Applications for Enrollment of Choctaw Newborn
## Act of 1905  Volume XI

Witnesses To Mark:
{ D Thomas
  Jno J Thomas

Subscribed and sworn to before me this  6  day of  April   , 1905.

                        Sam T Roberts Jr
                          Notary Public.

---

<u>Choc New Born 769</u>
    Adeline Hitcher   b.  11-1-02

                          7-2128

            Muskogee, Indian Territory, April 12, 1905.

Harrison Hitcher,
    Talihina, Indian Territory.

Dear Sir:

    Receipt is hereby acknowledged of the affidavits of Catherine Hitcher and Harrison Hitcher to the birth of Adeline Hitcher, daughter of Harrison and Catherine Hitcher, November 1, 1902, and the same have been filed with our records as an application for the enrollment of said child.

                      Respectfully,
                          T.B. Needles
                        Commissioner in Charge.

---

7-NB-768

            Muskogee, Indian Territory, July 29, 1905.

Harrison Hitcher,
    Talihina, Indian Territory.

Dear Sir:

    There is inclosed you herewith for execution application for the enrollment of your infant child, Adeline Hitcher.

## Applications for Enrollment of Choctaw Newborn
## Act of 1905   Volume XI

In the affidavits heretofore filed in this case, the date of birth of the applicant appears in the affidavit of the mother and father as November 1, 1902, while in the affidavits of Wallace Beames and Austin Billy, executed July 1, 1905, the date is given as November 1, 1903.

In the inclosed application the date of birth is left blank. Please insert the correct date, and when properly executed return to this office.

This matter should receive your immediate attention as no further action can be taken relative to the enrollment of your said child until the evidence requested is supplied.

        Respectfully,
        Tams Bixby
LM 1/29        Commissioner.

---

7 N B 769

        Muskogee, Indian Territory, August 14, 1905.

John J. Thomas,
  Talihina, Indian Territory.

Dear Sir:

Receipt is hereby acknowledged of your letter of August 11, transmitting affidavits of Catherin Hitcher and Wallace Beams and Austin Billy, to the birth of Adeline Hitcher, daughter of Harrison and Catherin Hitcher, November , 1903, and the same have been filed with the record in the matter of the enrollment of said child.

        Respectfully,
        Tams Bixby
        Acting Commissioner.

---

**BIRTH AFFIDAVIT.**

**DEPARTMENT OF THE INTERIOR.**
**COMMISSION TO THE FIVE CIVILIZED TRIBES.**

---

**IN RE APPLICATION FOR ENROLLMENT,** as a citizen of the  Choctaw  Nation, of Adeline Hitcher , born on the 1 day of November , 1902

Name of Father: Harrison Hitcher  a citizen of the Choctaw Nation.
Name of Mother: Catherine Hitcher  a citizen of the Choctaw Nation.

        Postoffice Talihina I.T.

# Applications for Enrollment of Choctaw Newborn
## Act of 1905   Volume XI

*Geo Benton Interpreter*

### AFFIDAVIT OF MOTHER.

UNITED STATES OF AMERICA, Indian Territory, }
Central                DISTRICT.

I,   Catherine Hitcher   , on oath state that I am   28   years of age and a citizen by   Blood   , of the   Choctaw   Nation; that I am the lawful wife of Harrison Hitcher   , who is a citizen, by Blood   of the   Choctaw   Nation; that a   Female   child was born to me on   1st day of   November   , 1902; that said child has been named   Adeline Hitcher   , and was living March 4, 1905.

                                     her
Witnesses To Mark:       Catherine x Hitcher
  { Jno J Thomas                   mark
  { George Benton

Subscribed and sworn to before me this   6 day of   April   , 1905

My commission expires Feb. 4, 1908
Commission from U.S. Court at So. McAlester I.T.      Sam T. Roberts Jr
MY OFFICE TALIHINA, I. T.                    Notary Public.

### AFFIDAVIT OF ATTENDING PHYSICIAN OR MID-WIFE.

UNITED STATES OF AMERICA, Indian Territory, }
Central                DISTRICT.

I,   Harrison Hitcher   , a   ———   , on oath state that I attended on Mrs.   Catherine Hitcher   , wife of   my wife   on the 1st day of November , 1902; that there was born to her on said date a   Female   child; that said child was living March 4, 1905, and is said to have been named   Adeline Hitcher

                                    his
Witnesses To Mark:       Harrison x Hitcher
  { Jno J Thomas                 mark
  { George Benton

Subscribed and sworn to before me this   6   day of   April   , 1905

                          Sam T Roberts Jr
                          Notary Public.

# Applications for Enrollment of Choctaw Newborn
## Act of 1905  Volume XI

*(The affidavit below typed as given.)*

United States of America,　　　　　Affidavit, in the matter of in-
Indian Territory,　　　　　　　　　rolement, of Adeline Hitcher, infant
Central District,　　　　　　　　　child of Harrison & Catherine Hitcher
　　　　　　　　　　　　　　　　　Choctaws by blood.

I, Wallace Beams, on oath state that I am 37 years of age, my post office is Talihina Indian Territory. That I am a citizen of the Choctaw Tribe of Indians by blood. That I know Harrison Hitcher, also his wife Catherine Hitcher and know them to be citizens of the Choctaw Nation by blood. I know that on the 1st day of November 1903, there was born to Catherine Hitcher a female child, that it is said to have been named Adeline Hitcher. That the said child was living on the 4th day of March, 1905, and is still living.
I am in no way related to any of the above named parties, and am not an interested party.

Witnessed by,　　　　　　　　　　Wallace Beams
George Benton

Subscribed and sworn to before me this the 1st day of July 1905.

My com expires　　　　　　　　　F.B. Lunsford
Feb. 4 1908　　　　　　　　　　　Notary Public.

---

*(The affidavit below typed as given.)*

United States of America,　　　　　Affidavit, in the matter of in-
Indian Territory,　　　　　　　　　rolement, of Adeline Hitcher, infant
Central District,　　　　　　　　　child of Harrison & Catherine Hitcher
　　　　　　　　　　　　　　　　　Choctaws by blood.

I, Austin Billy, on oath state that I am 30 years of age, my post office is Talihina Indian Territory. That I am a citizen of the Choctaw Tribe of Indians by blood. That I know Harrison Hitcher, also his wife Catherine Hitcher and know them to be citizens of the Choctaw Nation by blood. I know that on the 1st day of November 1903, there was born to Catherine Hitcher a female child, that it is said to have been named Adeline Hitcher. That the said child was living on the 4th day of March, 1905, and is still living.
I am in no way related to any of the above named parties, and am not an interested party.

Witnessed by,　　　　　　　　　　Austin Billy
George Benton

## Applications for Enrollment of Choctaw Newborn
## Act of 1905 Volume XI

Subscribed and sworn to before me this the 1st day of July 1905.

My com expires　　　　　　　　　F.B. Lunsford
Feb. 4 1908　　　　　　　　　　　　Notary Public.

---

**BIRTH AFFIDAVIT.**

### DEPARTMENT OF THE INTERIOR.
### COMMISSION TO THE FIVE CIVILIZED TRIBES.

---

　　IN RE APPLICATION FOR ENROLLMENT, as a citizen of the　　Choctaw　　Nation, of Adeline Hitcher　　, born on the　1st　day of　November　, 1903

Name of Father: Harrison Hitcher　　　　a citizen of the　Choctaw　Nation.
Name of Mother: Cathrine[sic] Hitcher　　a citizen of the　Choctaw　Nation.

　　　　　　　　　Postoffice　　Talihina, I.T.

---

**AFFIDAVIT OF MOTHER.**

UNITED STATES OF AMERICA, Indian Territory, }
　　Central　　　　　　　DISTRICT. }

　　I,　Cathrine Hitcher　, on oath state that I am　28　years of age and a citizen by　blood　, of the　Choctaw　Nation; that I am the lawful wife of　Harrison Hitcher　, who is a citizen, by　blood　of the　Choctaw　Nation; that a girl　child was born to me on　1st　day of　November　1903　, 1............; that said child has been named　Adeline Hitcher　, and was living March 4, 1905.

　　　　　　　　　　　　　　　　　her
　　　　　　　　　　　　　　Cathrine x Hitcher
Witnesses To Mark:　　　　　　　mark
　{ George Benton
　　Austin Billy

　　Subscribed and sworn to before me this　1$^{st}$　day of　July　, 1905

My Com expires　　　　　　　　　F.B. Lunsford
Feb. 4, 1908　　　　　　　　　　　Notary Public.

## Applications for Enrollment of Choctaw Newborn
## Act of 1905   Volume XI

**AFFIDAVIT OF ATTENDING PHYSICIAN OR MID-WIFE.**

UNITED STATES OF AMERICA, Indian Territory, }
Central             DISTRICT.

I, Harrison Hitcher, husband of Cathrine Hitcher, on oath state that I attended on Mrs. Catherine Hitcher, wife of Harrison Hitcher on the 1st day of November 1903, 1......; that there was born to her on said date a female child; that said child was living March 4, 1905, and is said to have been named Adeline Hitcher

                                                her
                                       Harrison x Hitcher
Witnesses To Mark:                    mark
   { George Benton
     Austin Billy

Subscribed and sworn to before me this 1$^{st}$ day of July, 1905

My Com expires                   F.B. Lunsford
Feb. 4, 1908                          Notary Public.

---

BIRTH AFFIDAVIT.    7 n B 769

**DEPARTMENT OF THE INTERIOR.**
**COMMISSION TO THE FIVE CIVILIZED TRIBES.**

---

IN RE APPLICATION FOR ENROLLMENT, as a citizen of the Choctaw Nation, of Adeline Hitcher, born on the 1st day of November, 1903

Name of Father: Harrison Hitcher      a citizen of the Choctaw Nation.
Name of Mother: Catherine Hitcher    a citizen of the Choctaw Nation.

                              Postoffice    Talihina Ind Ter

---

**AFFIDAVIT OF MOTHER.**

UNITED STATES OF AMERICA, Indian Territory, }
Central             DISTRICT.

I, Catherine Hitcher, on oath state that I am 28 years of age and a citizen by blood, of the Choctaw Nation; that I am the lawful wife of Harrison Hitcher, who is a citizen, by blood of the Choctaw Nation; that a female child was born to me on 1$^{st}$ day of November, 1903; that said child has been named Adeline Hitcher, and was living March 4, 1905.

## Applications for Enrollment of Choctaw Newborn
## Act of 1905 Volume XI

                                her
                        Catherine x Hitcher
                              mark

Witnesses To Mark:
  { J M Stevens
    Willard N Everett

    Subscribed and sworn to before me this  10$^{th}$  day of  Aug    , 1905

My Com exp Mch 30/09            Jno J Thomas
                                    Notary Public.

---

**AFFIDAVIT OF ATTENDING PHYSICIAN OR MID-WIFE.**

UNITED STATES OF AMERICA, Indian Territory, }
    Central                DISTRICT.}

                                                      *we are acquainted with*
    We    Wallace Beames and Austin Billy  , on oath state that ~~I attended on~~
Mrs.  Catherine Hitcher  , wife of  Harrison Hitcher  *and that* on  *or about* the  1$^{st}$
day of  Nov  ,1903; that there was born to her on said date a  female  child; that
said child was living March 4, 1905, and is said to have been named  Adeline Hitcher
*that we are not related to the applicant, nor in any manner* (illegible) *in said case*

                                  Wallace Beames
Witnesses To Mark:               Austin Billy
  {

    Subscribed and sworn to before me this  10$^{th}$  day of  Aug    , 1905

My Com exp Mch 30/09            Jno J Thomas
                                    Notary Public.

---

<u>Choc New Born 770</u>
      William M. Dilbeck  b. 5-2-03
      John L. Dilbeck, Jr.  b.  2-24-05

## Applications for Enrollment of Choctaw Newborn
## Act of 1905   Volume XI

## AFFIDAVIT OF ATTENDING PHYSICIAN OR MIDWIFE

UNITED STATES OF AMERICA
INDIAN TERRITORY
_____ DISTRICT

    I,   Mrs. E.J. Barnett   a   Mid Wife
on oath state that I attended on Mrs.   Alvrado[sic] Dilbeck   wife of   J L Dilbeck
on the  24   day of   February   , 190 5 , that there was born to her on said date a   male
child, that said child is now living, and is said to have been named   John F[sic] Dilbeck Jr

                                              Mid Wife        *M.D.*

        Subscribed and sworn to before me this, the   7th   day of
        March   190 5

WITNESSETH:                              Josh Clardy   Notary Public.
Must be two witnesses { Adam Ward
who are citizens          James Barnett

    We hereby certify that we are well acquainted with   Alvarada[sic] Dilbeck
a   Choctaw By Blood   and know _____ to be reputable and of good standing in the community.

    Jackson D Barnett

    Mary Ward

**NEW-BORN AFFIDAVIT.**

    Number..............

**...Choctaw Enrolling Commission...**

    IN THE MATTER OF THE APPLICATION FOR ENROLLMENT, as a citizen of the Choctaw   Nation, of   John L. Dilbeck Jr

born on the  24   day of   Feb   190 5

Name of father   J. L. Dilbeck          a citizen of    ~~United States~~
Nation final enrollment No. ——
Name of mother  Alvarado Dilbeck    a citizen of    Choctaw
Nation final enrollment No. 12353

                                              Postoffice   Womack I.T.

# Applications for Enrollment of Choctaw Newborn
## Act of 1905   Volume XI

### AFFIDAVIT OF MOTHER.

UNITED STATES OF AMERICA
INDIAN TERRITORY
_____ DISTRICT

    I   Alvarado Dilbeck   , on oath state that I am   34   years of age and a citizen by   blood   of the   Choctaw   Nation, and as such have been placed upon the final roll of the   Choctaw   Nation, by the Honorable Secretary of the Interior my final enrollment number being   12353   ; that I am the lawful wife of   J.L. Dilbeck   , who is a citizen of the   United States   ~~Nation~~, and as such has been placed upon the final roll of said Nation by the Honorable Secretary of the Interior, his final enrollment number being _____ and that a   Male   child was born to me on the   24   day of   Feb   190 5; that said child has been named   John L Dilbeck Jr   , and is now living.

Witnesseth.

Must be two Witnesses who are Citizens. } Mrs Mary Ward
                      Adam Ward

    Subscribed and sworn to before me this   4   day of   Mch   190 5

                                                   Josh Clardy
                                                           Notary Public.

My commission expires:   March 1$^{st}$ 1908

---

UNITED STATES OF AMERICA,
INDIAN TERRITORY,
SOUTHERN DISTRICT.

    Chris Wall, being duly sworn, states on oath that he is acquainted with John L. Dilbeck and Alvaredo[sic] Dilbeck; that a male child was born to them on the 2nd day of May 1905[sic]; that said child has been named William M. Dilbeck, and was living on the 4th day of March 1905, affiant further states that he is not related to the said John L. and Alvaredo Dilbeck either by blood or by marriage.

                                                                          Chris Wall

Subscribed and sworn to before me this   27 day of June 1905.

        My Commission Expires Jan. 30, 1907.                    J.C. Little
                                                                              Notary Public.

## Applications for Enrollment of Choctaw Newborn
## Act of 1905   Volume XI

UNITED STATES OF AMERICA,
INDIAN TERRITORY,
SOUTHERN DISTRICT.

John D. Edens, being duly sworn, states on oath that he is acquainted with John L. Dilbeck and Alvaredo[sic] Dilbeck; that a male child was born to them on the 2nd day of May 1903; that said child has been named William M. Dilbeck, and is still living, affiant further states that he is not related to the said John L. and Alvaredo Dilbeck either by blood or by marriage.

John D. Edens

Subscribed and sworn to before me this   27   day of June 1905.

My Commission Expires Jan. 30, 1907.                    J.C. Little
                                                        Notary Public.

---

**BIRTH AFFIDAVIT.**

### DEPARTMENT OF THE INTERIOR.
### COMMISSION TO THE FIVE CIVILIZED TRIBES.

---

**IN RE APPLICATION FOR ENROLLMENT,** as a citizen of the   Choctaw   Nation, of John L Dilbeck Jr   , born on the   24   day of   Feb   , 1905

Name of Father: J L Dilbeck            a citizen of the United States Nation.
Name of Mother: Alvarado Dilbeck       a citizen of the   Choctaw   Nation.

Postoffice   Womack Ind Ter

---

### AFFIDAVIT OF MOTHER.

UNITED STATES OF AMERICA, Indian Territory,
   Southern           DISTRICT.

I,   Alvarado Dilbeck   , on oath state that I am   34   years of age and a citizen by   blood   , of the   Choctaw   Nation; that I am the lawful wife of   J L Dilbeck   , who is a citizen, by   of the United States   Nation; that a   male   child was born to me on   24   day of   February   , 1905; that said child has been named John L Dilbeck   , and was living March 4, 1905.

Alvarado Dilbeck

Witnesses To Mark:

## Applications for Enrollment of Choctaw Newborn
## Act of 1905   Volume XI

Subscribed and sworn to before me this 4th day of April, 1905

Josh Clardy
Notary Public.

---

### AFFIDAVIT OF ATTENDING PHYSICIAN OR MID-WIFE.

UNITED STATES OF AMERICA, Indian Territory, }
Southern      DISTRICT.

I, E J Barnett, a mid wife, on oath state that I attended on Mrs. Alvarado Dilbeck, wife of J L Dilbeck on the 24 day of February, 1905; that there was born to her on said date a male child; that said child was living March 4, 1905, and is said to have been named John L Dilbeck Jr

E J Barntt[sic]

Witnesses To Mark:
{

Subscribed and sworn to before me this 4th day of April, 1905

Josh Clardy
Notary Public.

---

BIRTH AFFIDAVIT.

### DEPARTMENT OF THE INTERIOR.
### COMMISSION TO THE FIVE CIVILIZED TRIBES.

IN RE APPLICATION FOR ENROLLMENT, as a citizen of the Choctaw Nation, of William M Dilbeck, born on the 2 day of May, 1903

Name of Father: John L Dilbeck   a citizen of the United States Nation.
Name of Mother: Alvarado Dilbeck   a citizen of the Choctaw Nation.

Postoffice   Womack Ind Ter

---

### AFFIDAVIT OF MOTHER.

UNITED STATES OF AMERICA, Indian Territory, }
Southern      DISTRICT.

I, Alvarado Dilbeck, on oath state that I am 34 years of age and a citizen by blood, of the Choctaw Nation; that I am the lawful wife of John L Dilbeck, who is a citizen, by of the United States Nation; that a male

# Applications for Enrollment of Choctaw Newborn
## Act of 1905   Volume XI

child was born to me on  2   day of   May    , 1903; that said child has been named William M Dilbeck   , and was living March 4, 1905.

Alvarado Dilbeck

Witnesses To Mark:
{

Subscribed and sworn to before me this 4$^{th}$  day of   April   , 1905

Josh Clardy<br>Notary Public.

---

**AFFIDAVIT OF ATTENDING PHYSICIAN OR MID-WIFE.**

UNITED STATES OF AMERICA, Indian Territory, }
Southern            DISTRICT. }

I,   Delila Wall   , a   Mid-wife   , on oath state that I attended on Mrs.  Alvarado Dilbeck  , wife of  John L Dilbeck   on the 2  day of May , 1903; that there was born to her on said date a     male     child; that said child was living March 4, 1905, and is said to have been named William M Dilbeck

Delila Wall

Witnesses To Mark:
{

Subscribed and sworn to before me this  31   day of    March     , 1905

My Commission Expires Jan. 30, 1907.          J.C. Little
Notary Public.

---

*Duplicate*<br>7-NB-770.

Muskogee, Indian Territory, June 6, 1905.

John L. Dilbeck,
   Womack, Indian Territory.

Dear Sir:

Referring to the application for the enrollment of your infant children, William M. Dilbeck and John L. Dilbeck, Jr., born May 2, 1903, and February 24, 1905, respectively, it is noted that applications for both of these children were filed in this office on April 14,

## Applications for Enrollment of Choctaw Newborn
## Act of 1905   Volume XI

1905, while the application made to the Choctaw Commission was for John L. Dilbeck, Jr., only.

Before the matter of the enrollment of William M. Dilbeck, can be finally determined it will be necessary for you to file in this office the affidavits of two persons, who are disinterested and not related to the applicant, who have actual knowledge of the facts that the child was born, the date of his birth; that he was living on March 4, 1905, and that Alvarado Dilbeck is his mother.

Respectfully,

Commissioner in Charge.

7 NB 770

Muskogee, Indian Territory, June 30, 1905.

J. L. Dilbeck,
Womack, Indian Territory.

Dear Sir:

Receipt is hereby acknowledged of your letter of June 27, 1905, transmitting affidavits of Chris Wall and John D. Edens to the birth of William M. Dilbeck, son of John L. and Alvaredo[sic] Dilbeck, May 2, 1903, and the same have been filed with our records in the matter of the enrollment of said child. matter of the enrollment of said child.

Respectfully,

Chairman.

---

Choc New Born 771
    Maude Marine Jones   b. 2-13-04

## Applications for Enrollment of Choctaw Newborn
## Act of 1905   Volume XI

7-NB-771.

Muskogee, Indian Territory, May 31, 1905.

J. J. Jones,
    Chickasha, Indian Territory.

Dear Sir:

    Referring to the application for the enrollment of your infant child, Maude Marine Jones, born February 13, 1904, it is noted that the Notary Public omitted his seal from the affidavits heretofore filed in this office. It will, therefore, be necessary for you to have the enclosed affidavits executed and return them promptly to this office.

    In having these affidavits executed care should be exercised to see that all names are written in full, as they appear in the body of the affidavit, and in the event that either of the persons signing the affidavit are unable to write, signatures by mark must be attested by two witnesses. Each affidavit must be executed before a Notary Public and the notarial seal and signature of the officer must be attached to each separate affidavit.

    Respectfully,

    Chairman.

VR 31-4.

---

7 NB 771

Muskogee, Indian Territory, July 1, 1905.

J. J. Jones,
    Chickasha, Indian Territory.

Dear Sir:

    Receipt is hereby acknowledged of the affidavits of Mary Ellen Jones and E. L. Dawson to the birth of Maude Marine Jones, daughter of J. J. and Mary Ellen Jones, February 13, 1904, and the same have been filed with our records in the matter of the enrollment of said child.

    Respectfully,

    Commissioner.

Applications for Enrollment of Choctaw Newborn
Act of 1905   Volume XI

BIRTH AFFIDAVIT.

*DEPARTMENT OF THE INTERIOR.*
## COMMISSION TO THE FIVE CIVILIZED TRIBES.

IN RE APPLICATION FOR ENROLLMENT, as a citizen of the   Choctaw   Nation of   Maude Marine Jones   , born on the   13$^{th}$   day of   Feb   , 1904

Name of Father:   J. J. Jones        a citizen of the   United States   Nation.
Name of Mother:   Mary Ellen Jones   a citizen of the   Choctaw        Nation.

Postoffice   Chickasha, I.T.

### AFFIDAVIT OF MOTHER.

UNITED STATES OF AMERICA, INDIAN TERRITORY, }
Southern                DISTRICT.          }

I,   Mary Ellen Jones   , on oath state that I am   25   years of age and a citizen by ~~Choctaw~~   Blood   , of the   Choctaw   Nation; that I am the lawful wife of   J. J. Jones   , who is a citizen, ~~by~~ ........ of the   United States   Nation; that a   Female   child was born to me on   13   day of   Feby   , 1904, that said child has been named   Maude Marine Jones   , and is now living.

Mary Ellen Jones

WITNESSES TO MARK:
{

Subscribed and sworn to before me this   3d   day of   April   , 1905.

Ado Melton
Notary Public.

### AFFIDAVIT OF ATTENDING PHYSICIAN OR MID-WIFE.

UNITED STATES OF AMERICA, INDIAN TERRITORY, }
Southern                DISTRICT.          }

I,   E.L. Dawson   , a   Physician   , on oath state that I attended on Mrs.   Mary Ellen Jones   , wife of   J J Jones   on the   13$^{th}$   day of   Feby   , 190 4; that there was born to her on said date a   Female   child; that said child is now living and is said to have been named   Maude Marine Jones

E. L. Dawson M.D.

# Applications for Enrollment of Choctaw Newborn
## Act of 1905 Volume XI

WITNESSES TO MARK:

Subscribed and sworn to before me this 3ᵈ day of April , 1905.

Ado Melton
Notary Public.

**BIRTH AFFIDAVIT.**

## DEPARTMENT OF THE INTERIOR.
## COMMISSION TO THE FIVE CIVILIZED TRIBES.

IN RE APPLICATION FOR ENROLLMENT, as a citizen of the Choctaw Nation, of Maude Marine Jones , born on the 13 day of Feb , 1904

Name of Father: J.J. Jones  a citizen of the U. S. Nation.
Name of Mother: Mary Ellen Jones  a citizen of the Choctaw Nation.

Postoffice Chickasha Ind Ter

**AFFIDAVIT OF MOTHER.**

UNITED STATES OF AMERICA, Indian Territory,
Southern DISTRICT.

I, Mary Ellen Jones , on oath state that I am 23 years of age and a citizen by blood , of the Choctaw Nation; that I am the lawful wife of J.J. Jones , who is a citizen, ~~by~~ —— of the United States Nation; that a female child was born to me on 13 day of February , 1904; that said child has been named Maude Marine Jones , and was living March 4, 1905.

Mary Ellen Jones

Witnesses To Mark:

Subscribed and sworn to before me this 27 day of June , 1905

Ado Melton
Notary Public.

276

## Applications for Enrollment of Choctaw Newborn
## Act of 1905 Volume XI

### AFFIDAVIT OF ATTENDING PHYSICIAN OR MID-WIFE.

UNITED STATES OF AMERICA, Indian Territory, }
   Southern             DISTRICT.

    I, E.L. Dawson, a Physician, on oath state that I attended on Mrs. Mary Ellen Jones, wife of JJ Jones on the 13 day of February, 1904; that there was born to her on said date a female child; that said child was living March 4, 1905, and is said to have been named Maude Marine Jones

                                              E.L. Dawson M.D.

Witnesses To Mark:
{

    Subscribed and sworn to before me this 27 day of June, 1905

                                              Ado Melton
                                              Notary Public.

---

Choc New Born 772
    William J. P. Coleman b. 2-28-04

---

                                                      7-2493

                      Muskogee, Indian Territory, April 12, 1905.

Pinkney Coleman,
    Tomaha[sic], Indian Territory.

Dear Sir:

    Receipt is hereby acknowledged of the affidavits of Susie G. Coleman and A. T. Hill to the birth of William J. P. Coleman, son of Pinkney and Susie G. Coleman, February 28, 1904, and the same have been filed with our records as an application for the enrollment of said child.

                                    Respectfully,

                                                Commissioner in Charge.

## Applications for Enrollment of Choctaw Newborn
### Act of 1905 Volume XI

**NEW-BORN AFFIDAVIT.**

Number................

...Choctaw Enrolling Commission...

---

IN THE MATTER OF THE APPLICATION FOR ENROLLMENT, as a citizen of the Choctaw Nation, of William James Pinkney Coleman

born on the 28 day of __February__ 190 4

| | | |
|---|---|---|
| Name of father  P.A. Coleman | a citizen of | Intermarried |
| Nation final enrollment No. ——— | | |
| Name of mother  Susy G Coleman | a citizen of | Choctaw |
| Nation final enrollment No. 7234 | | |
| | Postoffice | Tamaha I.T. |

**AFFIDAVIT OF MOTHER.**

UNITED STATES OF AMERICA
INDIAN TERRITORY
Central     DISTRICT

I     Susy G Coleman     , on oath state that I am 31 years of age and a citizen by Blood of the Choctaw Nation, and as such have been placed upon the final roll of the Choctaw Nation, by the Honorable Secretary of the Interior my final enrollment number being 7234 ; that I am the lawful wife of P.A. Coleman , who is a citizen of the Choctaw Nation, and as such has been placed upon the final roll of said Nation by the Honorable Secretary of the Interior, his final enrollment number being ——— and that a Male child was born to me on the 28 day of February 190 4; that said child has been named William James Pinkney Coleman , and is now living.

Susie Coleman

Witnesseth.

Must be two Witnesses who are Citizens.   }   George L Wadley
Sam Fortner

Subscribed and sworn to before me this 4 day of Jany 190 5

W$^m$ B. Davidson
Notary Public.

My commission expires:
11/May/1907

## Applications for Enrollment of Choctaw Newborn
### Act of 1905   Volume XI

## AFFIDAVIT OF ATTENDING PHYSICIAN OR MIDWIFE

UNITED STATES OF AMERICA
INDIAN TERRITORY
   Central     DISTRICT

I, A. T. Hill a Physician on oath state that I attended on Mrs. Susie G Coleman wife of P.A. Coleman on the 28 day of February, 190 4, that there was born to her on said date a male child, that said child is now living, and is said to have been named William James Pinkney Coleman

                                            A.T. Hill MD

Subscribed and sworn to before me this, the 4 day of January 190 5

WITNESSETH:                               W$^m$ B. Davidson    Notary Public.

Must be two witnesses who are citizens { Sam Fortner

                       George L Wadley

We hereby certify that we are well acquainted with A.T. Hill a Physician and know him to be reputable and of good standing in the community.

    *(Name Illegible)*                           Sam Fortner

    *(Name Illegible)*                           George L Wadley

BIRTH AFFIDAVIT.

### DEPARTMENT OF THE INTERIOR.
### COMMISSION TO THE FIVE CIVILIZED TRIBES.

IN RE APPLICATION FOR ENROLLMENT, as a citizen of the Choctaw Nation, of William J. P. Coleman, born on the 28 day of February, 1904

Name of Father: Pinkney Coleman    a citizen of the United States Nation.
Name of Mother: Susie G. Coleman    a citizen of the Choctaw Nation.

                      Postoffice    Tamaha Ind Ter

## Applications for Enrollment of Choctaw Newborn
## Act of 1905   Volume XI

### AFFIDAVIT OF MOTHER.

UNITED STATES OF AMERICA, Indian Territory, }
Central            DISTRICT.

    I, Susie G. Coleman, on oath state that I am 31 years of age and a citizen by blood, of the Choctaw Nation; that I am the lawful wife of Pinkney Coleman, who is a citizen, by —— of the United States Nation; that a male child was born to me on 28 day of February, 1904; that said child has been named William J. P. Coleman, and was living March 4, 1905.

                                Susie G Coleman

Witnesses To Mark:
{

    Subscribed and sworn to before me this 3 day of April, 1905

                                OL Johnson
                                Notary Public.

### AFFIDAVIT OF ATTENDING PHYSICIAN OR MID-WIFE.

UNITED STATES OF AMERICA, Indian Territory, }
Central            DISTRICT.

    I, A. T. Hill, a physician, on oath state that I attended on Mrs. Susie G. Coleman, wife of Pinkney G[sic] Coleman on the 28 day of February, 1904; that there was born to her on said date a male child; that said child was living March 4, 1905, and is said to have been named William J.P. Coleman

                                A.T. Hill, MD

Witnesses To Mark:
{

    Subscribed and sworn to before me this 6 day of April, 1905

My Commission                 W$^{m}$ B. Davidson
Expires 11$^{th}$ May 1907            Notary Public.

## Applications for Enrollment of Choctaw Newborn
## Act of 1905   Volume XI

Choc New Born 773
    James Arthur Adams   b. 5-9-03

---

7-2699

Muskogee, Indian Territory, April 12, 1905.

Jason Adams,
    Chant City, Indian Territory.

Dear Sir:

    Receipt is hereby acknowledged of the affidavits of Margaret Adams and Missouri Allen to the birth of James Arthur Adams, son of Jason and Margret[sic] Adams, May 9, 1903, and the same have been filed with our records as an application for the enrollment of said child.

                              Respectfully,

                                Commissioner in Charge.

---

**BIRTH AFFIDAVIT.**

### DEPARTMENT OF THE INTERIOR.
### COMMISSION TO THE FIVE CIVILIZED TRIBES.

    **IN RE APPLICATION FOR ENROLLMENT,** as a citizen of the   Choctaw   Nation, of James Arthur Adams   , born on the   9th   day of   May   , 1903

Name of Father:  Jason Adams            a citizen of the United States Nation.
Name of Mother: Margaret Adams       a citizen of the   Choctaw   Nation.

                    Postoffice   Chant City Ind. Ter.

**AFFIDAVIT OF MOTHER.**

UNITED STATES OF AMERICA, Indian Territory, }
    Central                 DISTRICT. }

    I,   Margaret Adams   , on oath state that I am   24   years of age and a citizen by   blood   , of the   Choctaw   Nation; that I am the lawful wife of   Jason Adams   , who is a citizen, X................ of the   United States   Nation; that a   male   child was born to me on   9th   day of   May   , 1903; that said child has been named   James Arthur Adams   , and was living March 4, 1905.

                              Margaret Adams

## Applications for Enrollment of Choctaw Newborn
## Act of 1905   Volume XI

Witnesses To Mark:

{

Subscribed and sworn to before me this 5th day of April, 1905

OL Johnson
Notary Public.

---

**AFFIDAVIT OF ATTENDING PHYSICIAN OR MID-WIFE.**

UNITED STATES OF AMERICA, Indian Territory,
Central                    DISTRICT.

I, Missouri Allen, a midwife, on oath state that I attended on Mrs. Margaret Adams, wife of Jason Adams on the 9th day of May, 1903; that there was born to her on said date a male child; that said child was living March 4, 1905, and is said to have been named James Arthur Adams

                    her
           Missouri x Allen
Witnesses To Mark:     mark
{ Jas Friar
{ *(Name Illegible)*

Subscribed and sworn to before me this 7th day of April, 1905

Jas H Deets
Notary Public.

---

Choc New Born 774
    Dean McKinnon Wadley  b. 5-23-04

## Applications for Enrollment of Choctaw Newborn
## Act of 1905   Volume XI

7-2608

Muskogee, Indian Territory, April 11, 1905.

George L. Wadley,
    Tomaha[sic], Indian Territory.

Dear Sir:

    Receipt is hereby acknowledged of the affidavits of Beulah Wadley and Charles D. Dale to the birth of Dean McKennon[sic] Wadley, son of George L. and Beulah Wadley, May 23, 1904, and the same have been filed with our records as an application for the enrollment of said child.

        Respectfully,

        Commissioner in Charge.

**NEW-BORN AFFIDAVIT.**

Number _____

...Choctaw Enrolling Commission...

IN THE MATTER OF THE APPLICATION FOR ENROLLMENT, as a citizen of the Choctaw Nation, of Dean M$^c$Kinnon Wadley

born on the 23 day of __May__ 190 4

Name of father   George L Wadley      a citizen of   Choctaw
Nation final enrollment No. _____
Name of mother   Beulah Wadley      a citizen of   Choctaw
Nation final enrollment No. 7558

    Postoffice   Tamaha

**AFFIDAVIT OF MOTHER.**

UNITED STATES OF AMERICA
INDIAN TERRITORY
  Central     DISTRICT

    I   Beulah Wadley, on oath state that I am _____ years of age and a citizen by Blood of the Choctaw Nation, and as such have been placed upon the final roll of the Choctaw Nation, by the Honorable Secretary of the Interior my final enrollment number being ——; that I am the lawful wife of George L Wadley, who is a citizen of the Choctaw Nation, and as such has

# Applications for Enrollment of Choctaw Newborn
## Act of 1905   Volume XI

been placed upon the final roll of said Nation by the Honorable Secretary of the Interior, his final enrollment number being  ——  and that a   Male   child was born to me on the   23   day of   May     190 4; that said child has been named   Dean McKinnon Wadley   , and is now living.

Beulah Wadley

Witnesseth.

Must be two Witnesses who are Citizens.  } Sam Fortner
Susie Coleman

Subscribed and sworn to before me this   4   day of   Jany     190 5

W<sup>m</sup> B. Davidson<br>Notary Public.

My commission expires:
11<sup>th</sup> May 1907

## AFFIDAVIT OF ATTENDING PHYSICIAN OR MIDWIFE

UNITED STATES OF AMERICA
INDIAN TERRITORY
  Central     DISTRICT

I,   C.D. Dale   a   Physician on oath state that I attended on Mrs.   Beulah Wadley   wife of   George L Wadley   on the   23   day of   May   , 190 4 , that there was born to her on said date a   male   child, that said child is now living, and is said to have been named   Dean M<sup>c</sup>Kinnon Wadley

C.D. Dale M.D.

Subscribed and sworn to before me this, the            day of   January     190 5

WITNESSETH:                 W<sup>m</sup> B. Davidson    Notary Public.

Must be two witnesses who are citizens { Sam Fortner
Susie Coleman

We hereby certify that we are well acquainted with   C.D. Dale   a   Physician   and know   him   to be reputable and of good standing in the community.

(Name Illegible)                          Sam Fortner

Alec Burns                              Susie Coleman

# Applications for Enrollment of Choctaw Newborn
## Act of 1905   Volume XI

**BIRTH AFFIDAVIT.**

### DEPARTMENT OF THE INTERIOR.
### COMMISSION TO THE FIVE CIVILIZED TRIBES.

IN RE APPLICATION FOR ENROLLMENT, as a citizen of the     Choctaw     Nation, of Dean M$^c$Kinnon Wadley    , born on the    23 day of    May   , 1904

Name of Father: George L Wadley             a citizen of the Intermarriage Nation.
Name of Mother: Beulah Wadley             a citizen of the    Choctaw    Nation.

Postoffice    Tamaha Ind Ter

**AFFIDAVIT OF MOTHER.**

UNITED STATES OF AMERICA, Indian Territory, }
    Central             DISTRICT. }

I,    Beulah Wadley    , on oath state that I am    29    years of age and a citizen by    Blood   , of the    Choctaw    Nation; that I am the lawful wife of    George L Wadley    , who is a citizen, by    Intermarriage    of the ................................. Nation; that a    male    child was born to me on    23    day of    May    , 1904; that said child has been named    Dean M$^c$Kinnon Wadley    , and was living March 4, 1905.

Beulah Wadley

Witnesses To Mark:
{

Subscribed and sworn to before me this    7    day of    April    , 1905

W$^m$ B Davidson
Notary Public.

**AFFIDAVIT OF ATTENDING PHYSICIAN OR MID-WIFE.**

UNITED STATES OF AMERICA, Indian Territory, }
    Central             DISTRICT. }

I,    Charles D Dale    , a    Physician    , on oath state that I attended on Mrs.    Beulah Wadley    , wife of    George L Wadley    on the    23    day of    May   , 1904; that there was born to her on said date a    male    child; that said child was living March 4, 1905, and is said to have been named    Dean M$^c$Kinnon Wadley

Chas D Dale M.D.

Witnesses To Mark:
{

## Applications for Enrollment of Choctaw Newborn
## Act of 1905   Volume XI

Subscribed and sworn to before me this   7   day of     April     , 1905

W<sup>m</sup> B Davidson
Notary Public.

---

Choc New Born 775
    Perry Roberts   b. 9-29-03
    Irene Exodus Roberts   b. 1-31-05

7-3457

Muskogee, Indian Territory, April 12, 1905.

J. B[sic]. Roberts,
    Russellville, Indian Territory.

Dear Sir:

    Receipt is hereby acknowledged of the affidavits of Lillie M. Roberts and J. M. Turner to the birth of Irene Exodus Roberts, daughter of J. G. and Lillie M. Roberts, January 31, 1905; also affidavits of Lillie M. Roberts and A. B. Strange to the birth of Perry Roberts, son of J. G. and Lillie M. Roberts, September 29, 1903, and the same have been filed with our records as an application for the enrollment of said child.

Respectfully,

Commissioner in Charge.

**BIRTH AFFIDAVIT.**

**DEPARTMENT OF THE INTERIOR.**
**COMMISSION TO THE FIVE CIVILIZED TRIBES.**

**IN RE APPLICATION FOR ENROLLMENT,** as a citizen of the     Choctaw     Nation, of  Perry Roberts     , born on the 29th   day of   September   , 1903

Name of Father: J. G. Roberts                    a citizen of the   -------------   Nation.
Name of Mother: Lillie M. Roberts, nee Guess    a citizen of the   Choctaw   Nation.

Postoffice   Russellville, Indian Territory.

# Applications for Enrollment of Choctaw Newborn
## Act of 1905   Volume XI

**AFFIDAVIT OF MOTHER.**

UNITED STATES OF AMERICA, Indian Territory,  
Western DISTRICT.

I, Lillie M. Roberts, nee Guess, on oath state that I am 21 years of age and a citizen by blood, of the Choctaw Nation; that I am the lawful wife of J. G. Roberts, who is a citizen, by -------- of the ---------------- Nation; that a Male child was born to me on 29th day of September, 1903; that said child has been named Perry Roberts, and was living March 4, 1905.

Lillie M. Roberts

Witnesses To Mark:

Subscribed and sworn to before me this 3rd day of April, 1905

Guy A. Curry<br>Notary Public.

---

**AFFIDAVIT OF ATTENDING PHYSICIAN OR MID-WIFE.**

UNITED STATES OF AMERICA, Indian Territory,  
Western DISTRICT.

I, A. B. Strange, a Physician, on oath state that I attended on Mrs. Lillie M. Roberts, nee Guess, wife of J. G. Roberts on the 29th day of September, 1903; that there was born to her on said date a Male child; that said child was living March 4, 1905, and is said to have been named Perry Roberts

A.B. Strange M.D.

Witnesses To Mark:

Subscribed and sworn to before me this 5$^{th}$ day of April, 1905

J.D. Ward<br>Notary Public.<br>Central Dist

# Applications for Enrollment of Choctaw Newborn
## Act of 1905   Volume XI

**BIRTH AFFIDAVIT.**

## DEPARTMENT OF THE INTERIOR.
## COMMISSION TO THE FIVE CIVILIZED TRIBES.

IN RE APPLICATION FOR ENROLLMENT, as a citizen of the Choctaw Nation, of Irene Exodus Roberts, born on the 31st day of January, 1905

Name of Father: J. G. Roberts       a citizen of the ------------- Nation.
Name of Mother: Lillie M. Roberts, nee Guess   a citizen of the Choctaw Nation.

Postoffice   Russellville, I.T.

**AFFIDAVIT OF MOTHER.**

UNITED STATES OF AMERICA, Indian Territory,  
Western   DISTRICT.

I, Lillie M. Roberts, nee Guess, on oath state that I am 21 years of age and a citizen by blood, of the Choctaw Nation; that I am the lawful wife of J. G. Roberts, who is a citizen, by -------- of the --------- ------- Nation; that a Female child was born to me on 31st day of January, 1905; that said child has been named Irene Exodus Roberts, and was living March 4, 1905.

Lillie M. Roberts

Witnesses To Mark:

Subscribed and sworn to before me this 3rd day of April, 1905

Guy A. Curry  
Notary Public.

**AFFIDAVIT OF ATTENDING PHYSICIAN OR MID-WIFE.**

UNITED STATES OF AMERICA, Indian Territory,  
Western   DISTRICT.

I, J. M. Turner, a Physician, on oath state that I attended on Mrs. Lillie M. Roberts, nee Guess, wife of J. G. Roberts on the 31st day of January, 1905; that there was born to her on said date a FeMale[sic] child; that said child was living March 4, 1905, and is said to have been named Irene Exodus Roberts

J.M. Turner M.D.

Witnesses To Mark:

Applications for Enrollment of Choctaw Newborn
Act of 1905   Volume XI

Subscribed and sworn to before me this 1ˢᵗ   day of   April   , 1905

Guy A Curry
Notary Public.

Choc New Born 776
    Martha Danridge[sic]   b. 8-13-04

## NEW BORN AFFIDAVIT

No

### CHOCTAW ENROLLING COMMISSION

IN THE MATTER OF THE APPLICATION FOR ENROLLMENT as a citizen of the Choctaw Nation, of     Martha Dandridge     born on the 13ᵗʰ day of   August   190 4

Name of father   W.A. Dandridge    a citizen of  ——  ——    Nation, final enrollment No. ——     *now Dandridge*

Name of mother   Sarah Allison    a citizen of   Choctaw    Nation, final enrollment No. 11920

Calloway I.T.
Postoffice.

**AFFIDAVIT OF MOTHER**

UNITED STATES OF AMERICA
    INDIAN TERRITORY
DISTRICT   Central

    I   Sarah Allison now Dandridge  , on oath state that I am   24   years of age and a citizen by   blood   of the   Choctaw   Nation, and as such have been placed upon the final roll of the   Choctaw   Nation, by the Honorable Secretary of the Interior my final enrollment number being ................; that I am the lawful wife of   W.A. Dandridge  , who is a citizen of the   ——   Nation, and as such has been placed upon the final roll of said Nation by the Honorable Secretary of the Interior, his final enrollment number being —— and that a   Female   child was born to me on the   13ᵗʰ   day of   August   190 4; that said child has been named   Martha Dandridge  , and is now living.

289

## Applications for Enrollment of Choctaw Newborn
## Act of 1905   Volume XI

                                          her  
WITNESSETH:                Sarah Allison x now Dandridge  
  Must be two witnesses { Eastman Jacob      mark  
  who are citizens        Lewis Armstrong

Subscribed and sworn to before me this, the 22 day of February , 190 5

                               A.E. Folsom  
                                      Notary Public.  
My Commission Expires:  
Jan 9 - 1909

**BIRTH AFFIDAVIT.**

### DEPARTMENT OF THE INTERIOR.
### COMMISSION TO THE FIVE CIVILIZED TRIBES.

IN RE APPLICATION FOR ENROLLMENT, as a citizen of the Choctaw Nation, of Martha Dandridge , born on the 13$^{th}$ day of August , 1904

Name of Father: William A Dandridge    a citizen of the Choctaw Nation.  
Name of Mother: Sarah Dandridge nee Allison    a citizen of the Choctaw Nation.

                          Postoffice    Calloway I.T.

### AFFIDAVIT OF MOTHER.

UNITED STATES OF AMERICA, Indian Territory, }  
    Central               DISTRICT. }

    I, Sarah Dandridge , on oath state that I am 24 years of age and a citizen by blood , of the Choctaw Nation; that I am the lawful wife of William A. Dandridge , who is a citizen, by ................ of the United States Nation; that a female child was born to me on 13$^{th}$ day of August , 1904; that said child has been named Martha Dandridge , and was living March 4, 1905.

                                      her  
                              Sarah x Dandridge  
Witnesses To Mark:           mark  
  { WH Martin  
    JD Ward

## Applications for Enrollment of Choctaw Newborn
## Act of 1905 Volume XI

Subscribed and sworn to before me this 8<sup>th</sup> day of April , 1905

W.H. Angell
Notary Public.

---

**AFFIDAVIT OF ATTENDING PHYSICIAN OR MID-WIFE.**

UNITED STATES OF AMERICA, Indian Territory,
Central DISTRICT.

I, Effie Cole , a midwife , on oath state that I attended on Mrs. Sarah Dandridge , wife of William A Dandridge on the 13<sup>th</sup> day of August , 1904; that there was born to her on said date a female child; that said child was living March 4, 1905, and is said to have been named Martha Dandridge

her
Effie x Cole
mark

Witnesses To Mark:
- WH Martin
- J.D. Ward

Subscribed and sworn to before me this 8<sup>th</sup> day of April , 1905

W.H. Angell
Notary Public.

---

## *Affidavit of Attending Physician or Midwife*

UNITED STATES OF AMERICA,
INDIAN TERRITORY,
Central DISTRICT

I, Telphia Coal[sic] a Mid Wife on oath state that I attended on Mrs. Sarah Allison now Dandridge wife of W.A. Dandridge on the 13<sup>th</sup> day of August , 190 4, that there was born to her on said date a Female child, that said child is now living, and is said to have been named Martha Dandridge

her    *Mid wife*
Telphia x Cole    M.D.
mark

Subscribed and sworn to before me this the 24 day of February 1905

N.S. Fanner
Notary Public.

# Applications for Enrollment of Choctaw Newborn
## Act of 1905  Volume XI

WITNESSETH:

Must be two witnesses who are citizens and know the child. { Eastman Jacob
Lewis Armstrong

We hereby certify that we are well acquainted with Telphia Coal a Mid wife and know her to be reputable and of good standing in the community.

Must be two citizen witnesses. { Eastman Jacob
Lewis Armstrong

---

Choc New Born 777
Mary Magdaline Spain   b  2-23-03

BIRTH AFFIDAVIT.
## DEPARTMENT OF THE INTERIOR.
## COMMISSION TO THE FIVE CIVILIZED TRIBES.

**IN RE APPLICATION FOR ENROLLMENT,** as a citizen of the Chocktaw[sic] Nation, of  Mary Magdaline Spain  , born on the  23  day of  Feb , 1903

Name of Father: Andrew Spain            a citizen of the  Chocktaw  Nation.
Name of Mother: Allie May Spain         a citizen of the  Chocktaw  Nation.

Postoffice    Harrisburg I.T.

**AFFIDAVIT OF MOTHER.**

UNITED STATES OF AMERICA, Indian Territory,
Southern            DISTRICT.

I,  Allie May Spain  , on oath state that I am  20  years of age and a citizen by Intermarriage , of the Chocktaw Nation; that I am the lawful wife of Andrew Spain , who is a citizen, by Blood of the Chocktaw Nation; that a female child was born to me on 23 day of February , 1903, that said child has been named  Mary Magdaline Spain , and is now living.

Allie May Spain

# Applications for Enrollment of Choctaw Newborn
## Act of 1905   Volume XI

Witnesses To Mark:
{

    Subscribed and sworn to before me this  4   day of    April   , 1905.

                                      T.J. Nichols
                                      Notary Public.

---

**AFFIDAVIT OF ATTENDING PHYSICIAN OR MID-WIFE.**

UNITED STATES OF AMERICA, Indian Territory, }
    Southern                DISTRICT. }

    I,   W S Spears        , a    physician    , on oath state that I attended on Mrs.  Allie May Spain   , wife of   Andrew       on the   23   day of Feb , 1903; that there was born to her on said date a    female     child; that said child is now living and is said to have been named   Mary Magdaline Spain

                              W S Spears M.D.

Witnesses To Mark:
{

    Subscribed and sworn to before me this  4   day of    April   , 1905.

                                      T.J. Nichols
                                      Notary Public.

---

Choc New Born 778
        Walter Orr   b. 10-28-02

---

*Settle & Norwell,*
*Physicians and Surgeons*

OFFICE OVER SOUTHERN NATIONAL BANK
ROOMS 1 AND 2.

*Wynnewood, I. T.*_____ *190*

        To Whom This May Concern,
I do hereby certify up.[sic] my honor that I am a practicing Physician and that I attended Mrs. Catherine Orr during Labor on the 28<sup>th</sup> day of Oct 1902. And that there was borned to her on that day a son whose name is Walter Orr.

# Applications for Enrollment of Choctaw Newborn
## Act of 1905 Volume XI

Signed E.E. Norvell M.D. Sworn and subscribed to before me a Notary Public in and for the Southern Dist of Ind Ter. This the 2nd day of Nov. 1904.

Signed

Fred Tekarr
Notary Public

---

UNITED STATES OF AMERICA, INDIAN TERRITORY
SOUTHERN DISTRICT

O. C. Holder on oath state that I am 29 years of age and a citizen of the United States P.O. Address Duncan I.T. that I was personally acquainted with Catherine Orr, deceased, who was a citizen by blood of the blood of the Choctaw Nation and the lawful wife of William E. Orr, a citizen by intermarriage of the Choctaw Nation; that I know of my own knowledge that the male child born to her *about* October 28, 1902, and named Walter Orr, and was living on the 4th day of March, 1905, and is now living.

O. C. Holder

Subscribed and sworn to before me this 8$^{th}$ day of April A.D. 1905, at Ardmore, Indian Territory.

Fred Tekarr
NOTARY PUBLIC

---

UNITED STATES OF AMERICA, INDIAN TERRITORY
SOUTHERN DISTRICT

T. D. Sullivan on oath state that I am 47 years of age and a Citizen of the United States P.O. Address Duncan I.T. that I was personally acquainted with Catherine Orr, deceased, who was a citizen by blood of the blood of the Choctaw Nation and the lawful wife of William E. Orr, a citizen by intermarriage of the Choctaw Nation; that I know of my own knowledge that the male child born to her *about* October 28, 1902, and named Walter Orr, and was living on the 4th day of March, 1905, and is now living.

T. D. Sullivan

Subscribed and sworn to before me this 8$^{th}$ day of April A.D. 1905, at Ardmore, Indian Territory.

Fred Tekarr
NOTARY PUBLIC

## Applications for Enrollment of Choctaw Newborn
## Act of 1905 Volume XI

BIRTH AFFIDAVIT.

### DEPARTMENT OF THE INTERIOR.
### COMMISSION TO THE FIVE CIVILIZED TRIBES.

IN RE APPLICATION FOR ENROLLMENT, as a citizen of the Choctaw Nation, of Walter Orr , born on the 28$^{th}$ day of October , 1902

Name of Father: William E. Orr a citizen of the Choctaw Nation.
Name of Mother: Catherine Orr a citizen of the Choctaw Nation.

Postoffice Duncan, Indian Territory.

**Father**
AFFIDAVIT OF ~~MOTHER~~.

UNITED STATES OF AMERICA, Indian Territory,
Southern DISTRICT.

I, William E. Orr , on oath state that I am 42 years of age and a citizen by Intermarriage , of the Choctaw Nation; that I am the lawful ~~wife of~~ husband of Catherine Orr , who ~~is~~ was a citizen, by blood of the Choctaw Nation ^ and who died September 18th, 1904; that a male child was born to ~~me~~ her on 28$^{th}$ day of October , 1902; that said child has been named Walter Orr , and was living March 4, 1905.

William E. Orr

Witnesses To Mark:

Subscribed and sworn to before me this 8$^{th}$ day of April A.D. , 1905

Fred Tekarr
Notary Public.

See Separate Affidavit Attached -

---

Choc New Born 779
Margaret Virginia Sterrett
b. 3-4-05

Applications for Enrollment of Choctaw Newborn
Act of 1905   Volume XI

# NEW BORN
## CHOCTAW
## ENROLLMENT

MARGARET VIRGINIA STERRETT

(BORN March 4, 1905)

As Citizen of the
CHOCTAW NATION
Act of Congress
Approved March 3, 1905

REFUSED

June 22, 1905

Record forwarded department

June 22, 1905

Action approved by Secretary
of interior

July 22, 1905

Notice of departmentel[sic] action forwarded attorneys for Choctaw and
Chickasaw nations.

Aug. 1, 1905

Notice of departmental action
mailed applicant's Father

Aug. 1, 1905

## Applications for Enrollment of Choctaw Newborn
## Act of 1905   Volume XI

*(The letter below typed as given.)*

(Copy)

D. C. Strong M.D.,
105 Cajon St.

Telephones-

Sunset Red 231
Home, 336

To The Honorable Commission
of The Five Civilized Tribes.

Redlands, Calif., March 24 1905.

Gentlemen-  This is to vertify that I attended Mrs Frank M. Sterrett Jr in childbirth on the 4th day of March 1905  The child being borne between 11 & 12 A. M. Labor began early on the morning of the 3rd of March 1905. There was complet cervical dililation at midnight on the 3$^{rd}$ of March but owing a rigid peuneum *parineum* and uteune *uterine* metria *inertia* birth was delayed until the hour above mentioned.

Respectfully,

(signed) D. C. Strong M.D.

---

**BIRTH AFFIDAVIT.**   *(Copy)*

**DEPARTMENT OF THE INTERIOR.**
**COMMISSION TO THE FIVE CIVILIZED TRIBES.**

---

IN RE APPLICATION FOR ENROLLMENT, as a citizen of the     Choctaw     Nation, of Margaret Virginia Sterrett     , born on the  4th   day of March   , 1905

Name of Father: Frank M. Sterrett Jr.     a citizen of the   Choctaw   Nation.
Name of Mother:  Susan Sterrett            a citizen of the   Choctaw   Nation.

Postoffice   Redlands, California

---

**AFFIDAVIT OF MOTHER.**

*State of California*
~~UNITED STATES OF AMERICA, Indian Territory,~~
*County of San Bernardino* ~~DISTRICT.~~

I,   Susan Sterrett   , on oath state that I am  24   years of age and a citizen by Blood   , of the    Choctaw    Nation; that I am the lawful wife of    Frank M. Sterrett, Jr.    , who is a citizen, by Intermarriage   of the     Choctaw     Nation; that a   Female    child was born to me on  4th    day of    March     , 1905; that said child has been named  Margaret Virginia Sterrett    , and was living March 4, 1905.

# Applications for Enrollment of Choctaw Newborn
## Act of 1905   Volume XI

                             (Signed)   Susan Sterrett
Witnesses To Mark:
   O.M. Miller, Redlands, Calif.
   C.S. Chesnut, Redlands, Cal.

(Seal)

Subscribed and sworn to before me this  24th  day of  March  , 1905

                             (signed)  R.R. Richey
                                       Notary Public.

---

**AFFIDAVIT OF ATTENDING PHYSICIAN OR MID-WIFE.**

State of California
~~UNITED STATES OF AMERICA, Indian Territory,~~
County of San Bernardino ~~DISTRICT.~~

   I,   D.C. Strong M.D.   , a   Physician   , on oath state that I attended on Mrs.  Susan Sterrett  , wife of Frank M Sterrett, Jr.  on the 4th day of March  , 1905; that there was born to her on said date a   Female   child; that said child was living March 4, 1905, and is said to have been named  Margaret Virginia Sterrett

                             (Signed)   D.C. Strong M.D.
Witnesses To Mark:
   O.M. Miller, Redlands, Calif.
   C.S. Chesnut, Redlands, Cal.

Subscribed and sworn to before me this  24th  day of  March  , 1905

(Seal)

                             (signed)  R.R. Richey
                                       Notary Public.

---

*W.F.*
7-NB-779.

## DEPARTMENT OF THE INTERIOR,
## COMMISSION TO THE FIVE CIVILIZED TRIBES.

   In the matter of the application for the enrollment of Margaret Virginia Sterrett as a citizen by blood of the Choctaw Nation.

### --: DECISION :--

   It appears from the record herein that on April 14, 1905 application was made to the Commission for the enrollment of Margaret Virginia Sterrett as a citizen by blood of the Choctaw Nation.
   It further appears from the record herein and the records of the Commission that the applicant was born on March 4, 1905 and is a daughter of Susan Sterrett, a recognized

## Applications for Enrollment of Choctaw Newborn
## Act of 1905   Volume XI

and enrolled citizen by blood of the Choctaw Nation whose name appears as number 9151 upon the final roll of citizens by blood of the Choctaw Nation, approved by the Secretary of the Interior on February 4, 1903, and Frank M. Sterrett, Jr., a recognized and enrolled citizen by intermarriage of the Choctaw Nation.

The Act of Congress approved March 3, 1905 (Public No. 212) among other things provides:

"That the Commission to the Five Civilized Tribes is authorized for sixty days after the date of the approval of this act to receive and consider applications for enrollment of children born subsequent to September twenty-fifth, nineteen hundred and two, and prior to March fourth, nineteen hundred and five, and who were living on said latter date, to citizens by blood of the Choctaw and Chickasaw tribes of Indians whose enrollment has been approved by the Secretary of the Interior prior to the date of the approval of this act; and to enroll and make allotments to such children."

It is the opinion of this Commission that, inasmuch as the said Margaret Virginia Sterrett was not born prior to March 4, 1905, the Commission is without authority to receive or consider the application for her enrollment as a citizen by blood of the Choctaw Nation and that, therefore, the Commission should decline to receive or consider such application, under the provision of law above quoted and it is so ordered.

COMMISSION TO THE FIVE CIVILIZED TRIBES.

Tams Bixby
Chairman.

TB Needles
Commissioner.

C.R. Breckenbridge
Commissioner.

Muskogee, Indian Territory.
JUN 22 1905

7-NB-779

Muskogee, Indian Territory, June 22, 1905.

**COPY**

Frank M. Sterrett Jr.,
Redlands, California.

Dear Sir:

Inclosed herewith you will find a copy of the decision of the Commission to the Five Civilized Tribes, rendered June 22, 1905, declining to receive or consider the

## Applications for Enrollment of Choctaw Newborn
## Act of 1905 Volume XI

application for the enrollment of your infant child, Margaret Virginia Sterrett, as a citizen by blood of the Choctaw Nation.

The decision, with the record of proceedings in the case, is this day transmitted to the Secretary of the Interior for review. The final decision of the Secretary will be made known to you as soon as this office is informed of the same.

                Respectfully,
                SIGNED   *Tams Bixby*
Registered.                     Chairman.
Incl. 7-NB-779.

---

7-NB-779

Muskogee, Indian Territory, June 22, 1905.

**COPY**

Mansfield, McMurray & Cornish,
    Attorneys for Choctaw and Chickasaw Nations,
        South McAlester, Indian Territory.

Gentlemen:

Inclosed herewith you will find a copy of the decision of the Commission to the Five Civilized Tribes, rendered June 22, 1905, declining to receive or consider the application for the enrollment of Margaret Virginia Sterrett as a citizen by blood of the Choctaw Nation.

The decision, with the record of proceedings in the case, is this day transmitted to the Secretary of the Interior for review. The final decision of the Secretary will be made known to you as soon as this office is informed of the same.

                Respectfully,
                SIGNED   *Tams Bixby*
Incl. 7-NB-779            Chairman.

# Applications for Enrollment of Choctaw Newborn
## Act of 1905  Volume XI

Muskogee, Indian Territory, June 22, 1905.

**COPY**

The Honorable,
    The Secretary of the Interior,

Sir:

There is herewith transmitted the record of proceedings in the matter of the application for the enrollment of Margaret Virginia Sterrett as a citizen by blood of the Choctaw Nation, including the decision of the Commission, dated June 22, 1905, declining to receive or consider said application

Respectfully,
SIGNED

*Tams Bixby*
Chairman.

Through the
    Commissioner of Indian Affairs.

2 Incl. 7-NB-779.

---

DEPARTMENT OF THE INTERIOR,
WASHINGTON.

W.C.F.
FHE.

D.C.  36278-1905.
I.T.D.  8000-1905.

July 22, 1905.

Y.P.

Commissioner to the Five Civilized Tribes,
    Muskogee, Indian Territory.

Sir:

June 22, 1905, the Commission to the Five Civilized Tribes transmitted the record in the matter of the application for the enrollment of Margaret Virginia Sterrett as a citizen by blood of the Choctaw Nation, including its decision of the same date, refusing to receive or consider said application.

Reporting June 30, 1905, the Indian Office recommends that said decision be approved. A copy of its letter is inclosed.

The Department concurs in said recommendation, and the Commission's decision is hereby affirmed.

## Applications for Enrollment of Choctaw Newborn
## Act of 1905   Volume XI

Respectfully,

THOS. RYAN,
Acting Secretary.

1 inclosure.

---

Land.
48795-1905.

DEPARTMENT OF THE INTERIOR,
OFFICE OF INDIAN AFFAIRS,
WASHINGTON.

June 30, 1905.

The Honorable,
  The Secretary of the Interior.

Sir:

I have the honor to enclose a report from the Commission to the Five Civilized Tribes, dated June 22, 1905, transmitting the record of the application for enrollment as a citizen by blood of the Choctaw Nation by Margaret Virginia Sterrett.

June 22, 1905, the Commission decided adversely to the applicant.

cThe[sic] record shows that the applicant was born March 4, 1905, and is a daughter of Susan Sterrett whose name appears at No. 9151 on the final roll of citizens by blood of the Choctaw Nation approved by the Department February 4, 1903.

In view of the record and of the fact that the applicant was not born prior to March 4, 1905, as required by the terms of the act of March 3, 1905 (Public No. 212) the approval of the Commission's decision adverse to the applicant is recommended.

Very respectfully,
C. F. Larrabee
Acting Commissioner

M.M.M.
W.

## Applications for Enrollment of Choctaw Newborn
## Act of 1905  Volume XI

7-NB-779

Muskogee, Indian Territory, August 1, 1905.

**COPY**

Frank M. Sterrett Jr.,
    Redlands, California.

Dear Sir:

You are hereby notified that the Secretary of the Interior the Interior under date of July 22, 1905, affirmed the decision of the Commission to the Five Civilized Tribes, rendered June 22, 1905, declining to receive or consider the application for the enrollment of your infant child, Margaret Virginia Sterrett, as a citizen by blood of the Choctaw Nation.

                            Respectfully,
                            SIGNED

                            *Tams Bixby*
                            Chairman.

---

7-NB-779

Muskogee, Indian Territory, August 1, 1905.

Mansfield, McMurray & Cornish,
    Attorneys for Choctaw and Chickasaw Nations,
        South McAlester, Indian Territory.

Gentlemen:

You are hereby certified that the Secretary of the Interior under date of July 22, 1905, affirmed the decision of the Commission to the Five Civilized Tribes, rendered June 22, 1905, declining to receive or consider the application for the enrollment of Margaret Virginia Sterrett as a citizen by blood of the Choctaw Nation.

                            Respectfully,
                            SIGNED

                            *Tams Bixby*
                            Chairman.

## Applications for Enrollment of Choctaw Newborn
## Act of 1905   Volume XI

Choc New Born 780
   Oscar M. Krieger  b. 10-17-03

Choctaw 6703.

Muskogee, Indian Territory, April 12, 1905.

William Krieger,
   Kiowa, Indian Territory.

Dear Sir:

Receipt is hereby acknowledged of the affidavits of Margaret[sic] A. Krieger and Lee W. McMorries[sic] to the birth of Oscar M. Krieger, son of William and Margaret A. Krieger, October 17, 1903, and the same have been filed with our records as an application for the enrollment of said child.

Respectfully,

Commissioner in Charge.

*Affidavit of Attending Physician or Midwife*

UNITED STATES OF AMERICA,
INDIAN TERRITORY,
Central   DISTRICT

I, Dr. L W M$^c$Morris   a   Physician on oath state that I attended on Mrs. Margret A Krieger   wife of   William Krieger on the   17$^{th}$   day of October  , 190 3, that there was born to her on said date a   Male child, that said child is now living, and is said to have been named   Oscar M. Krieger

LW McMorriet[sic]   M. D.

Subscribed and sworn to before me this the   25$^{th}$   day of   Feby   1905

CC Culbertson
Notary Public.

WITNESSETH:
Must be two witnesses who are citizens and know the child.
{ Lee Pollock
  William E Krieger

Applications for Enrollment of Choctaw Newborn
Act of 1905   Volume XI

We hereby certify that we are well acquainted with    Dr L W McMorris   a   Physician   and know   him   to be reputable and of good standing in the community.

Must be two citizen witnesses. { Lee Pollock   William E Krieger

# NEW BORN AFFIDAVIT

No _____

## CHOCTAW ENROLLING COMMISSION

IN THE MATTER OF THE APPLICATION FOR ENROLLMENT as a citizen of the Choctaw Nation, of   Oscar M. Kreiger[sic]   born on the   17$^{th}$ day of   October   190 3

Name of father   William Krieger   a citizen of   Choctaw   Nation, final enrollment No.   574
Name of mother   Margret A Krieger   a citizen of   Choctaw   Nation, final enrollment No.   12985

Kiowa I.T.   Postoffice.

### AFFIDAVIT OF MOTHER

UNITED STATES OF AMERICA  
INDIAN TERRITORY  
DISTRICT   Central

I   Margret A Krieger   , on oath state that I am   36   years of age and a citizen by   Blood   of the   Choctaw   Nation, and as such have been placed upon the final roll of the   Choctaw   Nation, by the Honorable Secretary of the Interior my final enrollment number being   12985   ; that I am the lawful wife of   William Krieger   , who is a citizen of the   Choctaw   Nation, and as such has been placed upon the final roll of said Nation by the Honorable Secretary of the Interior, his final enrollment number being   574   and that a   Male   child was born to me on the   17$^{th}$ day of   October   190 3; that said child has been named   Oscar M Krieger   , and is now living.

Margret A Krieger

WITNESSETH:
Must be two witnesses who are citizens { Lee Pollock   William E. Krieger

## Applications for Enrollment of Choctaw Newborn
## Act of 1905 Volume XI

Subscribed and sworn to before me this, the 25<sup>th</sup> day of Feby, 190 5

C.C. Culbertson
Notary Public.

My Commission Expires: Dec 2<sup>nd</sup> 1905

---

**BIRTH AFFIDAVIT.**

### DEPARTMENT OF THE INTERIOR.
### COMMISSION TO THE FIVE CIVILIZED TRIBES.

---

IN RE APPLICATION FOR ENROLLMENT, as a citizen of the Choctaw Nation, of Oscar M. Krieger, born on the 17 day of October, 1903

Name of Father: William Krieger     a citizen of the Choctaw Nation.
Name of Mother: Margaret[sic] A Krieger     a citizen of the Choctaw Nation.

Postoffice    Kiowa I.T.

---

**AFFIDAVIT OF MOTHER.**

UNITED STATES OF AMERICA, Indian Territory,
Centl            DISTRICT.

I, Margaret A Krieger, on oath state that I am 36 years of age and a citizen by Blood, of the Choctaw Nation; that I am the lawful wife of William Krieger, who is a citizen, by marriage of the Choctaw Nation; that a Male child was born to me on 17 day of October, 1903; that said child has been named Oscar M Krieger, and was living March 4, 1905.

                               Her
                  Margaret A x Krieger
Witnesses To Mark:           mark
   JC Farley
   Charles O Ward

Subscribed and sworn to before me this 8 day of April, 1905

HB Rowley
Notary Public.

## Applications for Enrollment of Choctaw Newborn
## Act of 1905   Volume XI

**AFFIDAVIT OF ATTENDING PHYSICIAN OR MID-WIFE.**

UNITED STATES OF AMERICA, Indian Territory, }
Centl                    DISTRICT.

    I,   L W McMorries         , a   Physician       , on oath state that I attended on Mrs.   Margaret A Krieger    , wife of   William Krieger     on the   17   day of   October      , 1903; that there was born to her on said date a     male      child; that said child was living March 4, 1905, and is said to have been named   Oscar M Krieger

                                                  Lee W. McMorries MD

Witnesses To Mark:
{

    Subscribed and sworn to before me this   8 day of    April      , 1905

                                        HB Rowley
                                              Notary Public.

---

Choc New Born 781
    Hellen D. Dillard   b. 8-26-04

                                                                     Choctaw 3904.

                    Muskogee, Indian Territory, April 12, 1905.

Tandy W. Dilliard[sic],
    Caddo, Indian Territory.

Dear Sir:

    Receipt is hereby acknowledged of the affidavits of Virginnie Dilliard and W. J. Melton to the birth of Hellen D. Dilliard, daughter of Tandy W. and Virginnie Dilliard, August 26, 1904, and the same have been filed with our records as an application for the enrollment of said child.

                              Respectfully,

                                                Commissioner in Charge.

## Applications for Enrollment of Choctaw Newborn
## Act of 1905   Volume XI

7-NB-781.

Muskogee, Indian Territory, May 31, 1905.

Tandy W. Dillard,
    Caddo, Indian Territory.

Dear Sir:

    There is enclosed you herewith for execution application for the enrollment of your infant child, Hellen D. Dillard.

    In the affidavits filed in this office on April 14, 1905, the date of the applicant's birth is given as August 26, 1904, while in those filed in April 25, 1905, it is given as August 26, 1903. In the enclosed application the date of birth is left blank. Please insert the correct date and, when the affidavits are properly executed, return them to this office.

    In having these affidavits executed care should be exercised to see that all names are written in full, as they appear in the body of the affidavit, and in the event that either of the persons signing the affidavit are unable to write, signatures by mark must be attested by two witnesses. Each affidavit must be executed before a Notary Public and the notarial seal and signature of the officer must be attached to each separate affidavit.

                    Respectfully,

VR 31-10.                      [sic]

**NEW-BORN AFFIDAVIT.**

Number..............

...Choctaw Enrolling Commission...

IN THE MATTER OF THE APPLICATION FOR ENROLLMENT, as a citizen of the Choctaw Nation, of Hellen D. Dillard

born on the 26 day of ___August___ 190 3

Name of father  Tandy W. Dillard      a citizen of  Choctaw
Nation final enrollment No.  10984
Name of mother  Virginia Dillard      a citizen of  Choctaw
Nation final enrollment No.  361

                    Postoffice      Caddo IT

## Applications for Enrollment of Choctaw Newborn
## Act of 1905  Volume XI

### AFFIDAVIT OF MOTHER.

UNITED STATES OF AMERICA
INDIAN TERRITORY
Central    DISTRICT

I    Virginia Dillard    , on oath state that I am  33  years of age and a citizen by  Intermarriage  of the  Choctaw  Nation, and as such have been placed upon the final roll of the  Choctaw  Nation, by the Honorable Secretary of the Interior my final enrollment number being  361 ; that I am the lawful wife of  Tandy W. Dillard  , who is a citizen of the  Choctaw  Nation, as such has been placed upon the final roll of said Nation by the Honorable Secretary of the Interior, his final enrollment number being  10984  and that a  Female  child was born to me on the  26"  day of  August  190 3; that said child has been named  Hellen D Dillard  , and is now living.

Virginnie[sic] Dillard

Witnesseth.

Must be two Witnesses who are Citizens.    W.L. Ward
    CO Robinson

Subscribed and sworn to before me this  21"  day of  Jan  190 5

A.E. Folsom
Notary Public.

My commission expires:
9-Jan 1909

### *Affidavit of Attending Physician or Midwife*

UNITED STATES OF AMERICA,
INDIAN TERRITORY,
Central    DISTRICT

I,    W.J. Melton    a    Practicing Physician  on oath state that I attended on Mrs.  Virginnia[sic] Dillard  wife of  Tandy W Dillard  on the  26"  day of  August  , 190 3, that there was born to her on said date a  Female  child, that said child is now living, and is said to have been named  Hellen D Dillard

W.J. Melton    M. D.

Subscribed and sworn to before me this the  21  day of  Jany  1905

A.E. Folsom
Notary Public.

WITNESSETH:

Must be two witnesses who are citizens and know the child.    W.L. Ward
    CO Robinson

## Applications for Enrollment of Choctaw Newborn
## Act of 1905   Volume XI

We hereby certify that we are well acquainted with   Dr W.J. Melton a Physician   and know   him   to be reputable and of good standing in the community.

Must be two citizen witnesses. { WL Ward / CO Robinson }

Exp
9-Jan 1909

**BIRTH AFFIDAVIT.**

### DEPARTMENT OF THE INTERIOR.
### COMMISSION TO THE FIVE CIVILIZED TRIBES.

**IN RE APPLICATION FOR ENROLLMENT,** as a citizen of the   Choctaw   Nation, of Hellen D. Dilliard[sic]   , born on the   26   day of   August   , 1904

| Name of Father: Tandy W. Dilliard | a citizen of the   Choctaw   Nation. |
| Name of Mother: Virginia Dilliard | a citizen of the   Choctaw   Nation. |

Postoffice   Caddo I.T.

**AFFIDAVIT OF MOTHER.**

UNITED STATES OF AMERICA, Indian Territory,
Central   DISTRICT.

I, Virginia Dilliard   , on oath state that I am   34   years of age and a citizen by   marriage   , of the   Choctaw   Nation; that I am the lawful wife of   Tandy W Dilliard   , who is a citizen, by Blood   of the   Choctaw   Nation; that a Female   child was born to me on   26   day of   August   , 1904; that said child has been named   Hellen D. Dilliard   , and was living March 4, 1905.

Virginnie Dilliard

Witnesses To Mark:

Subscribed and sworn to before me this   6   day of   April   , 1905

J.T. Jackson
Notary Public.

## Applications for Enrollment of Choctaw Newborn
## Act of 1905 Volume XI

#### AFFIDAVIT OF ATTENDING PHYSICIAN OR MID-WIFE.

UNITED STATES OF AMERICA, Indian Territory,
   Central                       DISTRICT.

I,   Dr. W. J. Melton   , a  Physician   , on oath state that I attended on Mrs.   Virginnie Dilliard   , wife of   Tandy W. Dilliard   on the  26  day of  August  , 1904; that there was born to her on said date a   Female   child; that said child was living March 4, 1905, and is said to have been named   Hellen D. Dilliard

W.J. Melton M.D.

Witnesses To Mark:

Subscribed and sworn to before me this  7  day of   April   , 1905

J.T. Jackson
Notary Public.

**BIRTH AFFIDAVIT.**

#### DEPARTMENT OF THE INTERIOR.
#### COMMISSION TO THE FIVE CIVILIZED TRIBES.

IN RE APPLICATION FOR ENROLLMENT, as a citizen of the   Choctaw   Nation, of  Hellen D. Dillard   , born on the  26  day of  Aug  , 1903

Name of Father: Tandy W. Dillard         a citizen of the   Choctaw   Nation.
Name of Mother: Virginia Dillard         a citizen of the   Choctaw   Nation.

Postoffice   Caddo I.T.

#### AFFIDAVIT OF MOTHER.

UNITED STATES OF AMERICA, Indian Territory,
   Central                       DISTRICT.

I,   Virginia Dillard   , on oath state that I am  34  years of age and a citizen by   intermarriage   , of the   Choctaw   Nation; that I am the lawful wife of  Tandy W Dillard   , who is a citizen, by blood   of the   Choctaw   Nation; that a   female   child was born to me on  26th   day of   August   , 1903; that said child has been named   Hellen D. Dillard   , and was living March 4, 1905.

Virginia Dillard

Witnesses To Mark:

## Applications for Enrollment of Choctaw Newborn
## Act of 1905   Volume XI

Subscribed and sworn to before me this 3rd day of   June   , 1905

                        I L Rappolee
                        Notary Public.

---

**AFFIDAVIT OF ATTENDING PHYSICIAN OR MID-WIFE.**

UNITED STATES OF AMERICA, Indian Territory, }
   Central                 DISTRICT. }

    I,   W. J. Melton   , a ........................., on oath state that I attended on Mrs.   Virginia Dillard   , wife of   Tandy W. Dillard   on the 26th day of August   , 1903; that there was born to her on said date a   female   child; that said child was living March 4, 1905, and is said to have been named   Hellen D. Dillard

                        W.J. Melton M.D.
Witnesses To Mark:
{

Subscribed and sworn to before me this 3rd day of   June   , 1905

                        I L Rappolee
                        Notary Public.

---

<u>Choc New Born 782</u>
    Cecil A. Staples   b. 12-2-04

                        Choctaw 4703.

            Muskogee, Indian Territory, April 12, 1905.

Bras[sic] Staples,
    Kiowa, Indian Territory.

Dear Sir:

    Receipt is hereby acknowledged of the affidavits of Crystal E. Krieger Staples and Lee W. McMorries to the birth of Cecil A. Staples, son of Braz[sic] and Crystal E. Staples, December 2, 1904, and the same have been filed with our records as an application for the enrollment of said child.

                Respectfully,

                        Commissioner in Charge.

Applications for Enrollment of Choctaw Newborn
Act of 1905   Volume XI

# NEW BORN AFFIDAVIT

No ............

## CHOCTAW ENROLLING COMMISSION

IN THE MATTER OF THE APPLICATION FOR ENROLLMENT as a citizen of the Choctaw Nation, of   Cecile A Staples   born on the   $2^{nd}$ day of   December   190 4

Name of father   Braze Staples   a citizen of   United States   ~~Nation~~,
final enrollment No. ................
Name of mother   Chrystal[sic] E. Staples   a citizen of   Choctaw   Nation,
final enrollment No.   12986

Kiowa I.T.   Postoffice.

**AFFIDAVIT OF MOTHER**

UNITED STATES OF AMERICA }
INDIAN TERRITORY
DISTRICT   Central

*(nee Krieger)*

I   Chrystal E. Staples   , on oath state that I am   19   years of age and a citizen by   Blood   of the   Choctaw   Nation, and as such have been placed upon the final roll of the   Choctaw   Nation, by the Honorable Secretary of the Interior my final enrollment number being   12989   ; that I am the lawful wife of   Braze Staples   , who is a citizen of the   United States   ~~Nation~~, and as such has been placed upon the final roll of said Nation by the Honorable Secretary of the Interior, his final enrollment number being   ——and that a   Male   child was born to me on the   $2^{nd}$   day of   December   190 4; that said child has been named   Cecile A Staples   , and is now living.

Chrystal E Staples

WITNESSETH:
Must be two witnesses { T Colbert
who are citizens       { Riley Willis

Subscribed and sworn to before me this, the   $25^{th}$   day of   Feby   , 190 5

C C Culbertson
Notary Public.

My Commission Expires:   Dec $2^{nd}$ 1905

313

## Applications for Enrollment of Choctaw Newborn
## Act of 1905 Volume XI

*Affidavit of Attending Physician or Midwife*

UNITED STATES OF AMERICA,
INDIAN TERRITORY,
Central     DISTRICT

I,   Dr L.W. M$^c$Morris   a   Physician   on oath state that I attended on Mrs. Chrystal E. Staples   wife of Braze Staples on the   2$^{nd}$   day of December  , 190 4, that there was born to her on said date a   male child, that said child is now living, and is said to have been named   Cevile A. Staples

L.W. McMorriet     M. D.

Subscribed and sworn to before me this the   25$^{th}$   day of   Feby   1905

C.C. Culbertson
Notary Public.

WITNESSETH:
Must be two witnesses who are citizens and know the child.   { T. Colbert
Riley Willis

We hereby certify that we are well acquainted with   Dr. L.W. M$^c$Morris a   Physician   and know   him   to be reputable and of good standing in the community.

Must be two citizen witnesses.   { T. Colbert
Riley Willis

BIRTH AFFIDAVIT.

### DEPARTMENT OF THE INTERIOR.
### COMMISSION TO THE FIVE CIVILIZED TRIBES.

IN RE APPLICATION FOR ENROLLMENT, as a citizen of the   Choctaw   Nation, of Cecil A Staples   , born on the   2   day of   December  , 1904

Name of Father: Braz Staples           a citizen of the   US       Nation.
Name of Mother: Crystal E Staples      a citizen of the   Choctaw  Nation.

Postoffice   Kiowa I.T.

# Applications for Enrollment of Choctaw Newborn
## Act of 1905   Volume XI

### AFFIDAVIT OF MOTHER.

UNITED STATES OF AMERICA, Indian Territory, }
   Centl                DISTRICT.

    I, Crystal E Krieger now Staples, on oath state that I am 20 years of age and a citizen by Blood, of the Choctaw Nation; that I am the lawful wife of Braz Staples, who is *not* a citizen, by ............... of the Choctaw Nation; that a male child was born to me on 2 day of December, 1904; that said child has been named Cecil A Staples, and was living March 4, 1905.

                                      Crystal E. Krieger, now Staples

Witnesses To Mark:
  {

    Subscribed and sworn to before me this 8 day of April, 1905

                                      H B Rowley
                                        Notary Public.

### AFFIDAVIT OF ATTENDING PHYSICIAN OR MID-WIFE.

UNITED STATES OF AMERICA, Indian Territory, }
   Centl                DISTRICT.

    I, L W M$^c$Morries, a Physician, on oath state that I attended on Mrs. Crystal E Staples, wife of Braz Staples on the 2 day of December, 1904; that there was born to her on said date a male child; that said child was living March 4, 1905, and is said to have been named Cecil A Staples

                                      LW M$^c$Morriet M.D.

Witnesses To Mark:
  {

    Subscribed and sworn to before me this 8 day of April, 1905

                                      H B Rowley
                                        Notary Public.

## Applications for Enrollment of Choctaw Newborn
## Act of 1905  Volume XI

Choc New Born 783
    Spairs[sic] A. Manning  b. 3-2-04

Choctaw 3678.

Muskogee, Indian Territory, April 12, 1905.

Arthur F. Manning,
    Caddo, Indian Territory.

Dear Sir:

    Receipt is hereby acknowledged of the affidavits of Nannie H. Manning and W. J. Melton to the birth of Spears[sic] A. Manning, son of Arthur F. and Nannie H. Manning, March 7, 1904, and the same have been filed with our records as an application for the enrollment of said child.

        Respectfully,

        Commissioner in Charge.

# NEW BORN AFFIDAVIT

No ............

## CHOCTAW ENROLLING COMMISSION

IN THE MATTER OF THE APPLICATION FOR ENROLLMENT as a citizen of the Choctaw Nation, of Spairs[sic] A. Manning born on the 7$^{th}$ day of March 190 4

Name of father  Arthur F. Manning   a citizen of   Choctaw   Nation, final enrollment No.   11017
Name of mother  Nannie H. Manning   a citizen of   Choctaw   Nation, final enrollment No.   10400

        Caddo I.T.   Postoffice.

## Applications for Enrollment of Choctaw Newborn
## Act of 1905   Volume XI

### AFFIDAVIT OF MOTHER

UNITED STATES OF AMERICA  
INDIAN TERRITORY  
DISTRICT   Central

I   Nannie H. Manning   , on oath state that I am   23   years of age and a citizen by   Blood   of the ................... Nation, and as such have been placed upon the final roll of the   Choctaw   Nation, by the Honorable Secretary of the Interior my final enrollment number being   10400   ; that I am the lawful wife of   Arthur F. Manning  , who is a citizen of the   Choctaw   Nation, and as such has been placed upon the final roll of said Nation by the Honorable Secretary of the Interior, his final enrollment number being   11017   and that a   Male   child was born to me on the   7"   day of   March   190 4; that said child has been named   Speairs A Manning  , and is now living.

WITNESSETH:                             Nannie H Manning  
Must be two witnesses { L I Lawrence  
who are citizens      { Frank T Lawrence

Subscribed and sworn to before me this, the   7"   day of   February   , 190 5

A.E. Folsom  
Notary Public.

My Commission Expires:  
Jan 9 - 1909

### *Affidavit of Attending Physician or Midwife*

UNITED STATES OF AMERICA,  
INDIAN TERRITORY,  
Central   DISTRICT

I,   W.J. Melton   a   Practicing Physician on oath state that I attended on Mrs.   Nannie H Manning   wife of   Arthur F. Manning on the   7"   day of   March , 190 4, that there was born to her on said date a   Male   child, that said child is now living, and is said to have been named   Spears A. Manning

W. J. Melton            M. D.

Subscribed and sworn to before me this the   11"   day of   February   1905

A.E. Folsom  
Notary Public.

WITNESSETH:  
Must be two witnesses { L I Lawrence  
who are citizens and  
know the child.       { Frank T Lawrence

## Applications for Enrollment of Choctaw Newborn
## Act of 1905 Volume XI

We hereby certify that we are well acquainted with W.J. Melton a Physician and know him to be reputable and of good standing in the community.

Must be two citizen witnesses. { L I Lawrence
Frank Lawrence

**BIRTH AFFIDAVIT.**

### DEPARTMENT OF THE INTERIOR.
### COMMISSION TO THE FIVE CIVILIZED TRIBES.

IN RE APPLICATION FOR ENROLLMENT, as a citizen of the Choctaw Nation, of Speairs A. Manning, born on the 7$^{th}$ day of March, 1904

Name of Father: Arthur F. Manning a citizen of the Choctaw Nation.
Name of Mother: Nannie H. Manning a citizen of the Choctaw Nation.

Postoffice Caddo Indian Territory

**AFFIDAVIT OF MOTHER.**

UNITED STATES OF AMERICA, Indian Territory, }
Central DISTRICT.

I, Nannie H. Manning, on oath state that I am 23 years of age and a citizen by Blood, of the Choctaw Nation; that I am the lawful wife of Arthur F. Manning, who is a citizen, by Blood of the Choctaw Nation; that a Male child was born to me on 7$^{th}$ day of March, 1904; that said child has been named Speairs A. Manning, and was living March 4, 1905.

Nannie H Manning

Witnesses To Mark:
{

Subscribed and sworn to before me this 4 day of April, 1905.

J. T. Jackson
Notary Public.

## Applications for Enrollment of Choctaw Newborn
## Act of 1905 Volume XI

**AFFIDAVIT OF ATTENDING PHYSICIAN OR MID-WIFE.**

UNITED STATES OF AMERICA, Indian Territory, }
Central DISTRICT. }

I, Dr W.J. Melton , a Physician , on oath state that I attended on Mrs. Nannie H. Manning , wife of Arthur F. Manning on the 7 day of March , 1904; that there was born to her on said date a Male child; that said child was living March 4, 1905, and is said to have been named Speairs A Manning

W.J. Melton M.D.

Witnesses To Mark:
{

Subscribed and sworn to before me this 7 day of April , 1905

J.T. Jackson
Notary Public.

---

Choc New Born 784
    Arthur Lafate Henry b. 12-29-03

---

7-2845

Muskogee, Indian Territory, April 12, 1905.

Amos Henry,
    Lodi, Indian Territory.

Dear Sir:

Receipt is hereby acknowledged of the affidavits of Arian Henery[sic] and I. W. Yandell to the birth of Arthur Lafate Henery, son of Amos and Arian Henery, December 29, 1903, and the same have been filed with our records as an application for the enrollment of said child.

Respectfully,

Commissioner in Charge.

---

## Applications for Enrollment of Choctaw Newborn
## Act of 1905   Volume XI

**BIRTH AFFIDAVIT.**

### DEPARTMENT OF THE INTERIOR.
### COMMISSION TO THE FIVE CIVILIZED TRIBES.

IN RE APPLICATION FOR ENROLLMENT, as a citizen of the Choctaw Nation, of Arthur Lafate Henery, born on the 29 day of Dec, 1903

Name of Father: Amos Henery   a citizen of the Choctaw Nation.
Name of Mother: Arian Henery   a citizen of the Choctaw Nation.

Postoffice   Lodi Ind Ter

**AFFIDAVIT OF MOTHER.**

UNITED STATES OF AMERICA, Indian Territory,　}
Central   DISTRICT.

I, Arian Henry, on oath state that I am 30 years of age and a citizen by Blood, of the Choctaw Nation; that I am the lawful wife of Amos Henery, who is a citizen, by Blood of the Choctaw Nation; that a male child was born to me on 29 day of Dec, 1903; that said child has been named Arthur Lafate Henery, and was living March 4, 1905.

　　　　　　　　　　　　　　　　　　her
　　　　　　　　　　　　Arian Henery x
Witnesses To Mark:　　　　　　　　mark
  { J.Y. Ervin
  { Tobe Brown

Subscribed and sworn to before me this 6 day of April, 1905

　　　　　　　　　　　　L N Hunt
　　　　　　　　　　　　　　Notary Public.
My commission expires Jan 9 1908

**AFFIDAVIT OF ATTENDING PHYSICIAN OR MID-WIFE.**

UNITED STATES OF AMERICA, Indian Territory,　}
Central   DISTRICT.

I, I W Yandell, a Physician, on oath state that I attended on Mrs. Arian Henery, wife of Amos Henery on the 29 day of December, 1903; that there was born to her on said date a Male child; that said child was living March 4, 1905, and is said to have been named Arthur Lafate

　　　　　　　　　　　　I.W. Yandell

## Applications for Enrollment of Choctaw Newborn
## Act of 1905   Volume XI

Witnesses To Mark:
{ J.Y. Ervin

Subscribed and sworn to before me this 6 day of   April   , 1905

L N Hunt
Notary Public.

My commission expires Jan 9 1908

---

Choc New Born 785
　　Garlie Vincent  b. 3-13-04

~~7-126~~
7 NB 785

Muskogee, Indian Territory, July 1, 1905.

Charles S. Vincent,
　　Womack, Indian Territory.

Dear Sir:

　　Receipt is hereby acknowledged of your letter of June 27, 1905, asking if the enrollment of yourself and your child Garlie Vincent has been approved.

　　In reply to your letter you are advised that the application for the enrollment of yourself as an intermarried citizen of the Choctaw Nation is now receiving consideration and as soon as a decision is reached in this case you will be notified of the action taken therein.

　　You are further advised that the name of your child Garlie Vincent has been placed upon a schedule of citizens by blood of the Choctaw Nation prepared for forwarding to the Secretary of the Interior. You will be notified when her enrollment is approved.

Respectfully,

Commissioner.

## Applications for Enrollment of Choctaw Newborn
## Act of 1905 Volume XI

7-NB-785

Muskogee, Indian Territory, August 12, 1905.

Charles S. Vincent,
Womack, Indian Territory.

Dear Sir:

Receipt is hereby acknowledged of your letter of August 8, 1905, stating that you have received notice of the approval of your child Garlie Vincent and you wish to know how selection of allotment may be made for this child as you have not yet been approved by the Department and your wife is unable by reason of ill health to go to the land office.

In reply to your letter you are advised that if your wife is unable to appear at the land office in person bor[sic] the purpose of selecting allotment of Garlie Vincent, it will be necessary for you to be appointed guardian of said child by the United States Court in order to file for this child.

Respectfully,

Acting Commissioner.

---

**BIRTH AFFIDAVIT.**

### DEPARTMENT OF THE INTERIOR.
### COMMISSION TO THE FIVE CIVILIZED TRIBES.

---

IN RE APPLICATION FOR ENROLLMENT, as a citizen of the Choctaw Nation, of Garlie Vincent, born on the 14$^{th}$ day of March, 1904

Name of Father: Chas S. Vincent    a citizen of the Choctaw Nation.
Name of Mother: Lena Vincent    a citizen of the Choctaw Nation.

Postoffice    Womack I.T.

---

**AFFIDAVIT OF MOTHER.**

UNITED STATES OF AMERICA, Indian Territory,  
Southern DISTRICT.

I, Lena Vincent, on oath state that I am twenty nine years of age and a citizen by blood, of the Choctaw Nation; that I am the lawful wife of Chas S Vincent, who is a citizen, by marriage of the Choctaw Nation; that a Female child was born to me on 14$^{th}$ day of March, 1904; that said child has been named Garlie, and was living March 4, 1905.

# Applications for Enrollment of Choctaw Newborn
## Act of 1905   Volume XI

                                              Lena Vincent

Witnesses To Mark:
{

    Subscribed and sworn to before me this   6$^{th}$   day of   April   , 1905

                                                 Josh Clardy
                                                     Notary Public.

My commission expires Mar 1$^{st}$ 1908

---

**AFFIDAVIT OF ATTENDING PHYSICIAN OR MID-WIFE.**

UNITED STATES OF AMERICA, Indian Territory, }
................................................... DISTRICT. }

    I,   J H Howard   , a   M.D.   , on oath state that I attended on Mrs.   Lena Vincent   , wife of   Chas S. Vincent   on the 14   day of   March   , 1904; that there was born to her on said date a ........................... child; that said child was living March 4, 1905, and is said to have been named Garlie Vincent

                                            J.H. Howard M.D.

Witnesses To Mark:
{

    Subscribed and sworn to before me this   7 day of   ~~M~~   April   , 1905

                                              Jas M Gordon
                                              Notary Public.

My Term of office expires Mch 1907

---

Choc New Born 786
       Amanda Baken   b.  8-8-03
       Clarsey Baken   b.  3-2-05

       No. 1 Died  Oct 14-1904
       No. 1 Dismissed  Oct 6, 1905

# Applications for Enrollment of Choctaw Newborn
## Act of 1905   Volume XI

DEPARTMENT OF THE INTERIOR,
COMMISSIONER TO THE FIVE CIVILIZED TRIBES.

Record in the matter of the application for enrollment as a citizen by blood of the Choctaw Nation of:

AMANDA BAKEN                              7-NB-786.

---

**BIRTH AFFIDAVIT.**

DEPARTMENT OF THE INTERIOR.
**COMMISSION TO THE FIVE CIVILIZED TRIBES.**

---

IN RE APPLICATION FOR ENROLLMENT, as a citizen of the   Choctaw   Nation, of Amanda Baken   , born on the   8   day of   Aug   , 1903

Name of Father: Layman Baken        a citizen of the   Choctaw   Nation.
Name of Mother: Mollie Baken        a citizen of the   Choctaw   Nation.

Postoffice   Valliant I.T.

---

**AFFIDAVIT OF MOTHER.**

UNITED STATES OF AMERICA, Indian Territory, }
Central            DISTRICT.

I,   Mollie Baken   , on oath state that I am   24   years of age and a citizen by Blood   , of the   Choctaw   Nation; that I am the lawful wife of   Layman Baken   , who is a citizen, by Blood   of the   Choctaw   Nation; that a   Girl   child was born to me on   8   day of   Aug   , 1903; that said child has been named Amanda Baken   , and was living March 4, 1905. dodo *did*[sic]

                                    Mollie Baken

Witnesses To Mark:
{ W M Stanley
{ Jonas Taylor

Subscribed and sworn to before me this   8   day of   Aprile[sic]   , 1905

                                    H L Fowler
                                        Notary Public.

## Applications for Enrollment of Choctaw Newborn
## Act of 1905  Volume XI

**AFFIDAVIT OF ATTENDING PHYSICIAN OR MID-WIFE.**

UNITED STATES OF AMERICA, Indian Territory, }
Central                    DISTRICT.

   I,  Lucy Lake  , a ................., on oath state that I attended on Mrs.  Mollie Baken , wife of  Layman Baken  on the  8 day of  Aug  , 1903; that there was born to her on said date a  Girl  child; that said child was living March 4, 1905, and is said to have been named Amanda Baken *dide*[sic] *Oct 14 1904*

Lucy Lake

Witnesses To Mark:
{ W M Stanley
{ Jonas Taylor

   Subscribed and sworn to before me this 8 day of  Aprile[sic]   , 1905

H L Fowler<br>Notary Public.

---

7-NB-786.

Muskogee, Indian Territory June 10, 1905.

Mollie Baken,
    c/o Lymon Baken,
        Valliant, Indian Territory.

Dear Madam:

   In the matter of the application for the enrollment of your daughter Amanda Baken, born August 8, 1903, as a citizen by blood of the Choctaw Nation it appears from the affidavit of Lucy Lake on file in said case that said child died October 14, 1904.

   You are requested, therefore, to furnish proper proof of death of said child and a blank for said purpose is inclosed herewith.

   You will notice that there is a blank for the affidavit of a relative and of an acquaintance of the deceased. In having the same executed be careful to see that all blanks are properly filled, all names written in full and that the notary public before whom the affidavits are acknowledged, attaches his name and seal to each separate affidavit.

Respectfully,

D C                                                                                         Chairman.
Env.

Applications for Enrollment of Choctaw Newborn
Act of 1905   Volume XI

## DEPARTMENT OF THE INTERIOR.
## COMMISSION TO THE FIVE CIVILIZED TRIBES.

In the matter of the death of   Amanda Baken   a citizen of the   Choctaw Nation, who formerly resided at or near   Valliant   , Ind. Ter., and died on the   14$^{th}$   day of October , 1904

**AFFIDAVIT OF RELATIVE.**

UNITED STATES OF AMERICA, Indian Territory,
Central   DISTRICT.

I,   Lyman Baken   , on oath state that I am   34   years of age and a citizen by Blood , of the   Choctaw   Nation; that my postoffice address is   Valliant   , Ind. Ter.; that I am   The Father   of   Amanda Baken   who was a citizen, by   Blood   , of the   Choctaw   Nation and that said   Amanda Baken   died on the   14$^{th}$   day of October   , 1904

Lyman Baken

Witnesses To Mark:

Subscribed and sworn to before me this   16$^{th}$   day of   June   , 1905.

William Swink
Notary Public.

**AFFIDAVIT OF ACQUAINTANCE.**

UNITED STATES OF AMERICA, Indian Territory,
Central   DISTRICT.

I,   Jesse Christie   , on oath state that I am   40   years of age, and a citizen by B[sic]   of the Choctaw   Nation; that my postoffice address is   Valliant   , Ind. Ter.; that I was personally acquainted with   Amanda Baken   who was a citizen, by   Blood   , of the   Choctaw   Nation; and that said   Amanda Baken   died on the   14$^{th}$   day of October   , 1904

Jesse Christie

Witnesses To Mark:

## Applications for Enrollment of Choctaw Newborn
## Act of 1905  Volume XI

Subscribed and sworn to before me this 16<sup>th</sup> day of June , 1905.

William Swink
Notary Public.

*W.F.*
7-NB-786.

### DEPARTMENT OF THE INTERIOR,
### COMMISSION TO THE FIVE CIVILIZED TRIBES.

In the matter of the application for the enrollment of Amanda Baken as a citizen by blood of the Choctaw Nation.

----oOo----

It appears from the record herein that on April 14, 1905 there was filed with the Commission to the Five Civilized Tribes an application for the enrollment of Amanda Baken as a citizen by blood of the Choctaw Nation.

It further appears from the record herein and the records of this office that the applicant was born August 8, 1903; that she is a daughter of Lyman Baken and Mollie Baken (enrolled as Mollie Nakintaya), recognized and enrolled citizens by blood of the Choctaw Nation whose names appear opposite numbers 1358 and 1365, respectively, upon the final roll of citizens by blood of said nation, approved by the Secretary of the Interior on December 12, 1902; and that said applicant died October 14, 1904.

The Act of Congress approved March 3, 1905 (Public No. 212) among other things provides:

"That the Commission to the Five Civilized Tribes is authorized for sixty days after the date of the approval of this act to receive and consider applications for enrollment of children born subsequent to September twenty-fifth, nineteen hundred and two, and prior to March fourth, nineteen hundred and five, and who were living on said latter date, to citizens by blood of the Choctaw and Chickasaw tribes of Indians whose enrollment has been approved by the Secretary of the Interior prior to the date of the approval of this act; and to enroll and make allotments to such children."

It is, therefore, hereby ordered that the application for the enrollment of Amanda Baken as a citizen by blood of the Choctaw Nation be dismissed.

Tams Bixby  Commissioner.

Muskogee, Indian Territory,
OCT 6 - 1905

## Applications for Enrollment of Choctaw Newborn
## Act of 1905 Volume XI

7-NB-786

Muskogee, Indian Territory, October 6, 1905.

**COPY**

Lyman Baken,
Valliant, Indian Territory.

Dear Sir:

Inclosed herewith you will find a copy of the order of the Commissioner to the Five Civilized Tribes, dated October 6, 1905, dismissing the application for the enrollment of Amanda Baken as a citizen by blood of the Choctaw Nation.

Respectfully,
SIGNED

*Tams Bixby*
Commissioner.

Register.
7-NB-786.

---

7-NB-786

Muskogee, Indian Territory, October 6, 1905.

Mansfield, McMurray & Cornish,     **COPY**
    Attorneys for Choctaw and Chickasaw Nations,
    South McAlester, Indian Territory.

Gentlemen:

Inclosed herewith you will find a copy of the order of the Commissioner to the Five Civilized Tribes, dated October 6, 1905, dismissing the application for the enrollment of Amanda Baken as a citizen by blood of the Choctaw Nation.

Respectfully,
SIGNED

*Tams Bixby*
Commissioner.

7-NB-786.

## Applications for Enrollment of Choctaw Newborn
### Act of 1905  Volume XI

7-596

Muskogee, Indian Territory, April 12, 1905.

Lyman Baken,
Valliant, Indian Territory.

Dear Sir:

Receipt is hereby acknowledged of the affidavits of Mollie Baken and Lucy Lake to the birth of Amanda Baken daughter of Lyman and Mollie Baken, August 8, 1903, and the same have been filed with our records as an application for the enrollment of said child.

Respectfully,

Commissioner in Charge.

7 NB 786

Muskogee, Indian Territory, June 21, 1905.

Lyman Baken,
Valliant, Indian Territory.

Dear Sir:

Receipt is hereby acknowledged of your affidavit and the affidavit of Jesse Christie to the death of Amanda Baken which occurred October 14, 1904, and the same have been filed with our records as evidence of the death of the above named child.

Respectfully,

Chairman.

# Index

ABBOTT
  Elizabeth .................................... 196
  W E .................................... 196,197
  W E, MD .................................... 197
ACHIH, Nancy .................................... 46,49
ADAMS
  James Arthur .................................... 281,282
  Jason .................................... 281,282
  Margaret .................................... 281,282
  Margret .................................... 281
ALLEN
  Arthur Marmeduke .......... 108,110,111
  F B .................................... 127
  F P .................................... 101
  John C .................... 108,109,110,111
  L D .................................... 98,99
  Mary I .................... 108,109,110,111
  Maud .................................... 236,237,238
  Missouri .................................... 281,282
  Silvy Eltine .................................... 108
  Sylvia Eltine .................................... 108,109
  Sylvy Eltine .................................... 108
ALLISON, Sarah .................. 289,290,291
ANDERSON
  Barney Etta .................................... 70
  C J .................................... 165
ANGELL, W H ....... 115,119,120,290,291
ARMSTRONG
  J R .................................... 179,180
  Jos R .................................... 180
  Lewis .................................... 290,291,292
ARNOLD, S S .................................... 147
ATOKA, Simon .................................... 84
AUSTIN
  W C .................................... 146
  W G .................................... 145
  W G, MD .................................... 146

BABB
  Amanda .................................... 32,35
  Bele Zora .................................... 33
  Bellzora .................................... 33
  Belzora .................................... 32,33,34,35
  Berlzora .................................... 34
  G L .................................... 32,33,34,35
  Ocia .................................... 32,33,34
  Ocie .................................... 32,34,35

BAKEN
  Amanda ............ 323,324,325,326,327, 328,329
  Clarsey .................................... 323
  Layman .................................... 324,325
  Lyman .................................... 326,327,328,329
  Lymon .................................... 325
  Mollie .................................... 324,325,327,329
BARNES, T J .................................... 60,61,62
BARNETT
  E J .................................... 271
  Jackson D .................................... 268
  James .................................... 268
  Levicey .................................... 132
  Mrs E J .................................... 268
  Wysee .................................... 132,133
BARNTT, E J .................................... 271
BARTON, Lillie .................................... 257
BEAL
  Ada .................................... 15,16
  Ailcy .................................... 76
  Ailsey .................................... 75,80,81,82
  Ailsie .................................... 75,76,78,79
  Alsie .................................... 79
  Andrew P .................................... 79,80
  D E .................................... 16
  George .................................... 15,16
  Ina .................... 231,232,233,235,236
  Julious .................................... 78,79
  Julius .................... 75,76,80,81,82
  Minnie .................................... 232,235
  Mrs D E .................................... 16
  Pinckney .................................... 76,77
  Pinkney ............ 75,76,78,79,80,81,82
  R B .................................... 233,234
  Reuben .................................... 232,233,235
  Thomas T .................................... 79,80
  Willis Franklin .................................... 15,16
BEALEY, W H .................................... 111
BEALL, Wm O .................................... 218,219
BEAMES, Wallace .................................... 262,267
BEAMS
  John J .................................... 173,174
  Scion .................................... 160
  Wallace .................................... 262,264
BEATTY, R B .................................... 108
BECKETT

# Index

J B .................................................... 101
J B, MD ................................... 101,172
Jas B ............................................... 172
BELVIN
  Henry Harrison ............................ 176
  Henry Harrison J ............... 176,177,179
  Henry Harrison Jones ............. 177,178
  Mabel ........................ 176,177,178,179
  Watson ............................ 176,177,179
BENTON
  Beorge .......................................... 252
  Eliza ..................... 252,253,255,256,257
  Frances ........................................ 252
  Francis ......... 252,253,254,255,256,257
  Geo ................................ 256,257,263
  George ............. 252,253,254,255,257, 263,264,265,266
  Levi ............................................... 243
  Lillie ........................ 257,258,259,260
  Nelson ..................... 243,244,258,259
  Phebe ................................... 243,244
BETTS, Emerline ....................... 31,32
BILLY
  Austin ............... 248,249,251,262,264, 265,266,267
  Charles .................................. 160,163
BIXBY, Tams ........... 44,48,49,65,77,104, 105,113,123,124,159,187,217,221,262, 299,300,301,303,327,328
BLACK, Maggie E ......... 117,118,119,120
BLAYLOCK, Ruth .................... 202,203
BOBO
  Lacey P .................................. 216,223
  Lacy P ......................................... 224
BOHANAN
  Harriet .............................. 243,244,245
  Harriett ........................... 242,243,244
  Levi .............................................. 243
  Levi W ........................ 241,242,244,245
  Selina ..................... 241,242,243,244,245
  Thomas ................................. 163,164
BOHANNON
  Harriet ......................................... 260
  Harriett .................................. 243,244
  Levi ....................................... 243,244
  Selina ................................... 243,244
BOHANON

Harriet ............................................ 245
Levi W ............................................ 245
Selina ............................................. 245
BOND, E H ...................................... 103
BOONE, T L ............................... 215,231
BOWER, James .. 24,28,33,67,68,132,134, 153,154,188,191,206,207
BOYD
  E S ....................................... 147,148
  E S, MD ............................... 147,148
BRACKETT
  David A ............................... 180,181
  Henry A ............................... 180,181
  Laura A ................................ 180,181
BRASHEARS
  Benjamin ................................... 156
  Benjamin F ................................ 156
  Benjamin Franklin ................ 156,157
  Bessie .................................. 17,18,19
  Buster ..................................... 17,18
  Fadias ......................................... 17
  Isa May ................................ 156,157
  Myrtle .................................. 156,157
  Tobias ................................ 17,18,19
  Viola ..................................... 17,19
BRECKENRIDGE, C R ................. 299
BRINKLEY, Robert B ...................... 118
BROWN
  Alfred Earl ............... 172,173,174,175
  Annie ......................................... 204
  Annie E ....................... 201,202,203
  Charles ................... 201,202,203,204
  Dwight ........................................ 2,3
  Elum ....................... 172,173,174,175
  Ida B ........................................ 174
  Ida F ......................... 172,173,175
  Maud Mahalie ........... 201,202,203,204
  Tobe .......................................... 320
BRYANT
  Dan ............................................ 259
  Lillie Benton ............................. 258
  Nelson ............................. 257,258,260
  Raymon ..................................... 260
  Raymond ............................. 257,260
BURNS, Alec ................................... 284
BUTLER
  Henry C ............. 116,117,119,120,121

# Index

Henry Clide .................... 117,118
J M ............... 116,117,119,120,121
James M ........................ 117,118
Maggie E ...... 117,118,119,120,121
BYBEE, Nora ........................... 29

CADILL, Bertha ......................... 90
CAIN
   P L ................... 29,75,79,80,81,82
   P L, MD ............................. 29,79
   P S ......................................... 76
CALHOUN, M F ................. 163,164
CAMPBELL
   C M .................................. 126,127
   H G ........................................ 147
   William ..................................... 3
CANDILL, Henry A .................... 90
CARNEY
   Elsie ................................... 86,87
   M D .................................... 85,87
CARPENTER
   Joseph ................. 197,198,199,200
   Kitsy ..................... 197,198,199,200
   Soloman ............... 197,198,199,200
   Solomon ............................... 199
CARR
   D H ....................................... 148
   Daniel H ........................... 146,147
   Jessie Redman ....................... 148
   Jessie Redmon ....................... 148
   Jessie Redmond ............... 146,147
   Lillie ....................................... 148
   Lillie McClung ................. 146,147
   T G .......................................... 55
CASS, Osborne ..................... 37,38
CATHIE, J D ........................ 113,114
CAUDILL
   Anderson ............................... 93
   Bertha ............... 89,90,91,92,93,94
   Clarence ................................ 93
   Clarence Edward ...... 89,90,91,92,94
   Henry A .................... 89,90,91,92,94
CHESNUT, C S .......................... 298
CHOATE, Christopher C ........... 175
CHRISTIE, Jesse .................. 326,329
CHRISTY
   Adam .......................... 36,37,38,39

Adams ...................................... 36
Joshua .............................. 37,38,39
Miney ............................... 36,38,39
Sallie ................................ 36,37,38
Sally ........................................ 39
Wilson ............................ 36,37,38,39
CHUBBE, Miney .................... 36,38
CHUBBY, Miney .................... 36,37
CLARDY, Josh ....... 268,269,271,272,323
CLAYTON & BRAINARD .......... 239
CLEAVELAND
   Edmon Ree ........................... 171
   Mollie .................................... 171
CLEVELAND
   Edmon Ree ...................... 171,172
   Edward ............................ 171,172
   Mollie ............................... 171,172
COAL, Telphia .................... 291,292
COBB, Loren ................. 25,132,133
CODY
   R D ........................................ 107
   R D, MD ................................. 107
COFFER, R N ........................... 7,9
COLBERT, T ..................... 313,314
COLE
   Effie ...................................... 291
   Telphia ................................ 291
COLEMAN
   P A ................................. 278,279
   Pinkney ..................... 277,279,280
   Pinkney G .............................. 280
   Susie ..................................... 284
   Susie G ..................... 277,279,280
   Susy G ................................... 278
   William J P ................ 277,279,280
   William James Pinkney ..... 278,279
COLEY
   Anderson .................... 82,83,84,85
   Biney ........................... 82,83,84,85
   Carles ..................................... 84
   Carlos .................................... 82
   Charles ............................... 82,85
   Charlie ............................... 83,84
   Dave ....................................... 97
COLLINS, J D .................... 105,106
COOK
   J M .................................. 186,187,189

J M, MD ..................................187,189
COOPER
   Abel............................................... 68
   Ailey .............................................. 78
   Ailsey ............................................ 77
   Elliot............................................ 188
   Robert............................................ 99
   Roger.............................................. 97
COTTEN
   Cora J......................................137,139
   David Oscar...........................137,139
   Nellie ...............................134,137,139
   Oscar........................................134,137
COTTON
   Cora J......................................135,136,138
   David Oscar...............134,135,136,138
   Nellie ..............................134,135,136
   Oscar........................134,136,138,139
COVINGTON, W P .......................... 216
CROSS, John H..............................107,108
CROUTHAMEL, A H...................101,172
CROWDER
   Emily..........................................51,52
   Lisabeth .....................................51,52
   Martin S......................................51,52
   P C................................................ 52
   Rena............................................... 52
CRUZ, V V....................................203,204
CULBERSON
   James ......................................182,183
   Martha V .................................182,183
   Mary Catherine.......................182,183
CULBERTSON, C C......304,306,313,314
CURRY, Guy A............18,19,287,288,289
CURTIS
   Ella ..........................204,205,206,207
   Harry Edward ............190,191,192,193
   Luvicey................................190,191
   Luvicy......................190,191,192,193
   M C........................................190,191
   Marion C ..........................190,192,193
   Nancy ..................................191,192
   Nancy H.........................190,191,193
   Nealy Clarence ..........204,205,206,207
   Thomas.................................206,207
   Thomas A ..............................204,205

DABNEY
   Dr J A .......................................... 113
   J A...........................................112,115
   J A, MD..................................112,115
DALE
   C D .............................................. 284
   C D, MD...................................... 284
   Charles D................................283,285
   Chas D, MD................................. 285
DALTON, E M.................................. 69
DANDRIDGE
   Martha .............................289,290,291
   Sarah.................................289,290,291
   W A....................................289,291
   William A..............................290,291
DANRIDGE, Martha....................... 289
DARNEAL
   Bennie Alfred ..................96,97,98,99
   James.......................................97,99
   Mary.................................97,98,99
   Stephen....................................97,99
   Stephen C ..................................... 98
   Steven......................................97,99
DARNLL, Mary ................................. 98
DAVIDSON, Wm B......278,279,280,284,
285,286
DAVIS
   Alonzo ......................................... 167
   Alonzo M..................................... 166
   Daniel .......................................... 175
   Goldie Loma...........................166,167
   Lorena.....................................166,167
   Luther D ..................................16,146
   A R ............................................... 96
   Rev W M ..................................... 114
DAWSON
   E L .......................................274,275,277
   E L, MD.................................275,277
DECK, G F ...................................... 234
DEETS, Jas H.................................. 282
DICKEY, R P ................................73,74
DIFENDAFER, Chas T.............25,27,122
DILBECK
   Alvarada ..................................... 268
   Alvarado .............268,269,270,271,272
   Alvaredo .......................269,270,273
   Alvrado ...................................268,273

J L ..................... 268,269,270,271,273
John F, Jr ........................................ 268
John L ................ 269,270,271,272,273
John L, Jr ........... 267,268,269,270,271, 272,273
William M ... 267,269,270,271,272,273
DILLARD
   Hellen D ............. 307,308,309,311,312
   Tandy W ..................... 308,309,311,312
   Virginia ...................... 308,309,311,312
   Virginnia ................................................. 309
   Virginnie ................................................ 309
DILLIARD
   Hellen D ............................ 307,310,311
   Tandy W ............................ 307,310,311
   Virginia ........................................... 310
   Virginnie ................................ 307,311
DOBSON
   Albert D .......................................71,72
   Ollia ................................................71,72
   Thomas M ....................................71,72
DOWNING
   J H .................................................. 183
   S H ............................................89,178
DUDLEY, Irene ............................. 178,179
DUDLY, Irene ................................. 176
DUNCAN, Lewis .............................. 142
DURANT, Caroline ............................ 122

ECKELKAMP, W H ...... 210,212,229,231
EDENS, John D ............................ 270,273
ELKINS, O C ................................. 112,116
ERVIN, J Y ..................................... 320,321
ETHEREDGE, A G ................... 120,121
EVERETT, Willard N ...................... 267
EVERIDGE
   Lula ........................... 152,153,154,155
   Martin V ........................................... 155
   Robert T ........................................... 152
   Robert Thomas ............................. 152
   Robert Turner ....................... 154,155
   Robt T ...................................... 153,154
   Sofia Ann ................................ 153,154
   Sophiraan ..................... 152,154,155
   Sophiram ....................................... 152

FALLMER, Demmer ........................... 55

FANNER, N S ...................................... 291
FANNIE, E J ....................................... 105
FANNIN, E J ............. 65,66,106,113,114, 233,234
FARLEY, J C ...................................... 306
FAULK, A A ................................ 170,171
FINTON, Mamie ....................... 63,65,66
FIRZGERALD
   Mable .............................................. 238
   Maud ............................................... 238
   T A .................................................. 238
FITZGERALD
   Mable ............................... 236,237,238
   Maud ................................ 236,237,238
   Thomas A ............................... 236,237
   Thos A ..................................... 237,238
FLEMING
   J T .................................................. 8,9
   M A ................................................ 7,9
FOLLMAR, Demmer .................... 53,55
FOLSOM
   Ben ......................................... 150,151
   A E .......... 41,42,112,118,290,309,317
   John ......................... 191,192,206,207
   Noel ....................................... 150,151
FORBES, Nellie Ida ....................... 60,62
FORTNER, Sam .................. 278,279,284
FOSTER, John E ................................. 67
FOSTER & DALTON ....................... 62
FOWLER
   D A .............................................. 10,11
   H L ........................................ 324,325
FRANKLIN
   I A ........................................ 240,241
   Wirt ....................... 18,20,35,192,205
FRAZIER, Thomas H .................. 254,255
FREE, Fannie ..................................... 206
FRIAR, Jas .......................................... 282

GAFFORD, T T .................................. 148
GARDNER
   Basil ..................................................... 3
   D H ............................................. 41,42
   E J .................................................... 56
GARLAND
   Frank ............................................... 37
   John A ........................................ 53,54

# Index

John Arthur ..................... 53,55
Joseph ............................... 187
Quay ............................ 53,54,55
Sarah Annie ............... 52,53,54,55
Sarrah Annie ..................... 55
W G .................................. 187
GARVIN, D W ..................... 127
GAYLORD
  J W ................................. 167
  W N ................................ 167
GIBBINS, I M ..................... 128
GIBSON
  Claude ...................... 193,194,195
  Laura ........................ 193,194,195
  Mitchell ...................... 194,195
  W T .......................... 193,194,195
GILBERT, W J ..................... 103
GILL
  J J, MD ............................. 85
  Jno J ................................ 84
  Jno J, MD .......................... 84,85
  John J .............................. 82
GIVENS, J I ..................... 198,200
GOBEN
  H G .................................. 1,3
  H G, MD ............................. 2,3
GOINGS
  Lena ............................... 88,89
  Nicholas ............................ 88
  Nicholas .......................... 88,89
  Zora ............................. 87,88,89
GOLD, S M ....................... 173,174
GOODNIGHT, Jno H .................. 22,23
GORDON, Jas M ...................... 323
GUESS, Lillie M ............... 286,287,288

HALLOWAY, Minnie ................... 233
HAMILTON
  Dr N J .............................. 41
  N J ......................... 40,41,43,44,45
  N J, MD ......................... 40,41,43
HAMPTON
  John W ...................... 232,235,236
  P J ................................. 184
  P J, MD ............................ 185
HARBISON, J E ...................... 74
HARDY

J J ........................ 149,150,151,152
J J, MD ......................... 150,152
HARKINS, Isaac ..................... 54
HARPER, C W .................... 185,186
HARRIS
  Elizabeth C ................... 182,183
  R P ................................. 183
HARRISON
  Edga Lee ........................... 128
  J C ............................. 126,127
  Joseph C ....................... 124,125
  Joseph Colbert ............. 123,124,128
  Juanita ............................ 126
  Leola ......................... 123,124,128
  Lyman ........................... 247,249
  Ruth Juanita ............ 123,124,125,128
  Ruthie Juanita ..................... 126
HAYES, S W ......................... 70,71
HENDERSON
  Benjaman Franklin ................. 185
  Benjaman F ........................ 184
  Benjamin F .................. 183,184,185
  E E ................................ 184
  Edna E ......................... 184,185
  Edner E ............................ 185
  J H ............................ 184,185
HENERY
  Amos .......................... 319,320
  Arian ......................... 319,320
  Arthur Lafate ................. 319,320
HENRY
  Amos .............................. 319
  Arthur Lafate ..................... 319
  Mathew ............................. 37
  Pat ............................... 77,78
HERNDON, E B ...................... 10,11
HICKMAN, Eugene A ............... 238,239
HILL
  C W ............................... 155
  A T ........................... 277,279,280
  A T, MD ........................ 279,280
HINES
  Della May ......................... 73,74
  G M .............................. 73,74
  Oma ................................ 73
  Oma McLellan ....................... 73
  Oma Mclellan ....................... 74

HINSLEY, T M .................. 91,92,94,95
HITCHER
   Adeline ........ 261,262,263,264,265,266
   Catherin ................................................. 262
   Catherine ..... 261,262,263,264,266,267
   Cathrine ....................................... 265,266
   Harrison ............. 253,254,255,257,260, 261,262,263,264,265,266
HITHER
   Adeline ................................................. 263
   Catherine ............................................. 263
   Harrison ................................................ 263
HODGES
   Dave .................................. 103,104,107
   E F ........................................................... 72
   E F, MD ................................................... 72
   Henry .................................. 104,105,106
   Henry C ......................................... 104,107
   Myrtle ............................................ 104,107
HOLDER, O C ..................................... 294
HOLLOWAY, Minnie ................ 233,234
HOLMAN, Chas R ..................... 57,58,59
HOMER
   Ana ........................................................ 46
   Dana ........................... 46,47,48,49,50
   A H .......................................................... 46
   Kizzie ............................................... 47,48
   Nancy .................................. 46,47,48,50
   Sophia ...................... 46,47,48,49,50
   Willie ..................................................... 50
HONOBA, Malenunine ...................... 22
HONOBBEE
   Fanine ................................................... 24
   Fannie ................................................... 24
HONUBBEE
   Maleunine ............................................ 22
   Melvina ................................................. 27
HONUBEE, Maleunine ....................... 21
HORN, Eliza ............................... 242,245
HOUNEBBY, Fanny .......................... 24
HOWARD
   J H ....................................................... 323
   J H, MD ............................................... 323
HOWERTON, W W ................... 194,195
HUGGINS
   J J ...................................................... 1,2,3
   Lula E ............................................... 1,2,3

Ola .................................................... 2,3
Olla ....................................................... 1
HUME
   Dr W M ................................................ 142
   J S ......................................................... 144
   W M .................................... 141,142,144
   W M, MD ................................... 142,144
HUNT
   Annette ............................................ 95,96
   Ennett .................................................... 95
   James .............................................. 95,96
   L N ............................................... 320,321
   Louisa ................................................... 96
   Wilburn ........................................... 95,96
IMPSON
   Flora ................................... 40,41,42,45
   Flora A ................................ 39,42,43,44
   Flore R ................................................. 45
   M M .................................................. 41,42
   Troy Silvester .......... 39,40,42,43,44,45
   Troy Silvister .................................... 39
   Troy Sylvester ....................... 41,42,46
   W D ...................................................... 46
   William B ............................................ 45
   William D .................... 39,40,42,43,44
   Wm D ............................................. 41,42
IRETON
   Henry ........................................ 129,130
   Laura ................................................. 130
   Ollie Birgil ........................................ 129
   Ollie Virgil ............................... 129,130
   Ollie Virgin ....................................... 129
ISH, W W ............................................ 87

JACKETT
   W B ..................................................... 167
   W B, MD ............................................ 167
JACKSON
   Edmon ............................................... 241
   J T ........................... 310,311,318,319
   Mary .................................................. 240
JACOB, Eastman ................... 290,291,292
JAMES, S W ......................................... 22
JEFFERSON
   Bicey ............................................. 86,87
   Joseph .......................................... 86,87

# Index

Thomas ..............................85,86,87
JEFFRIES, E F .....................237,238
JENKINS, O O ........................... 101
JOHN, Susan ............................... 54
JOHNICO
   John ............ 20,21,22,23,24,25,26,27
   Locay ........................................ 23
   Lucy ............ 20,21,22,23,24,25,26,27
   Ole ............. 20,21,22,23,24,25,26,27
JOHNSON
   Dr E ......................................... 97
   E97,98
   E, MD ....................................97,98
   Geo F ................................136,139
   Henry ..................... 160,164,255,256
   O L ............ 26,27,72,101,122,132,171,
   237,280,282
JONES
   C C ....................38,39,187,189,190
   Cham .................................13,14,15
   J J .............................274,275,276,277
   Mary Ellen ...............274,275,276,277
   Maude Marine .... 273,274,275,276,277

KANEHTA, Annette ......................... 95
KANICTOBE, Cele ........................60,62
KING, Lizzie .........................121,122
KIRKPATRICK, J C ..................153,154
KITZMILLER
   J H ............................................ 71
   J H, MD .................................... 71
KREIGER, Oscar M .......................... 305
KRIEGER
   Chrystal E ................................ 313
   Crystal E .................................. 315
   Margaret A ......................304,306,307
   Margret A .........................304,305
   Oscar ....................................... 304
   Oscar M ...........................304,306,307
   William ............................304,305,306
   William E .........................304,305
   Willim ..................................... 307

LABOR
   Pheby ....................................... 29
   Wm .......................................... 28
LABORS, Phoeba ......................27,30

LAKE, Lucy .........................325,329
LANE, Mary .......................89,90,92,94
LARRABEE, C F ......................... 302
LAWRENCE
   Frank ...................................... 318
   Frank T ................................... 317
   L I ....................................317,318
LEE
   Robert E ................................... 84
   Robt E ................................... 136
LEEDTKE, Wm C .......................... 231
LEEFTKE, Wm C ......................... 229
LEFLORE
   J W ..............................202,203,204
   Mack H ...............................83,84
LEMONS, C E ................................. 8
LEWIS
   Belle ..............................150,151
   Frank ..................................... 157
   James L .................................. 203
   Jas L ..............................202,204
LITTLE
   Albert L ................................... 35
   J C ......................................269,270,272
LLOYD
   J B ........................................... 30
   J W .................................31,32,47
   Joe ........................................... 32
LONG
   Dr Thomas ............................... 118
   F F ........................................... 30
   T J ...................................117,119,121
   T J, MD ...............................118,121
   Thomas ................................... 118
LOOMER, Werley .....................194,195
LOONEY
   Dr Robert E ............................ 137
   Robt E, MD ............... 135,137,138,139
LOWDER, M A ...........................11,12
LUNSFORD, F B ... 163,164,165,255,256,
264,265,266

MADDOX, E H ............................ 144
MAHAR
   C H ................................18,19,157
   Charles H ................................ 156
   Charles H, MD ...................18,19,157

MANNING
  Arthur F .................. 316,317,318,319
  Nannie H .................. 316,317,318,319
  Spairs A ................................ 316
  Speairs A ................ 316,317,318,319
MANSFIELD, MCMURRAY &
  CORNISH ............ 218,231,300,303,328
MARTIN
  M J ....................................... 66
  W H .................................. 290,291
MATHEWS, M B ........................ 149
MATHIES
  C C ....................................... 34
  A L ....................................... 34
MAYES, Leola ............................ 127
MAYS, Leola .................. 125,126,127
MCALLEN, F A ...................... 30,40,43
MCARTHUR, Claire L ................ 137
MCBRIDE
  E C ...................................... 241
  Emmett C ............................. 240
  Willis Owen ..................... 239,240
  Winnie ............................ 239,240
MCCARTY, Jennie .................... 108
MCDANIEL, Thomas .................. 250
MCDONNELL, J T ..................... 167
MCENTIRE
  F B ..................................... 106
  F B, DD .............................. 106
MCFERRAN
  Bennie ................... 102,140,141
  Isabel ................................. 102
  Isabell ............................... 140
  Walter .......................... 102,140
MCGEE
  Emily ............................ 121,122
  Lizzie ........................... 121,122
  Swinney ...................... 121,122
MCINTOSH
  Alex .................................. 253
  Francis ........................ 246,248
MCKEOWN, Tom D ................... 111
MCMANUS, M E ......................... 34
MCMORRIES
  L W .............................. 307,315
  Lee W ........................... 304,312
  Lee W, MD .......................... 307

MCMORRIET, L W, MD ..... 304,314,315
MCMORRIS, Dr L W .......... 304,305,314
MEADOWS, J V ............................ 32,47
MEASHINTUBBY
  Abe .................................. 246,247
  Andrew ..................... 246,247,249,250
  Jackson ..................... 246,247,249,250
  Lizzie ....................... 246,247,249,250
MEDELL
  Albert ................................... 31
  Everet Lee ........................... 31
  Lula ..................................... 31
MELTON
  Ado .............................. 275,276,277
  Dr W J .......................... 310,311,319
  W J ............... 307,309,312,316,317,318
  W J, MD ........... 309,311,312,317,319
MIEASHINTUBBY, Jackson ............. 246
MILLER
  H C ................................. 138,139
  O M .................................... 298
MISCHENBUTTI
  Andrew .............................. 251
  Jackson ............................. 251
  Lizzie ................................. 251
MISCHENTUBBI
  Abe .................................... 248
  Andrew ............................... 250
  Jackson ........................ 248,250
  Lizzie ............................. 248,250
MISCHINTUBBI
  Abe .................................... 246
  Andrew .............................. 246
  Jackson .............................. 246
  Lizzie .................................. 246
MISCHUNTUBBI
  Andrew .............................. 251
  Jackson .............................. 251
  Lizzie ................................. 251
MITCHELL
  Charles T ............................ 95
  E J ..................................... 109
  Mary ......................... 57,59,60,61
MONTGOMERY
  S K .............................. 13,14,15
  S K, MD ......................... 13,14
MOORE

# Index

Ada Bell.................................145,146
F B........................................145,146
Laura L.................................238,239
Mary Eunice................................ 145
MORGAN
  Jno B........................................... 195
  Jno B, MD ................................. 195
  John B.......................................... 193
MORRIS
  Belle ........................ 149,150,151,152
  John N ..................... 149,150,151,152
  John W......................................... 149
  Thelma..................... 149,150,151,152
MUNKUS
  Beverly C...............................102,103
  Beverly D ................................... 102
  Lillie May...............................102,103
  Ollie Lee.................................102,103
  Sillie May .................................... 102

NAKINTAYA, Mollie..................... 327
NASH, D S ..................................... 250
NEEDLES, T B .....................6,261,299
NERO
  Delia ....................... 212,213,215
  Hallie ...................... 212,213,215
  Henery ........................................ 213
  Henry...................... 212,213,215
  Jane............. 208,209,210,211,212,214,
  215,216,217,219,220,222,223,224,227
  ,228,229,230,231
  Jimmie........ 208,209,211,213,219,222,
  223,224,226,227,228
  Jimmy ......... 208,210,211,212,213,214,
  215,216,217,218,220,222,223,224,225
  ,226,227,229,230,231
  Joseph .......... 208,209,210,211,212,213,
  214,215,216,217,218,219,220,221,222
  ,223,224,225,226,227,228,229,230,
  231
  Nancy .......... 209,211,213,221,228,231
NICHOLS, T J................................. 293
NORVELL, E E, MD ...................... 293

OAKES, Geo W .......................153,154
O'DONBY, W J................................. 82
ODONBY, W J................................... 1

ORR
  Catherine ........................ 293,294,295
  Walter.............................. 293,294,295
  William E ..............................294,295
OTT
  Johnson.................................142,143
  Samuel A .................................... 142
PARISH
  Bethena.................................27,29,30
  James Otto ...........................27,29,30
  R M......................................180,181
  Ramson......................................27,29
  Ransom......................................... 30
PARKE
  Frank E ......................................... 96
  Roy .............................................. 96
PARKER
  Gabe George................................ 4,5
  Gable E......................................... 4,5
  Gabriel E.......................................... 4
  Louise E........................................ 4,5
PARO, Jane ...............................214,231
PARRISH
  Bethana........................................ 28
  Bethena................................28,29,30
  James Ottis ................................28,29
  James Otto ................................... 27
  Ransom.....................................28,29
PATTERSON
  John Walton......................12,13,14,15
  Martha J..............................13,14,15
  Walton ................................13,14,15
PEBWORTH, Henry ..................142,143
PHILLIP, Nancy............................... 50
PHILLIPS, W H ....................150,151,152
PICKENS
  J L..........................................33,34
  W C ......................................33,34
PILGREEN, James B ....................... 131
PITCHLYN, Susan.....................247,250
PITCHLYNN, E P......................255,256
POLLOCK, Lee.........................304,305
POPE, Will..................................... 47
PORTLOCK, Ella C........................ 130
PRIMROSE, James T............212,213,215
PRUNER

# Index

Burney Etta..................70,71
Charles B......................70,71
Walter Leonard............70,71
PUSLEY
  A B................................... 28
  John B................................ 200
  Nannie................................ 198
  Osborn............................... 200

RAPPOLEE, I L.................. 312
REASER, J M................79,80,81
REASOR, J M...................... 29
REEDER, J G....................... 75
REESE
  W I..................................6,8,9
  W I, MD............................ 8,9
  W O................................... 7
RICE, T J............................ 175
RICHARDS, W................... 169
RICHERSON, Maggie F...... 103
RICHEY, R R...................... 298
RIDDLE
  Jane.................................. 221
  Jimmie............................. 221
  Jimmy.............................. 221
  Joseph.............................. 221
  Steward...................210,221,229
  Tokee.......................210,221,229
RIGGS, J J......................193,206
ROACH
  Dr R W........................168,170
  Dr Robert W................... 170
  Joanna..........................168,170
  Lorena Pearl........167,168,169,170
  Robert W..................168,169,170
ROBERTS
  Irene Exodus.................286,288
  J B.................................. 286
  J G............................286,287,288
  Lillie M......................286,287,288
  Perry............................286,287
  Sam T.............................. 252
  Sam T, Jr........... 161,162,163,244,245,
  248,249,251,256,257,260,261,263
ROBINSON, C O................309,310
ROCKMAN
  J E............................186,187,188

Joseph E..........................186,189
Lizzie........................186,187,188,189
Montie J.....................186,187,188,189
ROGERS
  C....................................112,113
  Nettie.............................51,52
ROGGERS, Nettie................ 52
ROWLEY, H B.................306,307,315
RUCKER, G M................... 147
RUSSELL
  Eda..............................153,155
  Elum M..........................68,69
  Elum M, MD................... 69
  Ida................................. 152
  Scopia............................ 100
RUTHERFORD
  B C................................. 4,5
  B C, MD........................... 5
RYAN, Thos........................ 302

SAM, Morris....................83,84
SCOTT
  Cephus............................. 39
  Sampson......................... 178
SETTLE & NORVELL...... 293
SHIPLEY, Sam................... 169
SHIPPEY
  Dr E E.........................205,206
  E E................................. 204
  E E, MD.......................... 206
SHONEY, W A............3,10,11,54,92,93
SHULER, James L...........235,236
SIMMONS, O A................. 180
SIMPSON, R L..............229,230,231
SKAGGS, J H..................... 103
SMITH
  L J................................. 238
  L J, MD.......................... 237
  Lee J.............................. 239
  Lee J, MD...................... 238
SNEED, Myrtle..............104,105,106
SOCKEY
  Dora................................ 25
  Ned................................. 84
SPAIN
  Allie May.....................292,293
  Andrew........................292,293

# Index

Mary Magdaline .................. 292,293
SPAULDING, G C ................. 57,58,59
SPEARS
  W S ........................................... 293
  W S, MD ..................................... 293
STANLEY, W M ....................... 324,325
STAPLES
  Bras ............................................ 312
  Braz ................................ 312,314,315
  Braze ..................................... 313,314
  Cecil A ............................ 312,314,315
  Cecile A ................................. 313,314
  Chrystal E ............................. 313,314
  Crystal E .......................... 312,314,315
  Crystal E Krieger ......................... 312
STATON
  Pheby C ............................... 172,175
  Phoby ........................................ 174
  Phoeby C .................................... 174
STEPHENS, Mary ........................ 88,89
STERRETT
  Frank M, Jr ............... 297,298,299,303
  Margaret Virginia ..... 295,296,297,298,
  299,300,301,302,303
  Mrs Frank M, Jr .......................... 297
  Susan ........................... 297,298,302
STEVENS, J M ............................. 267
STIGLER, J S ................................. 68
STONE
  C L ...................................... 140,141
  W B ..................................... 233,234
STRANGE
  A B ...................................... 286,287
  A B, MD .................................... 287
STRONG, D C, MD .................... 297,298
SULLIVAN
  T D ........................................... 294
  T M ............................................. 52
SWINK, William ....................... 326,327

TACKETT, W B ............................ 166
TALBERT, M E ............................. 201
TALBURT, M E ................... 202,203,204
TALLEY
  I C ............................................ 140
  Isham C ............................... 102,141
TAYLOR

Absalom James ................. 56,58,59,60
Absolom James ............................ 58
Ellis .................................... 57,58,59
Jonas ................................... 324,325
Melvina ................... 56,57,58,59,60,61
Milton Nelson ....................... 56,57,61
Simon ..................... 56,57,58,59,60,61
TECUMSEH
  Houston ................. 23,24,131,132,133
  Ida ............................... 131,132,133
  Jesse ............................ 22,132,133
  Julia ............................ 131,132,133
TEKARR, Fred ........................ 294,295
THOMAS
  D ...................... 248,249,251,261
  Jno J ..................... 247,261,263,267
  John J .............................. 258,262
  O ..................................... 112,113
THOMPSON
  Clemmie ....................... 141,143,144
  Clmmie ..................................... 142
  Cyrus R .................... 141,142,143,144
  Daisy M .................... 141,142,143,144
  Elias ......................................... 118
TUCKER
  Bertha ................................ 112,115
  Earnest ..................................... 115
  Ernest ..................... 111,112,113,114
  John E ...................................... 115
  John E, Jr .................................. 111
  John J ................................. 111,112
TUEY, L C .................................. 100
TURNER
  J M ..................................... 286,288
  J M, MD .................................... 288
  W A .......................................... 108
VARNER, T T ............................. 65,66
VEACH, Horatio ......................... 92,93
VERNER
  Frank .................................. 6,7,8,9
  Mrs Frank ..................................... 8
  Nettie ................................. 6,7,8,9
  Pearl ................................ 5,6,7,8,9
VINCENT
  Charles S ............................ 321,322
  Chas S ................................ 322,323

Garlie ............................ 321,322,323
Lena ........................................ 322,323

WADE, Daniel F ................. 178
WADLEY
   Beulah ............................. 283,284,285
   Dean McKennon ........................ 283
   Dean McKinnon ........ 282,283,284,285
   George L ............. 278,279,283,284,285
WALKER, Will T ........................ 173,174
WALL
   Chris .......................................... 269,273
   Delila ................................................ 272
WALTON, Nancy ................. 198,199,200
WARD
   Adam .......................................... 268,269
   Bertha .......................................... 113,114
   Charles O ......................................... 306
   David ......................... 191,192,206,207
   J D ...................................... 287,290,291
   Mary .......................................... 268,269
   W L ............................................. 309,310
WASHINGTON, George ..................... 54
WATKINS, W .................................. 23,24
WEAVER, L M ................................... 111
WEBSTER, J M ................................. 147
WELCH, C A ............................... 249,250
WELCH & WELCH ........................... 247
WIER
   H B .................................................. 183
   J B ................................................... 183
WILHELM, P E .................................. 104
WILLIAMS
   B W ............................................... 5,181
   Charles R ........................................... 68
   Charley R ...................................... 63,67
   Charlie R .............................. 62,63,68,69
   Elizabeth ..................................... 195,197
   Elum M ............................................. 62
   Ike ..................................... 157,158,160
   J E .............................. 70,109,129,130
   Josep ............................................... 164
   Joseph ... 159,160,161,162,163,164,165
   Julia ................................................. 196
   Julia A ...................................... 196,197
   Kelsey ............ 62,63,64,65,66,67,68,69
   Lula Pearl ................................... 100,101
   Mamie ......................... 62,63,67,68,69
   Molsy ............................................. 159
   Motsy .... 159,160,161,162,163,164,165
   Robert ...................................... 196,197
   S F ................................................... 155
   Sarah .......... 157,158,159,160,161,162, 163,165
   Sarah E ..................................... 100,101
   Senora W .................................. 100,101
WILLIS
   Benjamin ........................................ 160
   Riley ......................................... 313,314
WILSON
   Elenor Jane .................................. 10,11
   Ellenor Jane ............................ 10,11,12
   Emma J .................................. 10,11,12
   Raphael F ............................... 10,11,12
WINGATE
   Mrs N M ........................................... 16
   N M .................................................. 16
WISHART, J C .................................. 8,9
WOODS, J A .................................... 169
WYNNS, W B ................................... 126

YANDELL, I W .......................... 319,320

www.ingramcontent.com/pod-product-compliance
Lightning Source LLC
Chambersburg PA
CBHW020241030426
42336CB00010B/567